Sufi Talks

Sufi Talks

Teachings of an American Sufi Sheikh

Robert Frager,
Sheikh of the Halveti-Jerrahi Order

QUEST
BOOKS

Theosophical Publishing House
Wheaton, Illinois • Chennai, India

Quest Books
Theosophical Publishing House
P. O. Box 270
Wheaton, IL 60187-0270
www.questbooks.net

Chapter Two, *Transforming Our Egos*, is adapted from an interview that originally appeared in the Spring 2000 issue of the magazine *What Is Enlightenment?*

Cover design by Kirsten Hansen Pott
Typesetting by Wordstop Technologies, Inc.

Library of Congress Cataloging-in-Publication Data

Frager, Robert.
Sufi talks: teachings of an American sufi sheikh / Robert Frager.
  p. cm.
Includes index.
ISBN 978-0-8356-0893-0
1. Sufism—Miscellanea.   I. Title.
BP189.23.F73 2012
297.4—dc23   2012001179

5 4 3 2 1 * 12 13 14 15 16

Printed in the United States of America

To my wife Ayhan, for all her devoted support,
and to all my extraordinary sheikhs, whose
teachings and stories form the backbone of this book.

Table of Contents

Acknowledgments

Many thanks to Leila Samrad and Gwendolyn Wagner for transcribing these talks and to Kenan Frager, Richard Smoley, and Phil Catalfo for editing them. I am also deeply grateful to a Sufi sheikh who wishes to remain anonymous. He has meticulously gone over the manuscript, corrected many errors, and added from the richness of his own experience. Of course, any errors in this book are my own and remain in spite of my editors.

In addition, I am deeply grateful to my Sufi Community in Redwood City, California, without whom these talks would never have occurred.

To Learn More

For more information on Islam and Sufism, contact:
http://jerrahi.com/california/

Introduction

This book is a collection of Sufi talks, called *sohbets* in Turkish. The word *sohbet* is related to the Arabic term *sahaba,* which refers to the companions of the Prophet§ (see the author's note on page xvii for an explanation of symbols used throughout this book when referring to the Prophet Muhammad and other revered figures). The teachings of early Islam were relayed orally from the Prophet§ to his companions, men and women who left their homes and risked everything for Islam. These faithful companions sat in the Prophet's company whenever they could and tried their best to live according to his teachings.

In Sufism, a *sohbet* is a conversation about spiritual topics. Sufi teachers often make formal *sohbets* in training their dervishes, or Sufi students. The *sohbet* provides guidance and inspiration for those dervishes who take to heart their teacher's words. Some Sufi teachers say that the *sohbet* is even more important than the *zikr,* the basic Sufi practice of Remembrance of God. In *zikr,* the dervishes occupy themselves with a practice. In *sohbet,* the dervishes occupy themselves with their sheikh. The relationship between sheikh and dervish underlies all of Sufism.

Years ago, a young American woman asked my master, Muzaffer Efendi, about the earthy nature of our *zikr.* She said the rhythmic, breathy chanting reminded her of the sounds of lovemaking. My sheikh was somewhat surprised. I'm sure he had never been asked that particular question before. But he gave a wonderful, deep laugh and answered without hesitation. His answer is a wonderful description of the spiritual power of the *sohbet.*

"Yes, it is like sex," he said, "but the organs are different. In Sufism, there is a transmission from the sheikh's mouth to the dervish's ear. If the dervish sincerely takes in the sheikh's words, a child is born to the dervish. It is a child of the heart, the birth of the dervish's spiritual being."

My sheikh continued, "When physical lovemaking is over, the lovers usually roll over and go to sleep. Physically satisfied, they forget each other. On the other hand, the relationship between sheikh and dervish continually deepens until we never forget each other—in this life or in the next."

The relationship between sheikh and dervish creates profound *sohbets*, living communications from heart to heart. I have often prepared a topic for a *sohbet* and found myself discussing a completely different topic. And dervishes have frequently commented that my *sohbets* have precisely addressed issues they needed to hear that week. They often felt the *sohbets* were addressed to them personally.

I still remember vividly the first time I heard my Sufi master, Muzaffer Efendi. At the end of his *sohbet*, I was surprised to see there were other people in the room. I had forgotten that anyone else was there. It felt as if he and I were the only ones present.

Muzaffer Efendi told two stories that day. The stories were about destiny, and they dramatically illustrated the principle that whatever is meant to come to us *will* come to us. That night I reflected deeply on these stories, and the next day I told Muzaffer Efendi, "Those were really profound stories. If I remember them, it will change my life." He looked deeply into my eyes and replied, "You will never forget them." He was right. I have never forgotten those stories, and they have changed my life. My introduction to Sufism was through the power of *sohbet*.

A Sufi Order has been described as a *silsilah*: a chain in which each sheikh is connected to his or her own teacher. The chain reaches, unbroken, to the founder of each Order, to great Sufi saints of the past, and all the way back to Hazreti Muhammad§ (the Turkish term *Hazreti*, from the Arabic *Hadrat*, is a title of respect similar to "Your Holiness"). I also think of an Order as a pipeline in which each sheikh is a section of pipe connected to those who come before and after. The wisdom and the blessings of the Order flow through the pipeline. What flows through the pipeline is not from the sheikh. The sheikh is a channel for something greater than any individual. That energy and wisdom often flows through the sheikh's *sohbets*.

Beginnings

Our California Sufi group began in 1981, when twelve of us were initiated by Muzaffer Efendi, the head sheikh of the Halveti-Jerrahi Order. Muzaffer Efendi was visiting the Institute of Transpersonal Psychology (ITP; now Sofia University), a graduate school I had founded in 1975. The school is dedicated to the interface between psychology and spirituality, and we often invited teachers from different spiritual traditions to speak.

ITP is based on the premise that psychology should include personal as well as intellectual development, and this study should involve the whole person—including physical, emotional, intellectual, creative, social, and spiritual aspects. We developed the ITP curriculum to help students grow as human beings and become more effective in whatever they choose to do.

In the spring of 1980, Muzaffer Efendi and a group of his Turkish dervishes visited ITP for several days as part of a tour of the United States. Muzaffer Efendi gave a series of talks at ITP. Each day, dozens of guests came to ITP to hear him and to be in his presence. He and his dervishes also performed a public *zikr* at Stanford University.

The next year, Muzaffer Efendi returned to ITP. Once again we enjoyed his profound talks and deeply moving *zikr*. Many guests asked questions about Sufism or Islam. One guest asked Muzaffer Efendi if someone living in America could become one of his dervishes. I'm sure she had read stories about Sufism and other mystical traditions, stories in which a seeker had to spend weeks or months on probation and years in training sitting at a teachers' feet.

Muzaffer Efendi answered that he would accept Americans as dervishes, and I was immediately moved by the possibility of becoming his dervish. I knew that I had found a teacher with profound wisdom and integrity, a teacher I could trust to guide my spiritual life. I had trained with many spiritual teachers from many different traditions, and I had learned a great deal from them. But I had never been moved to make this kind of commitment before.

I asked first to become a dervish, and so I became the senior Halveti-Jerrahi dervish in California. The Halveti-Jerrahi Order (also known as the Jerrahi Order) is a Turkish branch of the Halveti Order. The Halveti Order was founded in the fourteenth century. It is one of the oldest and most famous Sufi Orders. Hazreti Pir Nureddin al Jerrahi founded the Halveti-Jerrahi Order in Istanbul in 1703. Today, there are branches of the Halveti-Jerrahi Order in Europe, Canada, the United States, Mexico, South America, and Saudi Arabia.

No one in our little group of new dervishes knew much about Sufism. We had fallen in love with Muzaffer Efendi and with his teachings, so we started this path with enthusiasm and ignorance.

After our initiation, we began to meet weekly. We were drawn to each other and to exploring our newfound path together. Many of our early meetings consisted of discussion of what we had gotten ourselves into. What did it mean to be a dervish, to be a Muslim? Did we actually become Muslims as part of our initiation? Did we have to give up alcohol? What about prayer and visiting mosques? How much obedience did we owe to our sheikh? How much did we need to change our lives? None of us were quite sure, and we all experienced various levels of resistance to the path we had somehow chosen (or rather, the path that had chosen us.)

We have been meeting ever since—for thirty years and counting. At first we met once a week, and in a few months we began meeting for Friday prayers as well. Later we added weekly practices of Turkish Sufi music, an integral part of the Jerrahi *zikr*. In 1984 we bought a house in Redwood City, California, which has been our center ever since. (For more information, contact us at jerrahi.com/california/.)

In 1985 I was initiated as a sheikh at our Istanbul center by head sheikh Safer Efendi. (Muzaffer Efendi had passed away that year, and Safer Efendi had become his successor.) Four years is a very short time to become a sheikh. However, I had been leading our group for all this time, and in many ways I had already been functioning as a sheikh.

My new status was a great help as a spiritual guide. Before becoming a sheikh my *sohbets* were taken almost verbatim from Muzaffer Efendi's writings. After becoming a sheikh I was encouraged to give my own *sohbets*, which have been taken primarily from what I have learned over the years from my teachers.

There were esoteric benefits as well. When he initiated me, Safer Efendi taught me how to interpret dreams according to our tradition. Then he recited a prayer and blew into my mouth. When I returned to California I found I was able to interpret the dervishes' dreams in ways I had never before imagined in my psychological training. The California dervishes were convinced that in some mysterious way I had been truly transformed into a sheikh.

The talks that make up this book have been transcribed from the *sohbets* I have given weekly at our center. I have edited and compiled a selection of talks taken from the past ten years. They are examples of the living discipline of Sufism as we have been practicing it in the United States.

The thread of these discussions is rarely linear. The flow of the ideas found here is more of a spiral, circling around a topic and examining it from different perspectives. I have not striven for that nonlinear style. It is what generally emerges from this form of discourse.

Some of the stories and quotations are repeated in different talks. That is no accident or oversight. Years ago Muzaffer Efendi advised, "Tell these stories over and over again. You can tell them ten thousand times and people will still benefit from them."

I have learned a great deal in preparing and giving these *sohbets,* the dervishes have learned from listening to them, and I hope you will learn from reading them about the principles and practices of Sufism as understood in our Jerrahi Order.

The first few talks (chapters 1, 2, and 3) focus on working with the obstacles on the spiritual path, especially dealing with the ego, which is called the *nafs* in Sufism. Chapters 4, 5, 6, and 7 discuss the process of seeking God in our hearts and souls and in the world around us. Chapter 8 recounts many of the stories and legends of Ibrahim bin Adhem, one of the great Sufi saints, who gave up his kingdom to become a dervish. In chapters 9, 10, 11, 12, and 13, I discuss some of the basic practices of Sufism, particularly courtesy, service, and hospitality. Chapters 14, 15, 16, and 17 are talks given during various holidays and on special occasions, including the month of Ramadan, the holy Night of Power during Ramadan, New Year's Eve (when we traditionally meet and hold *zikr* practice), and on the evening of a wedding ceremony that I performed at our center. Chapters 18, 19, 20, and 21 describe the great Sufi virtues of inner poverty, generosity, dedication to our own spiritual lives, and nonattachment to the world.

Author's Note

Throughout this book, I use many terms that come from Arabic, Turkish, or other languages. Some of these words, like *sheikh* and *dervish*, have actually made their way into contemporary English (and so are not italicized in the text), but others will likely be unfamiliar to many readers. Where a more unfamiliar term first appears, I have defined it; and I have provided a glossary to help the reader recall the meaning of those and other terms when they reappear later.

Muslims (including Sufis) traditionally use a reverential expression when referring to the Prophet Muhammad: *salli allahu alayhi wa salam,* which, in Arabic, means "God's peace and blessings be upon him." In English, this expression is usually represented by the parenthetical abbreviation "(saws)," added immediately after the reference to the Prophet. For other divine Messengers, we traditionally add "(as)," which stands for *allayhi salam,* or "God's peace be upon him." For certain holy women and men, we usually add "(ra)," which stands for (for women) *radi Allahu-anha* or (for men) *radi Allahu-anhu,* or "May God be pleased with her or him." Lastly, when referring to certain saints, we use "(ks)," which stands for *kudduse sirruhu,* or "May his/her soul be sanctified." In this book, to make the text less mysterious or difficult for the lay reader, I use the symbol § to signify "(saws)"; ‡ to signify "(as)"; ∫ to signify "(ra)"; and ◊ to signify "(ks)."

In some of the chapters, I have included excerpts from question-and-answer segments that often take place during my talks. While the texts of my talks have been edited to be readable and intelligible outside the context of an oral address, the Q&A segments are included more or less "as is," because those dialogues serve to amplify the talks, and the exchanges between dervish and sheikh are also illustrative of the special relationship between the two.

Throughout the book, I quote from the Holy Qur'an. Where I refer to a specific passage, I provide a reference to that passage, citing first the *sura* (chapter), then the verse. So, for example, "50:16" means "*sura* 50, verse 16." As I use more than one translation of the Qur'an in my studies and teaching, in the text immediately following each quotation I indicate in parentheses the source of its translation. Translators I have used include Muhammad Asad, Thomas Cleary, and Tarif Khalidi; full publishing information for each is listed in the bibliography.

Obstacles on the Path

hy is the Sufi path so difficult and time consuming? According to an old Turkish Sufi saying, "The path of Sufism is like chewing an iron chickpea." (The Turks love roasted chickpeas as a snack, like we do peanuts.) Our jaws become sore, our teeth wear down, and the iron chickpea seems unchanged. This path requires tremendous patience. It is also a path of great joy and inner satisfaction for those who love God. (The choice of *Allah* or *God* to refer to our Creator is a matter of some debate among translators and Muslim scholars. I have chosen to use *God* in part to remind Western readers that we all worship the same Truth. In the Middle East, many Christians and Jews use *Allah* when they speak Arabic and *God* when they speak English.)

Seeking God

Consider the *hadith qudsi*, the divine revelation, in which God said, "I was a hidden treasure and I wished to be known, and so I created Creation."[1] If there were no obstacles between us and God, there would be no process of knowing. Creation is like a great treasure hunt, and God is the hidden treasure. We are invited to play a divine game, and it is an invitation we need to take seriously.

God wants us to come to know divine Truth. The *process* of seeking
and finding God is the essence of the spiritual path. Part of the fundamental nature of Creation is that God is hidden and must be sought.
Actually, God is more than hidden; God is beyond our comprehension.

As human beings, we have free will and can use our will to change
for the better—or for worse. We can choose to come closer to God, or
we can choose to become more separate. We can choose to submit our
individual will to God's will, or we can rebel. We can rise higher than
the angels, or we can sink lower than the animals.

To succeed in this path, we have to work hard and long. We have to
make what George Gurdjieff, a teacher strongly influenced by Sufism,
called "super efforts." There is a great difference between running a
marathon and driving a car across the finish line. There is not much
challenge to driving as opposed to running, nor does driving provide
us the benefit of using our will and our own physical energy. Similarly,
the challenges of following the Path of Truth are an important part of
the path itself—as many have noted, "The journey is the destination."

If we ask others when they feel happiest, most people will conclude
they are happiest while working toward important goals. Our greatest
happiness is not at the finish line but in the striving itself. The joy is
in the doing of it, not in accomplishing it.

It is also true there is nowhere to go. God says in the Holy Qur'an,
"We are closer to him [humanity] than his jugular vein." (50:16,
Cleary) In other words, God is closer to us than we are to ourselves.
It may feel as if we are moving closer to God, but God is already fully
present within us.

Moses and the Children of Israel

According to my teachers, Moses‡ once asked God to transform the
children of Israel. He was tired of the continual battle to free them

from the attitudes and values they had learned as slaves. Moses‡ was said to be so fiery and passionate that when he got angry or excited, the hair on his arms would stand on end and go right through his clothing. He would even argue with God.

Moses‡ complained, "God, You can do anything. Why don't You cleanse my people of their self-centered egos? I left them for a few days, and the moment I was away, they worshipped a golden calf. They have no faith, and they are not grateful for all You have done for them."

Moses‡ asked, "God, You can do anything. Please change them."

And God replied, "You see how egotistical your people are with all their faults. Could you imagine how arrogant they would be if I cleansed their faults?"[2]

We are just like the children of Israel. Time and time again, God delivers us from disasters, and yet we almost immediately forget. When the Israelites were in the desert, God sent down manna every day, but the manna did not last overnight; it could not be hoarded. And so the children of Israel worried about their next meal. Some also complained that the food was always the same. And so God no longer sent down manna, and the children of Israel had to find their own food from then on.

Don't we worry and complain in the same ways? Even though God has continually nourished and supported us every day of our lives, we are afraid God will not continue to do that tomorrow. We are not content with what we have. This is a sign of the weakness of our faith.

We are not perfect, and we are not going to become perfect. But we can improve. We have to work with our faults and learn from our mistakes. In the process of seeking God, we have to confront our limitations, and then we learn how much we need God's blessings to succeed at anything.

The children of Israel were the slaves of the pharaoh, just as we are slaves of our own "inner pharaoh"—an inner, oppressive ego that tries to enslave us and run our lives. The first goal of Sufism is to free ourselves from the tyranny of our narcissistic egos. Luckily we have a great ally in this struggle. God has placed within us an inner Moses, our own inner liberator. It is our soul, calling to us to follow the Path of Truth.

The liberation of the Israelites can be understood as a rich metaphor for self-liberation. It was a long-term process. It began with plague after plague, suffering after suffering. In a sense, the children of Israel had to be "birthed" out of Egypt and out of slavery. We all experience similar birth pains as we struggle to loosen the grip our egos have on us.

It took a good amount of courage to flee from Egypt and to walk toward the Red Sea pursued by the pharaoh's army. After the miracle of the parting of the Red Sea, each day in the desert brought new tests of faith. The making of the golden calf was an attempt to return to the idol-worshipping culture that had enslaved the Israelites for generations. They were still addicted to the culture of their oppressors.

If we make sincere intentions and act on them, God will aid and assist us. This is what happened to the children of Israel. They had no hope of overcoming the might of the pharaoh's army. They had been slaves for generations and had no idea how to fight. The legions of the pharaoh included archers, chariots, and armored warriors. These highly trained soldiers were pitted against a group of slaves who had probably never even held a weapon in their hands.

As they fled, the children of Israel came up to the Red Sea, a seemingly impassible barrier. God did not immediately part the waters before them. Scholars have pointed out that the waters did not part until the Israelites actually stepped into the water. In fact only when the water came up to the first person's chin did the sea begin to part. What a wonderful example of faith. It is also a reminder of the importance of action. The children of Israel acted without any certainty they would be successful. They followed their prophet.

These are teachings for today, not merely interesting historical stories. God has parted the Red Sea for us in our own lives, and we can discover many examples of divine help if we examine our own lives. We have all experienced miracles in our lives, miracles in which God has removed obstacles for us when we could not possibly have succeeded by ourselves. But we forget very quickly. We are like the pharaoh who changed his mind about freeing the Israelites after each plague was over. That is the work of our egos, our inner pharaoh. We forget. We are ungrateful. We complain, "God, what have You done for me lately?" And we worship what is tangible and material, our own golden calves.

When we hear stories like this, we can go beyond their historical significance and the obvious moral lessons. Haven't we experienced similar stories in our own lives?

Remember, the children of Israel had to spend forty years, or two generations, in the desert. Most of those who emerged from the desert were the grandchildren of the slaves who fled Egypt. The grandchildren were free of any trace of slavery.

How can we free ourselves? It took the Israelites two generations to enter the Promised Land, but we don't have that kind of time. How can we emancipate ourselves from the state of slavery to our egos and self-centeredness? How can we transform our lives and leave that enslaved state?

In their forty-year-long desert retreat, the children of Israel were constantly taught by Moses‡, one of God's great Messengers. That is what it took to transform a people.

Their goal was to enter Canaan, the land of milk and honey, just as our goal is to attain a state of inner contentment and serenity. Inner calm and peace are essential foundations for our spiritual lives. We have to decide whether to follow our inner Moses or our inner pharaoh. It is not always easy to follow our inner liberator. Our egos play

God—as if they were the pharaoh—and constantly work to distort the truth and turn sound advice or spiritual teachings into something useless or unhelpful.

This reminds me of another story about Moses‡ in the desert. This story comes from Rumi's spiritual classic, the six-volume *Mathnawi*. One day, when Moses‡ came down from Mount Sinai, someone asked, "Would you please invite God for dinner?"

Moses‡ replied angrily, "You can't invite God to dinner. God doesn't eat dinner! God is infinite, beyond any need for food. Besides, God has no mouth. God is beyond any human form! God is not like you and me. God is everywhere and everything."

"Are you sure you can't invite God to dinner?"

"Yes!"

When Moses‡ returned to Mount Sinai, God asked him about the invitation. Moses‡ replied, "I told them that You don't eat."

God said, "No, Moses. Go back and tell them to prepare a feast tomorrow evening, and I will come."

Can you imagine how Moses‡ must have felt? He had to return and tell his people that he was wrong, that God was coming to dinner after all. And this after his diatribe about how God did not have a mouth, God did not eat or drink, and God should not be thought of as another person. It must have been very hard on him.

Everyone was tremendously excited, and they prepared a wonderful feast the next day. The cooks made their finest dishes. Everybody was involved in the feast preparation.

In the middle of all the commotion, an old man came in from the desert. He asked if he could get something to drink and to eat. Moses‡ said, "God is coming to dinner. Wait until God gets here. Nobody is going to eat before God!" The cooks put him to work fetching water.

Dinnertime came and went, but God did not show up. It got later and later. The food got cold. Of course everyone criticized Moses‡:

"First you said God doesn't eat, then you said God was coming to dinner, and now God hasn't shown up. What kind of a prophet are you, anyhow?" Poor Moses‡ did not know what to say.

The next day, Moses‡ went to Mount Sinai and complained. "O God, I told them You do not eat. Then You said You were coming, but You didn't come."

"I did come. I was thirsty and hungry, but no one gave me anything to drink or to eat. The old man who came in from the desert was one of my servants, and when you feed my servants you feed Me; when you serve my servants, you serve Me."

This is a wonderful lesson. By serving God's creatures we serve God, and that service is worship.

The story also reminds us that whatever image of God we hold is imperfect. Whatever ideas we have of God are limited, inadequate, and distorted by our own limitations. Whatever concepts we have regarding God are more wrong than right.

While the children of Israel were busy getting ready for a special event, they failed to see what was right in front of them. They are mirrors for us. We are not Moses‡ in these stories! We are the confused children of Israel, and we struggle with limited faith and limited understanding.

▸ 2 ◂

Transforming
Our Egos

There are two approaches to dealing with the ego. One is to seek to transform it, and the other is to try to "drop" it. I believe that we have to begin by transforming our egos. Some spiritual seekers can reduce their egos to almost nothing, but that is only possible after years of inner work. Many people try to drop their egos much too soon. Safer Efendi once explained that the ego only falls away at the final stage of spiritual development. He said, "It's very, very hard to take the 'I' out of oneself."

Very few spiritual traditions admit young children into the monastery. Why not? After all, if they did, the children would be surrounded by spiritual teachers and spiritual discipline, instead of being surrounded by worldly people and secular life.

One reason they don't is to give the children a chance to develop their personalities, to mature enough so that they can come to the monastery with a personality—even though that personality has developed in the world. We have to let kids experience the world and mature to a certain extent, because only then could they make an informed choice to pursue a spiritual life. In other words, people are only admitted into religious life after they have developed their egos and their personalities.

Many years ago, my Zen teacher, Kennett Roshi, pointed out, "In Buddhist iconography, there is a statue of Maitreya, the Buddha to come, sitting on a fierce beast. The Buddha is larger than the beast— bigger and stronger. He hasn't killed the beast but he *sits on it* and he controls it. That beast represents the ego."

This image beautifully illustrates the most effective way to work with the ego. The goal is not to kill the ego or give up our personality. The goal is to control the ego rather than letting it control us.

Now, to control the ego doesn't mean to beat it or starve it. The ego might argue, "I'm being abused." But then, who believes the ego? The goal is to develop ourselves as spiritual beings so that our egos are only a small part of us—and, ideally, are transformed and become a mature part of our psyches.

The term *ego strength* is popular in psychology today. It refers to self-confidence and the ability to cope with challenges. It is seen as an indicator of success in life. Some psychologists tend to focus on building ego strength in patients with low self-esteem. They believe, "We have to work *just* on developing our patients' egos if they lack self-confidence." I would argue that the best way is to work on developing our egos in the context of "sitting" on them. We can't simply say, "Let me feed this beast and let it run free, even though I imagine by the time it has grown big and strong I'm going to have a hell of a time taming it." That's not very smart! What we can do is *train* the beast compassionately, with love and understanding. Sufi masters have compared training the ego to training a dog or a horse, with caring and compassion. Developing our egos without a context of spiritual discipline is just pandering to the ego. It is a foolish mistake.

From a Sufi perspective, service is an important component of the struggle to develop ourselves—service to humanity and service to the world, to all of Creation. One of the essential tools we use in service is our personality structure, *including our ego*. Letting go of our separate sense of self and attaining a state of unity is the last stage of spiritual development. Paradoxically, we need to use our ego well in order to get to this stage.

In the Sufi tradition, the greatest saints experience union and then return to the world of duality to serve. In order to serve, they must have an intact personality structure. But the difference between them and us is that their personality is firmly under their control. It is a tool that they can use. It is not their master.

Some spiritual seekers *do* lose their personalities and their sense of self. They become unbalanced or "God intoxicated," often unable to care for themselves. Instead of serving others, people have to serve them. They are stuck at this point, and further growth is impossible. It is a paradox that the ego, which is an obstacle on the spiritual path, is also an essential element on that path.

The great saints have had their own unique and interesting personalities, which were formed around a sense of separate self. The sense of self is essential in human development. We can't develop without it. Without that sense of self, we would probably be feral humans without much intelligence.

Like other people, these saints developed their personalities as they grew up and matured. They learned to relate to others with love and compassion. After they transformed themselves, the saints still retained their old personality structure, which allowed them to understand the problems of people who came to them for help and advice.

But in the saints, the personality ultimately becomes a structure imbued with the Divine. It no longer has the capacity to throw them off, to distort their experience in the way it used to. And yet, that personality structure did grow up from a sense of "I" and an ego. In the course of human development, we develop an ego and a personality structure. And in the course of human *spiritual* development, we begin to transcend ego and personality and incorporate them within something larger.

Pandering to our egos is self-defeating. On the other hand, avoiding ego development is not the answer. We can hold ego development in the context of the spiritual. It's tricky because we are talking about two different kinds of development: One is the normal maturation and growth of the ego. The other is spiritual development in which our ego is reduced and our sense of union increases. This latter comprises another level and another dynamic of human development.

On the spiritual path, personal development is held in a larger context. Maturation and growth occur, but they are part of a larger whole. C. G. Jung believed there are two centers of the personality. The ego is the center of consciousness, and the Self is the center of the psyche, including the conscious and unconscious. But the ego pretends to be the center of the psyche, and it tries to get us to ignore the Self.

We have to say to our egos, "Remember, you're only a *part* of the psyche. Don't become inflated. You're useful, but you're not in charge of this system. There is a greater Self, and I may not be fully conscious of it now, but it's what I'm seeking to connect with." That is one way of understanding how these two aspects fit together. It's a matter of context.

What Is Ego?

When Freud's writings were translated into English, the term that was translated as "the ego" is, in his original German, *das Ich*, which means "the I." So our modern theories of personality are built on this understanding that ego is the *I*; it's our sense of who we are.

Sufism would very much agree with this definition. Sufism explains that our sense of self, called in Sufism the "personal soul," is an outgrowth of our capacity to objectify ourselves, to see ourselves as objects as if observing ourselves from the outside. Our capacity to do this gives us power to act, to plan; it gives us tremendous control of the world around us. But the problem is that when we begin to say, "Here *I* am, an object," then by definition we are also separating ourselves from the world. If we say, "I" or "me," we create dualism. Where there is *I*, there has to be *other*. But from the Sufi point of view, we're seeking *unity*—and that powerful sense of dualism is one of the greatest blocks to attaining unity. Who wants to give up *I*? We don't want to give "ourselves" up; we're terribly attached to our sense of identity.

So, our ego is fundamentally rooted in our individuality, our sense of separateness. We identify with this separateness instead of identifying with the Self and its sense of unity. We identify with our ego instead of identifying with the Divine within us. And, to the extent that we remain attached to our self-concept or self-image or separateness, that keeps us from truly pursuing a spiritual path. It holds us back from our deepest mystical experiences, because in those experiences the sense of a separate self dissolves. One of my old colleagues once commented, "Everybody wants God but fights like the devil to avoid union!"

The Stages of the Nafs

Sufi teachers speak of the *nafs*, the ego or separate self, as evolving through various stages. The lowest level of the *nafs* is the *nafs ammara*, the tyrannical self. This includes all those forces in us that lead us astray. This term is mentioned in the Qur'an. The prophet Joseph‡ asked the pharaoh to clear his name of the accusation that he tried to rape Zuleika, the wife of his master when he was a slave. On investigation, the pharaoh found Zuleika guilty of trying to seduce Joseph. After he was declared innocent, Joseph admitted he was not blameless.

He said, "I do not declare my soul [*nafs*] innocent: the soul ever urges to evil, except when my Lord shows mercy." (12:53, Khalidi) The great prophet admits that he too has to struggle with his lower self. And he reminds us that this struggle will only succeed with God's help.

At this lowest level we are unconscious of our faults and our tendencies to evil. We are in denial that these tendencies exist, very much like an alcoholic who says, "I have no problem with alcohol. I just have a little drink with breakfast, a little with lunch, a little something in between. But I don't have a drinking problem." Our unconsciousness and denial makes the tyrannical *nafs* incredibly powerful. And many of us live in this stage more than we'd like to think. It's a stage that we can easily slip into, for example, when somebody cuts us off on the freeway, or when someone is rude, or when someone hooks our pride or makes us angry. We descend to that level of unconsciousness. So it's incredibly powerful.

The second level is called the "self-blaming *nafs*" or the "regretful *nafs*." This stage is also mentioned in the Qur'an. God says that on the Day of Resurrection, "I call to witness the accusing voice of man's own conscience [the self-blaming *nafs*]." (75:2, Asad) At this stage, we have become more aware of our ego, but we're still caught by it. We say to ourselves, "I know I'm going to say the wrong thing, I hope I can stop . . . oh damn, here I go . . . ," and we *know* we should shut up, but we can't. We just blurt out what we should never have said. At this stage, at least we realize that we're wrong. We're in the grip of something that is not our best self, but we still let ourselves act badly.

We come to see our *nafs* more clearly as we work on ourselves. We become more conscious; we begin to replace bad habits and actions with positive ones. We slowly weaken these negative forces and move out of their domination. But even these forces can become reawakened in certain situations. We may not be under their control most of the time, but they're still present. As one of my teachers said, these negative forces are like seeds in our psyches. They may sprout and lead to pain and tragedy unless we roast them in the fires of wisdom, service, and spiritual experience.

There is a classic story of the Prophet Muhammadﷺ in which he goes out in the desert late at night to pray. His young wife, Aishaʃ, thinks he's going out to meet another woman. As he walks into the silence of the desert, she follows him. He looks at her and realizes she was following him out of jealousy. He asks, "Aisha, have you brought your little Satan with you?"

Aishaʃ asks, "What little Satan?"

"Every human being has an imp, a little devilish part, their lower *nafs*."

"Even you, O Prophet of God?"

"Yes, even me. However, I made mine a Muslim."

Another translation of the Prophet's answer is, "I brought my *nafs* into submission," because *Muslim* means "one who submits." Only the greatest saints and prophets have achieved this accomplishment. Others may exhibit the most extraordinary patience and self-control in extremely challenging situations, but the potential to be tempted is still there. The "seeds" are dormant but not dead.

The temptations change as we grow. After the regretful *nafs*, the next stage is the "inspired *nafs*." In the inspired *nafs*, the wisdom of the heart begins to enter our personality and our consciousness. Now, for the first time, we have powerful alternatives to the forces of the ego—discernment, intuition, inner guidance. However, the ego is still active. The reign of the ego is not by any means over, and the biggest danger is that the ego can begin to use our wisdom and intuition for self-aggrandizement, for ego inflation.

Ideally, we learn to say, "This light, this wisdom, isn't mine; it comes *through* me, from a divine source." But the ego claims, "This is *my* wisdom. *I* know."

Some seekers and teachers get stuck at this stage. In many ways it is the most dangerous stage. Once the ego experiences light and wisdom it's very hard to change, because the light and wisdom are real. The problem is that the ego begins to attribute these qualities to itself, not to something greater than itself. And so the ego becomes inflated. We want the opposite; we want the ego to become more transparent, less domineering—lighter.

The saints have their personalities, but their personalities no longer run them. They run their personalities. Another way to put it is that their personalities are beautified. They have become permeated with light and love. They still have a personality; the great sheikhs and saints don't become generic. Each is different. But there's a beauty there, because their personalities have become vessels that hold the Divine. Like a clay pot that absorbs some of its contents, in holding the Divine a saint's personality becomes permeated with the divine qualities of love, light, generosity, and compassion.

One of my teachers said, "First, you have to get your life in order and begin to live a life of calmness, stability, service, and honesty, all the while attending to your religious duties. Otherwise, it's like having a cow that eats organic grass and gives wonderful organic milk, but when you milk that cow, the milk goes into a pail with a couple of small holes in the bottom." You waste all that "milk." The personality is very much like that pail. Habits like dishonesty, greed, or anger are like holes in our "pail" that keep it from holding the state of love of the Divine. But while we lose it, the great ones don't. They are more whole than we are.

What drives the ego? There are two answers. One is self-survival. The ego is afraid of deep mystical experience and transformation, because, from its point of view, that kind of major change is death. The *nafs ammaara* is not capable of faith in God. It is totally materialistic. It does not believe in anything but itself. The ego fears that it isn't going to survive spiritual transformation—and it may not. Our inner resistance is a survival mechanism. It is the part of all of us that wants to stay the same, a kind of inertial component in all of us that says, "Don't change."

The second answer is that the ego is arrogant and believes it is separate from the rest of the world. Sufis often describe the ego as connected to the devil. Carl Jung describes "the shadow" in similar terms. Jung's shadow is that which we don't see and can't accept in ourselves, but Jung also writes that it is connected with negative cosmic forces, what we might call "satanic forces." And no one likes to talk about this. I taught a course in spiritual psychology to a "new thought" religious group that is very focused on positive thinking, and whenever I brought this up, it was like I had poked one of their sacred cows. They complained, "How can you say evil exists? The universe is good, God is good!" I tried to explain, "Whenever there is light, there is shadow."

My Sufi teachers have referred to the *nafs* as though it is motivated and conscious, like a person. On one level, it's a metaphor, but on another level, it seems to behave like an entity. My sheikh Tosun Bayrak has often referred to the *nafs* as a "thief" who wishes to steal away what is beautiful and valuable in our lives. It's as if the *nafs* is a servant of Satan whose job is to test our faith, to see if we can hold onto it. In fact, my teacher has said to us, "Be especially careful after you've been on *hajj* [pilgrimage to Mecca] or after you've accomplished other spiritual work, because thieves usually don't go to empty houses. But if there's something there . . ." When we begin to grow spiritually, our inner resistance becomes activated.

So how do we guard ourselves against our egos? Sheikh Tosun asked, "What do you do when a thief comes into your house at night? You're in your bedroom and you hear the thief skulking around; you hear the silver candlesticks going into the thief's bag. If you rush downstairs with a knife in your hand, the thief will also have a knife. If you have a gun in your hand, the thief will have a gun. No matter what weapons you have, the thief is going to have the same. It's going to mirror whatever force you use against it." So what do you do?

The answer my sheikh gave is this: "You turn the light on! The thief is a coward, and if you shine the light of awareness on the process, the thief will flee." You don't fight. Fighting with Satan is the stupidest thing in the world. There are lots of great stories in Sufism and elsewhere in which someone tries to fight with Satan, and Satan always wins. It's a very bad idea.

There is a famous story in which Muhammad§ was returning from a battle and said to his followers, "Now we have returned from the lesser *jihad* [war] to the greater *jihad*." When asked what was the greater *jihad*, Muhammad§ pointed to his breast and answered, "The struggle against our *nafs*. The war on the battlefield has a beginning and an end. The war with the *nafs* never ends."

It was a perfect teaching for that particular time. The Muslims had just come back from fighting the Meccans, who had more warriors, more cavalry, better equipment, better armor, and better weapons. But, by means of faith, dedication, and God's Grace, they won. They came back exhausted but feeling proud of their achievements. It was at that point that Muhammad§ said, "Now we're going to an even greater war!" He was addressing their pride and reminding his followers that their spiritual efforts were more important than their worldly successes. Safer Efendi once commented, "The wars going on in the outside world are nothing compared to the wars going on within us."

This inner struggle is far more complex than outer warfare. It is not always easy to discern good and bad, black and white. In a war, you know who your allies and enemies are. But the spiritual path is much more subtle. The *nafs* never says to you, "I am your enemy. I'm going to try and mislead you from your spiritual path. I want you to pray and remember God less. I want you to love the world more." It says something else: "You've been working hard, so why don't you take it easy? Don't exhaust yourself. Instead of praying, get a little more sleep. Sleep is good for your health. I'm your friend. I have your best interests at heart." You see how complicated this business is.

Unfortunately, words like *jihad* are generally misunderstood by the general public—and also by many so-called Muslims. The term *jihad* literally means "struggle" or "effort," not "war." So the term "inner *jihad*" can be misleading. In many ways, working to control your ego is more like inner training—the way you would train a beautiful, intelligent dog or horse or even a child. I think "transformation through love" is a far more sane and sensible way to describe this process than "war," with its violent connotations.

Relationship between Sheikh and Dervish

According to an old Turkish Sufi saying, "If you have a cut, you can bandage yourself, but you cannot take out your own appendix." In other words, we can make trivial changes in ourselves, but we cannot bring about fundamental inner change without help. We can't see our ego and our resistance clearly enough. A sheikh can help with fundamental change and transformation. We can do many things for ourselves, but there are certain levels of inner transformation we just can't attain by ourselves.

Some people today think that we don't need spiritual teachers—that we don't need anyone to tell us how to live our spiritual lives. However, in my experience, real spiritual teachers don't tell their students what to do. My teachers have been wonderful guides and role models. I had to do the work myself: I had to say my own prayers. A wonderful yoga teacher named Haridas Baba explained this beautifully when he wrote, "I can cook for you, but you have to eat for yourself."[1] A teacher can serve us a banquet of wisdom, but we have to digest it for ourselves. Can we do that with the "banquet" that's available in all the spiritual paperbacks at $12.95 and $19.95?

Some people would say yes, but I think that those who try will get spiritual indigestion. Without a guide, we will choose those teachings and practices we *like*, not those we *need*. Our egos will encourage us to choose those teachings and practices that will keep us as we are. Rumi indicated this when he wrote, "Without a guide, it will take you two hundred years for a journey of two years."

I have been deeply inspired by my teachers. I would not have had the patience to stay with this path for so many years if not for the love, acceptance, and example of my teachers. I would not have had the courage to see myself honestly and clearly if they hadn't seen me clearly and still loved and accepted me.

But, even more fundamentally, a teacher is a powerful role model, an example that transformation is *possible*. We know this because we can see in the teacher someone whose personality has been transformed, whose inner nature has been permeated by light and love.

There are more esoteric aspects as well. Certain practices don't have any power unless they've been given by a teacher. This business about being your own teacher ignores the importance of transmission, lineage, and initiation. The spiritual path is not purely logical or mechanical. It's not psychological or spiritual muscle building. It's much more subtle, an energetic connection with the teacher. In Sufism this is called the *rabita al kalb,* the "connection of the heart."

There have been rare cases in which a connection was established without a living teacher. St. Francis of Assisi did that with Jesus‡. But how many of us are St. Francis? Very few. Also, Sheikh Tosun has said, only semi-humorously, that it is much better to have a dead teacher than a live one, because dead teachers don't give us much trouble—they don't speak up, they don't criticize. All they do is teach in generalities: "Love, be happy, have faith." What else can they teach a general audience? They can't say, for example "You are a bit of a hypocrite. Why don't you try to be more sincere?" or "You are too stingy. Practice generosity, and then tell me what you have learned."

When it comes to dealing with the subtle tricks of the ego, it is very useful to have a teacher. Some people start to stray from the spiritual path and don't know it. We need someone to say, "Wake up! You just took a ninety-degree turn and you need to go back."

Fasting from dawn to dusk during the month of Ramadan is one of the greatest blessings of Islam, because fasting reveals our *nafs*. We get short-tempered. We say, "I don't want to fast. I don't want to get up an hour before dawn." Or, "I have to drive today. Maybe I shouldn't fast." We begin to hear the voice of the *nafs*. And one of the great blessings of fasting—or doing any ascetic practice—is to begin to hear the voice that's opposing our efforts, saying, "Don't do this practice. I don't like this."

It's a bit like encountering the wizard in *The Wizard of Oz*. We hear a convincing, powerful voice and we think, "Well, obviously I have to follow *that*." But as we become more conscious, we begin to become aware of the ego's tricks. And then we hear a weaker voice pleading, "Ignore the little man behind the curtain." The more clearly we see our egos, the more we realize that the ego is a trickster, the less power it has. But we have to *see* it.

Ascetic practices alone don't allow us to do that. Purohit Swami, one of the renowned Indian teachers of the twentieth century, commented that he had met many practitioners of hatha yoga who had developed great capacities and powers—and very powerful egos in the process. So if we just engage in ascetic practices without understanding that these are practices of looking at ourselves, we are likely to feed our egos—"*I* fasted for a month!" It is interesting that in Islam we are required to stop fasting at the end of the month of

Ramadan. This helps curb ego inflation, since everyone is doing the same. Otherwise, some people might boast, "Well, *you* only fasted for twenty-nine days, but *I* fasted for thirty-five!" Asceticism has great potential for ego inflation. On the other hand, if we practice with an attitude of, "Watch what's going on, watch the process, observe both your inspiration and your resistance," then spiritual practice can reduce the ego tremendously.

There is an old system in Sufism focused on reducing the ego. It's called the *Malami* tradition, "the path of blame." The Malamis know the ego wants to be known and thought well of, so they hide their practice from other people. For example, the Malamis never wear special Sufi clothing. They don't have a special meeting place. They avoid all outer trappings, because they know that the ego loves trappings.

I have an old friend who is a highly respected teacher in this tradition—a wonderful, brilliant Sufi teacher. I have seen him enter our Sufi center in Istanbul looking like a visitor who just walked in from the street, not a distinguished visiting teacher. Many Sufis have this quality—as opposed to *showing* their practice to others, they hide it. They do their prayers where others can't see them. In a sense, this is like a very sophisticated war against the ego. It's like saying to the ego, "Whatever you want, I am going to go do the opposite. You want to look good? I'm going to look *bad*. You want to be seen? I'm going to be invisible. And any time I'm going to be visible, I'm going to make sure I don't look the way you want me to look." It's a rigorous discipline—and it requires a guide, because it is too easy either to overdo the practice or to become proud of it.

I honestly think most people are under the domination of their tyrannical *nafs* most of the time. To return to the metaphor of the pharaoh as inner tyrant: who is the most effective ruler? It's not the ruler who constantly calls out the troops to maintain order, but the ruler who commands and everybody responds, "We must obey."

That is, it's the ruler whose authority isn't questioned. Until we enter the spiritual path, the inner tyrant has it easy, because there's no real opposition.

But when we start on the spiritual path, we begin an inner rebellion. When we try to transform ourselves, the forces of the tyrannical self oppose our efforts. The troops of the ego become mobilized. Forces that have been underground, unrecognized, suddenly become revealed. That revealing actually weakens their power because they are no longer unconscious and unrecognized. But, paradoxically, when we start on the spiritual path, we suddenly see the ego's power and we think, "Oh, my God! I'm in much worse shape than I thought I was." The truth is that we just didn't know what bad shape we were in before. Our egos were dominating our lives, and we weren't resisting. So when we begin to see our *nafs*, we are shocked.

New dervishes often have dreams with frightening images—for example, a large snake coming out of one's body. The snake may represent the dreamer's *nafs*. (The sheikhs of my Order often interpret dreams, but there is no general meaning for dream symbols that fits everyone. Dream interpretation is based on the inspiration received by the sheikh as the dream is told.) It is frightening to see that snake and to realize it has been living within us. The good news is that the snake is leaving.

▸ 3 ◂

Reducing Our & *Narcissism*

hy are we here? From a Sufi perspective, we are here to
learn two things: to be less selfish and to love. The two
are related. As we become less selfish, less full of self, we
become more capable of love and closer to God.

In one sense, the essence of human development is the loss of narcissism or egotism. We begin life as pure narcissists. At birth, we do not understand that there is a world out there separate from ourselves. For the infant it is all *me*. Eventually the infant separates the world into *me* and *not-me*, a dichotomy only a relatively few spiritual seekers overcome when they experience unity.

As infants become older, they become more sophisticated about the world, mainly in order to manipulate it more effectively (to obtain nourishment and comfort). As we grow up, we become more effective narcissists. Unfortunately, that is considered normal human development.

Some years ago, a book by Robert J. Ringer entitled *Looking Out for #1* became a best seller. The popularity of such books is a sad commentary on modern society. In our society, "Number One" is not God; it is the ego. We are told that our egos, needs, and desires are

Number One. No wonder there are so many divorces and so much crime, from unethical bankers and politicians on down.

This is one meaning of the Qur'anic verse, "We have made man in the finest order [the best of forms], and then we return him to the lowest of the low, except for those who believe and do good works." (95:4-5, Cleary) The path of Sufism is a path of human maturation—a path of acquiring faith and development and the capacity for service. Our goal is to become real human beings, to grow out of the narcissism we were born with, to grow out of our sense of separateness to a sense of unity with our Creator.

Human Development

The great Sufi sage Jelaluddin Rumi described our evolutionary development as follows:

> I died to the inorganic state and became endowed with growth,
> And (then) I died to (vegetable) growth and attained to the animal.
> I died from animality and became Adam (man):
> Why, then, should I fear? When have I become less by dying?
> At the next remove I shall die to man,
> that I may soar and lift up my head amongst the angels;
> And I must escape even from (the state of) the angel:
> *everything is perishing except His Face.*
> Once more I shall be sacrificed and die to the angel:
> I shall become that which enters not into the imagination.[1]

In this poem, Rumi lyrically illustrates the Sufi system of "souls," or levels of consciousness. At the first level, the developing embryo is much like a plant. It has simple, instinctual, biological—we might say "vegetative"—responses. As the fetus develops, it begins to function more like an animal.

There is no real sense of love in the *plant soul*. Plants love the sun, but that is more an instinctual response to sunlight than love. We cannot discern love in the world of the fish, either. They spawn eggs, but there is no real connection between mates or between parent and offspring.

Love begins to develop with the *animal soul*. God created mammals, which give birth to young that need care. In the animal world, love is necessary for species survival; otherwise young mammals would never survive. God could certainly have created animals so that care of the young was not necessary. That course has worked extremely well for fish and insects.

So with the development of the animal soul, we have the beginning of love and altruism. Animals will sacrifice themselves for their children, or for their mates; for example, a mother bird will risk her life to lead predators away from her nest.

Narcissism develops with what I call the *prehuman soul*, the level that develops after the animal soul. Narcissism arises with the growth of intelligence and reasoning. However, intelligence can develop without love or compassion. There are many people whose hearts are closed, who cannot love or even feel empathy for others. To Sufis, these people are not yet fully human, no matter how intelligent they are.

The fictional character Hannibal Lector from the novel and film *The Silence of the Lambs* is a stark example of someone who is brilliant, but has absolutely no heart, no compassion. He is human in form, but his development is so stunted he is really less than an animal.

The ego develops at this stage as we learn to perceive and manipulate the world around us. It evolves with the development of our senses and our ability to understand our surroundings. The ego uses this understanding in order to satisfy the demands of what Freud called the *id*, which is much like the animal soul. The id is completely devoted to its own wants and needs. (It is important to remember that the terms *ego* and *id* refer to complex processes within us; they are not tangible, static *things*.)

For Freud, the ego is "the representative of the outer world to the id."[2] That is, the ego's concern is coping with the outer world. The id is devoted to the *pleasure principle*, the satisfaction of our inner drives. The ego is associated with reason, while the id belongs to the passions.

The fundamental problem with the ego is its perception of separateness. The ego never loses that sense of separation. In a sense, the ego is steeped in *shirk*, which is worshipping anything other than God and denying the essential unity of God. *Shirk* is the opposite of the classic Islamic statement of *tawhid*, or unity—*la ilaha illa Allah*, "There is no god but God." That is, there is one God, one Reality underlying the multiplicity of perceived reality.

I believe there are two fundamental, opposing processes in evolution: movement toward separation and movement toward unity. In the process of separation, the ego develops, and we deepen our sense of being a distinct individual in the world. Hence the ego is a force within us that operates to keep us from developing a sense of unity. We always have two choices: moving toward separation or moving toward unity. Once we move toward separation, we get further and further away from Truth. As Rumi has written, a broken mirror reflects hundreds of images of the same scene, but if we could repair the mirror it would reflect only a single image. Sufism provides treatment to mend our broken hearts, which are Rumi's broken mirrors.

Once a young dervish was sitting in his Sufi lodge, listening to his sheikh. The man who had collected everyone's shoes as they entered the lodge came into the room with a single sandal in his hand. He said, "I can't find the other one. The other sandal seems to have disappeared."

The young dervish jumped up and exclaimed, "That's *my* sandal! Where is the other one? Who took it?"

The sheikh said, gently but firmly, "My son, perhaps you should leave us. There is no room in this business of ours for *me* and *mine*."

Ego processes provide powerful tools to help us survive in the world, but we have to overcome its limitations. Unfortunately, most human beings remain stuck in an ego-based sense of separateness. Their lives are rooted in the perspective of *me* and *mine*. In Sufism, traditionally we do not use words such as *me* and *mine*, because these words reinforce our ego's sense of separateness.

The opposing fundamental process—the movement that leads us toward unity—is based on love. The capacity for love grows with the development of the *human soul*. Human infants require more care for a longer period of time than the young of any other species, so more love is required of us. My sheikhs have taught that our capacity to love is rooted in God's love for us. Like other forms of energy, love moves from the place of greatest concentration (God) to areas of lesser concentration (creation). Our children nourish our capacity for love. I believe that God designed the human family as a place in which we learn to love, a place in which human beings develop. God created families and communities for all humanity, and also for the animals and birds. "There is no animal on earth, nor yet a bird on the wing, but forms communities like you." (6:38, Cleary) We all grow up in a family. For some people it is an extended family, for some a single-parent family; but the family has been fundamental to human development throughout human history.

As we learn to love, we begin to overcome our narcissism; we begin to put others' needs before our own. For many of us, learning to put others first does not occur until we fall in love or until we become parents. I often think that having children is God's version of shock therapy, designed to cure us of focusing solely on ourselves. After the birth of a child, fathers and mothers who love to sleep all night suddenly find themselves getting up every few hours. Their lives begin to revolve around their child, and they take great joy in it. (Unfortunately, there are still many immature parents who see their children mainly in terms of gratifying their own egos. Tragically, their children generally become insecure, wounded adults.)

Ideally, children grow up in loving families, surrounded by care, support, and nurturing. Spiritual seekers grow in spiritual communities, which—again, *ideally*—are like healthy families. Throughout the world, the model for a spiritual community has been the family. This includes the monastery in Christianity, the ashram in India, the Zen temple in Japan, and the Sufi centers throughout the Islamic world.

The teacher is the father or mother. The word "abbot," for example, comes from *abba*, or father (in Greek and Aramaic). A common term for a Sufi teacher is *baba*, which also means father. The ideal of a spiritual community is to create a healthy spiritual family that will continue the development process of becoming a mature human being.

I think there is often too much focus on the sheikh in Sufism. Our relationship with our sheikh is important, but so is our relationship with all the members of our Sufi family. Our community is a place to develop our capacity to serve, love, and learn from each other. The relationship between sheikh and dervish is our most important single relationship in Sufism, but we can all learn a tremendous amount from our brother and sister dervishes as well.

We are here to serve, learn from, learn to be patient with, and love each other in spite of our faults. In fact, as dervishes we are taught to see the good in each other, not the faults. God did not make any of us perfect. It would be easy if we never made any mistakes, but then, any idiot can love a perfect person. The challenge is to deal with those who are less than perfect—that is, all of us.

Our capacity for love is greater than any other species, but so is our capacity for egotism, narcissism, and separation from God. And so we can rise higher than the angels or sink lower than the animals.

Animals are less separate from God than many humans are, because they do not have a clever ego telling them how unique they are. They cannot descend to the levels of self-centered human narcissism.

As we grow up, both these forces in us increase. In a nurturing, loving environment, our capacity for love develops at the same time our ego develops. The force of separateness and the force of unity both become stronger. These two great forces are far larger than we are. They are not simply personal tendencies within us. They are evolutionary forces, and both forces are active within each of us today. Rumi graphically described the human condition when he wrote that, in creating human beings, God tied an angel's wing to a donkey's tail in hopes that the angelic would transform the animal.

We can act from selfish motivations or out of love and service. We may start from a place of love and service and unconsciously lose sight of our original intentions. We have all experienced this. All too often, our best intentions become hijacked by our egos.

We may not realize that we have forgotten our original intention until it is too late. In my own field, education, I have seen many instructors enter the teaching profession because they want to teach— they love their subject matter and want to contribute to their chosen field and serve their students. However, many teachers forget their initial motivations over the years. Their classes become a duty instead of a joy, and they have no nourishing connection with their students. They have forgotten their intentions for teaching and only go through the motions. Some may eventually realize they have been living a lie, thinking they are dedicated teachers when in fact they have forgotten their love of teaching and their desire to serve students.

In many ways, our whole university system has institutionalized this failure to stay true to our intentions. In most universities, teaching is barely given lip service. Faculty members are promoted on the basis of research and publications, and most university administrators have never taught. When academic administrators do not understand good teaching, their decisions are likely to weaken the teaching process instead of strengthening it. And yet, universities and their faculties still cling to the myth that they are bastions of learning and teaching. It would be far more honest to call them *educational factories,* designed to turn out thousands of graduates a year.

The ego is always working, trying to get us to forget our intentions of love and service and to act instead out of egotism and self-service. The essence of the ego is selfishness. The *nafs* might best be called the narcissistic ego. There is certainly a wide variety of meanings of the term *ego,* but when we say *narcissistic ego,* the meaning is clear. This force is continually pushing us to act selfishly. As I mentioned earlier, in the Qur'an the prophet Joseph‡ says, "I do not declare my soul [*nafs*] innocent: the soul ever urges to evil, except when my Lord shows mercy." (12:53, Khalidi) This force within us compels us, drives us toward evil. It is harmful to us and to others.

This force is one of the basic challenges of the human condition. We must rise from conditional caring to unconditional caring and from selfishness to service. Can I love you even if you don't do what I want?

If we were perfect, we would not need this path. More than anything else, Sufism is medicine for our imperfections. Show me a "perfect" sheikh or dervish and I will show you a hypocrite pretending perfection. Even the great saints were not perfect.

We are here to forgive and learn from each other when we make mistakes. If another's faults really bother us, it is probably because they remind us of our own faults. The Prophet§ taught, "The believer is the mirror of the believer."[3] That is, we can see in another believer our own best qualities—faith, love, devotion, sincerity, etc. However, we can also see our faults in others, and it may be more useful at times to see in others the negative qualities we cannot clearly see in ourselves. If we look at a mirror we may see some dirt on our nose, which will motivate us to wash it off. Without a mirror we won't know the dirt is there. So a mirror can be invaluable.

A mirror provides a way for us to see ourselves; it is also a means for learning from each other's mistakes. There is probably no mistake anyone else has made that we have not made ourselves or been tempted to make, but we hate to admit that. Most of us think we only make minor mistakes. Certainly we would never make the kinds of mistakes some others make! As a result we become heedless, unconscious of what we are actually saying and doing.

Our egos may try another trick by claiming our mistakes are even worse than those of anyone else. We are actually boasting that we are *better* than anyone else—better at making mistakes, better at being imperfect. By giving ourselves this kind of undeserved credit, we avoid change. After all, if I am so much worse than anyone else, how can I possibly hope to change?

In a sense, the family and the Sufi community are laboratories meant to teach us to love. In our community, we are recreating the family, which God created millennia ago, so that we might learn to grow, love, be patient, and forgive. A Sufi community is a spiritual family in which we feel safe enough to risk changing and growing.

The well-known psychologist Carl Rogers pointed out that growth only occurs under conditions of psychological safety. We all need to feel loved and accepted. Rogers stressed that the most important element in any successful counseling or therapy is *unconditional positive regard* by the counselor for the client. As dervishes, we have to learn to care for others unconditionally. As noted earlier, our capacity *to* love comes from *being* loved. Our model is our sheikh. A mother or father does not cease to love her or his children when they misbehave. So too, the sheikh loves us despite our faults.

Muzaffer Efendi was once visited by two American psychiatrists, who asked him how he worked with dervishes. He replied, "When someone comes, we look at them. Everyone, no matter how bad his or her actions and attributes might be, has at least one worthy point. We find that point and build on it. The rest takes care of itself."

Most of our caring is not real love; it is horse-trading. "I love you because you are handsome or beautiful." "I love you because you do things for me, and the more you do for me the more I love you." That is not unconditional love.

Unfortunately, some parents only love their children *conditionally.* These children quickly learn that they only experience love when they are charming, successful at sports, or good at school. They learn that they are only loved for their achievement—that they are not inherently loveable. We have to let our children know that we love them no matter what. We may disagree with their choices, we may get angry with them, or we may have to forcibly stop them from doing something harmful. But ideally we never stop loving them, and they should know that.

I hope we feel unconditional love and caring here in our Sufi community. No matter what happens, I hope we love and care for each other and can forgive each other's mistakes unconditionally. If we cannot do this, we have not developed out of our childlike narcissism, that position of separation from everyone else and concern only for oneself.

This path is a struggle. We have to keep going back to our original intentions; we have to examine our relationships with others and keep reevaluating them. Our Sufi community is a laboratory, a place to try to overcome our tendencies toward selfishness. Even if most of us forget to make this effort, hopefully someone will remember. And, please God, the one who remembers will wake the others up. This is one of the functions of a spiritual community. Some people remember, and they can be the mirror of the believer, reflecting faith, love, and service. Their example helps us resist our tendencies toward separation and ego gratification.

To return the larger evolutionary scheme, we grow from the mineral to vegetable to animal, then to the prehuman or egoic. The soul at each of these stages is tied to the physical body. With the development of the *human soul*, we go beyond the physical. The human soul is located in the *qalb*, the spiritual heart. This is the level of the full development of unselfish love, compassion, and mercy. Love exists in a more basic form in the animal soul, in the love and caring animals have for their offspring. Love and compassion are more completely developed in the human soul, in mature human beings.

The physically rooted souls do not go with us when we leave this world. The animal soul is located in the physical heart, and that physical heart does not survive death. What is located in the skeleton will be buried with the skeleton. What is located in the brain will be buried with the brain. But what is located in the spiritual heart cannot be buried, because the spiritual heart is not a physical organ.

The saints have developed themselves so that they pass easily to the next world. But those who completely invest themselves in the earlier levels of functioning are tied to the body, which is mortal and will end up in a box in the ground. We become so attached to our bodies that we are fearful because they will not last. If instead we become attached to our hearts and souls, we will begin to lose our fear of death.

Our human development involves the growth of love, of unconditional love, and service, and love of God. We never fully achieve this. We only work toward it.

Beyond the human soul is the *angelic soul*. The angels are in constant prayer, in constant Remembrance of God. Deep in our spiritual hearts, we all have angelic souls. We have the potential to live in constant remembrance, at the level of the greatest saints and prophets.

The seventh and final level is the *sultan soul* (also called the *royal soul* or the *secret of secrets*). At this level there is no dualism. Even at the level of the angelic soul, there is a distinction between the one re-membering and the One who is remembered. In the final stage, there is unity; there is no *I* anymore. That transcendent soul is within us as well. Muzaffer Efendi used to say there is a spark in us that is a spark of God, a spark of the infinite. This spark within us transcends this universe and could instantly set the whole of Creation afire.

It is important for us to remember that God breathed this spark of the divine soul into us, to know God is present at the core of our being. Can we connect with this deepest part of ourselves? Can we begin to unveil the Divine within us? Not by ourselves. Only by God's blessing can we begin to get even a tiny glimpse.

In our community, we are attempting to develop ourselves toward the level of becoming mature human beings, as God wishes us to be. Our Sufi community is a laboratory for developing in ourselves that which is eternal, that which goes with us into the next life. My sheikhs said that we are in this world to prepare for the next.

Zikrullah means Remembrance of God. We practice the Sufi cer-emony of *zikrullah* every week, singing and chanting God's names together. The ceremony gives us a taste of these higher souls. How-ever, if we have many wonderful experiences of *zikrullah* but have not developed love and service, the experiences will dissipate, like milk poured into a bucket that has a hole in the bottom. A loving life filled with service is very important on this path. As we learn to become less selfish and more loving, the vessel of our consciousness becomes less leaky. In time we can hold on to the inspiration of prayer and maintain the joy of *zikr*.

To use a different metaphor, at first it is as though we are a bat-tery that cannot hold a charge. We keep "charging" ourselves with spiritual practices, but the spiritual energy never lasts. Life becomes a succession of spiritual peaks and valleys, because the high points cannot be sustained. Tosun Efendi explained that someone is only ready to become a sheikh when they have developed the capacity to hold a spiritual "charge." A sheikh is someone who can also "recharge" others.

Our job is to become whole. When we are whole, we can hold a charge. We no longer dissipate our spirituality in the distractions of daily life. We learn to maintain our state of remembrance and inspiration, until eventually we can inspire others. Until that point is reached, we are always in need; we keep running to our spiritual teachers and spiritual practices to get recharged and re-inspired. But we cannot hold it, so we run back again. It becomes a kind of spiritual addiction.

Some people practice "guru hopping." They run to a teacher, devote themselves to a particular practice, then they become disappointed in their lack of progress. They run to another teacher and another practice. They will always be frustrated. They do not realize that they are making no spiritual progress because they have never developed the capacity to hold a spiritual charge. No system works for them, and hopping from system to system guarantees that nothing will work to change them. Growth requires patience and heedfulness. Our current head sheikh, Tuğrul Efendi, asked a group of European dervishes, "What is the beginning of the path?" When no one answered, he said, "It is listening." Then he asked, "What is the end of the path?" No one could answer, and he said, "It is listening."

How can we become capable of "holding a charge"? By loving and nurturing each other, by developing simple, homely acts of service in our daily lives. To switch back to the earlier metaphor, it may be more dramatic to take one's bucket and travel halfway around the world to get holy water from the Ganges or the holy well of Zamzam in Mecca (which is located beside the Kaaba, the focus of all Muslim prayer). But in order for that to do any good, we first have to heal the cracks and holes in our bucket. The holiest waters will leak out unless our bucket is whole.

So we start at home. Many of us have gone to Mecca and returned with containers full of Zamzam water, as well as the wonderful inspiration that comes from being in a holy place. Then, all too soon, our experience begins to fade. This is one level of meaning of the *hadith*, the teaching of Hazreti Muhammad§, "Some people fast and all they get is hunger. Some people travel to Mecca and all they get is tourism."

In Sufism we begin by developing a stable, solid everyday life, a life of honesty, compassion, and service. Then we will become able to hold on to our spiritual experiences. The solution is not to go to a bigger waterfall, study with a "holier" teacher, or adopt a "better" practice. That is not going to do it. There are thousands of students out there who suffer from this misconception. They are focused on what they can take in without thinking about their capacity to hold it.

Muzaffer Efendi used to say some sheikhs are like Niagara Falls and other sheikhs are like a dripping faucet. And some students have only a small cup, while others have a bucket or even a barrel. But the important thing is to take our cup or bucket or barrel, make sure it is whole, and keep it under a source of water until it is full. If our bucket is intact, it will fill up eventually. If we run to Niagara Falls, we may enjoy the drama of the huge rush of water. However, little of that water may get into our vessels. If we try to fill a cup with a fire hose, almost all the water will spill over. The experience may be very exciting, but it does not do much in the long run.

Our path requires patience. It is a long-term process. Of course, we could all stay up all night several times a week and do special practices for hours on end. But these things do not work in the long run. In fact, they tend to feed the ego. Of course, it is a wonderful blessing to do more, to stay up all night once in a while and perform extra worship. But it should be in a context of patience. And we should always remember that if we do grow and develop, it is not so much because of our own efforts, but because of God's Grace.

▶ 4 ◀

Our Hearts Are Mirrors

azreti Mohammad§ said, "Everything in the world that rusts has a polish, and the polish for the heart is Remembrance."[1] Remembrance is the medicine that keeps our hearts healthy.

The Sufi saint 'Abd al-Qadir Al-Jilani wrote, "Your heart is a polished mirror. You must wipe it clean of the veil of dust which has gathered upon it, because it is destined to reflect the light of divine secrets."[2] The function of a mirror is to reflect something. What do our hearts reflect? What is "the light of divine secrets"?

A "Polished" Heart

In the *Mathnawi*, Rumi tells of a great art competition. Two teams of artists were the finalists. The team from China created the most exquisite art, combining intricate designs and detailed miniatures. The artists from Greece created artwork that was simple but elegant. (In some ways this story reflects the Muslim love of Greek philosophy and thought. Many Muslim scholars studied the Greek philosophy and were especially fond of Aristotle, whose works were translated into Arabic in the ninth century.)

The two groups were each given a palace wall, facing each other, on which to paint their masterpieces. The Chinese artists filled their wall with the most incredibly rich and complex art. They kept asking for more gold leaf, gems, and rare pigments for their artwork. The Greeks put a curtain in front of their wall. Instead of gems and fancy pigments, the Greek artists asked for sandpaper, pumice stone, and other cleaning agents.

Finally, the sultan came to judge their art. He first viewed the Chinese artists' wall. They had created an absolutely exquisite masterpiece. The whole wall was alive with sparkling scenery, animals and plants, water and mountains. It was breathtakingly beautiful. The sultan exclaimed, "This is exquisite. I've never seen anything as beautiful."

Then the Greeks took down the curtain in front of their wall. There was nothing on the wall, but the wall was so perfectly polished that it reflected the art of the other wall. Somehow this reflection was even more exquisite than the original.

This story illustrates the importance of polishing ourselves to remove inner dust and dirt. We usually emphasize *adding* things—accumulating more, doing more, applying more paint to the wall, gilding the lily. The Greek artists in this story remind us that we can instead strive to cleanse ourselves so our hearts become pristine, perfect mirrors. There is nothing more beautiful than hearts that reflect God's Presence.

A mind that has become a perfect mirror has been also described as a lake that is absolutely still. Any reflection in that lake is perfect, but if you drop a single pebble in the lake the reflection becomes distorted. To be a perfect mirror requires inner stillness and calm.

Can our hearts become that calm? Can we be in the world without attachment to our own agendas and preconceptions? Can our calm hearts reflect accurately whatever is in front of us?

According to an old saying, "The dervish is the child of the moment." If we could be truly in the moment, our hearts would become flawless mirrors. But it is not easy to be without expectations, without desires, without attachments to our beliefs and opinions.

Heart Connections

If our hearts are clear, we can truly understand others. We can develop heart connections with others. In Sufism we often talk about the *rabita al kalb*, the connection of the heart, an essential element in the relationship of dervish and sheikh.

Heart connections develop from love and caring. On our path we seek to develop a compassionate heart, one that can empathize with the hearts of others. Our hearts are usually distracted with thoughts of the past and expectations of the future. They are filled with all the things we desire; there is no room for compassion or even for love of God.

We can remember God throughout the day by keeping in mind that God is in the hearts of everyone we encounter. When we know this, interacting with others is not a distraction from remembering God, but a practice of remembrance.

This practice deepens when we think of serving others and having compassion and respect for them. My sheikh used to say, "Always respect others. If you are with someone older than you are, respect them because they have had more time to pray. And respect those who are younger than you because they've had less time to sin."

In other words, we should always assume that others are better than we are. That is an excellent practice, but it is not an easy one. We tend to do the opposite. Our *nafs* insists that we are better than everyone else. We say to ourselves, "Well, they're not as old as I am. I'm sure they aren't as smart or as spiritual as I am." Or, "They're older than I am, and I'll bet they have sinned more." Our egos do this all the time.

But to be a dervish is to serve others, to remember that their hearts are divine mirrors and that there is a spark of God in their hearts. If we love and respect others, we will also be able to learn from them.

Our love for others is the foundation for our love of God. Seeing God in others is the daily polishing of the heart that is Remembrance of God.

If a TV screen shows the same static picture on the screen for a long while, that image will become burned into the screen. Then, that image will overlay everything else. Similarly, if we can keep the image of God in our hearts, this image will overlay everything else.

The more God's image becomes ingrained in our hearts, the more our hearts reflect divine light from everything around us and our remembrance becomes automatic. According to an old Turkish Sufi saying, "First you do the *zikrullah*, then the *zikrullah* does you, and then there is only the *zikrullah*." First, we must use our will to remember God. Then, remembrance goes on by itself. It has a life of its own, and the mirrors of our hearts become filled with the image of God. If our hearts only reflect God, that image deepens. Finally, the mirrors of our hearts come to reflect God constantly, in all circumstances.

Heart Lessons

The word *mirror* has an interesting connotation in English. To mirror another is to imitate them. We can mirror another's movements, language, or posture. That is one of the most important ways we learn—from observing others. How does a child learn language? By mirroring the way his or her parents speak. Within a few months after birth, children begin to babble in the sounds of their parents' language. The babbling of a French child is different than the babbling of an American child or the babbling of a Japanese or an Arab child.[3]

It is important to choose carefully whom we are mirroring. We need to mirror what is best in the world around us, to find inspiring role models. That is why most dervishes traditionally lived in a Sufi center with other dervishes and their sheikhs. New dervishes lived in an atmosphere where positive spiritual qualities were mirrored in everyone around them. They learned almost automatically from their elders. We have a greater challenge today, because we don't live together any more. It is harder to find inspiring role models.

Ideally, we will mirror the believer in others, imitate those who inspire our development as dervishes and as human beings. It is easy to look around us and criticize one dervish for being short-tempered, another for being lazy, etc. It is much better to focus on the best in others: the beautiful voice of one dervish, the patience of another, and so on.

Our hearts reflect what we see and hear and how we think and feel. It is important to consider what we are putting into our hearts. What habits of the heart are we developing?

We can leave the driest firewood in the sun and it will not catch fire. However, if we use a mirror to focus the rays of the sun, the wood may catch fire. For us that mirror is the one who can help our souls catch fire, who can intensify God's Light so that it will transform us.

How can we allow that divine energy to transform us? Any sincere believer can be the mirror that helps our souls come alive. We can learn a tremendous amount from those around us, especially the senior dervishes. But anyone can teach us, because God is present in every heart.

There is a blessing in learning to relate from the heart. We can ask ourselves, "Can I turn the mirror of my heart into a mirror that can reflect the other, that can connect deeply with the other?" That intention can transform us.

CHAPTER 4

Conscious Conversations

Most conversations are extremely superficial. Most people barely listen to the words others speak. But our conversations can be much deeper; they can include more silence and reflection.

One of my Japanese graduate students commented on the poor quality of conversations in the United States. "In Japan, we would never step on the end of someone else's sentence. After someone else has stopped speaking, we take at least a few breaths before we speak. Those who are truly polite wait for five breaths." That kind of pause gives each speaker a sense that we have truly listened to him or her. It gives us a chance to listen more deeply.

We can learn to take time to listen. We can also ask ourselves, "What is the heart connection here? How can my heart *feel* what has been said? Can my heart relate to the other person's heart?" All too often, our heads are full of our own thoughts, and we are just waiting for others to finish speaking so we can make our own speech. Then there's no real connection, just a poor imitation of real conversation.

These imitation conversations are like two monologists appearing together on stage. One person goes through his or her monologue, while the other is busy rehearsing his or her own lines. As a result, the two monologues have almost nothing to do with each other.

A real dervish listens with the heart. A tremendous amount of information lies beyond the spoken words. If we listen sincerely and compassionately, our conversations will become far deeper and more meaningful.

Even intelligent people find it difficult to have a real conversation. I often think of one couple I counseled. Both husband and wife were CEOs of companies they had founded. They were very intelligent, successful people who had a good marriage. However, for months they kept repeating the same argument. She wanted to go to Europe

44

that summer, and he was worried about the cost of the trip. Neither one really listened to the other. She would assert, "I really want to go to Europe." He would respond, "I'm afraid we may not have enough money to go to Europe."

I used the simplest communication techniques with them. I said, "What we are going to do is slow everything down. I want each of you to repeat what the other one says."

The wife began, "Look, I really want to go to Europe this summer. We can use a vacation, and I think we should go to Sweden [he was Swedish] and visit your hometown. It would be good for us to get away. I also want to go to Paris . . ."

I said to the husband, "Okay, now repeat what she said."

He said, "Let's see, you said you want to go to Europe and we could go to my hometown." Although he is a very smart, successful man, he remembered only a fraction of what she said.

Then I said to the wife, "Okay, did he get it?"

She replied, "No."

I told her to repeat half of what she had just said, and then he could repeat her points back one by one.

Then I said to the husband, "Okay, now what do *you* want to say?"

He said, "I'm really worried about our financial situation. My company has a cash flow problem right now, and we don't have nearly as much money in the bank as I would like."

It took some time for the wife to repeat what he said. I kept the conversation going, slowly, until at one point she exclaimed, "Oh. You're really worried about our financial situation. You're *not* saying you don't want to go to Europe!"

He replied, "No, I never said I don't want to go to Europe. I've always said that I'm worried about our financial situation."

Finally, the husband said, "Yes, I'd really like to go to Europe."

"You'd *like* to go to Europe?"

"Yes! But I'm worried about money."

"I'm concerned about money, too. You know I am financially responsible."

"I just thought you wanted to go to Europe without even considering our financial situation."

"No, I would never do that."

Eventually the husband said, "Well, you know, if we can accumulate $5,000 in savings, I think we can go without any problems."

"Oh! Well. That makes sense. Sure, terrific. If we can put together $5,000, then we'll go."

"Yes, absolutely."

"Oh, that's terrific!"

This was the resolution of six months of miscommunication. We accomplished it in less than half an hour. All I did was to slow their conversation down and make sure they actually listened to and understand each other. This is what I mean about being heedless and unconscious. Until I intervened, neither had truly heard the other. And these are very intelligent people in a happy, long-term relationship. We all get stuck like this from time to time.

It does take work to communicate well. One of the fundamentals of good communication is being aware and not allowing our thoughts or projections to get in the way. Also, we have to let go of our attachment to our own opinions so we can hear what the other person is saying. That doesn't mean giving up our opinions; it just means giving up our attachment to them.

Our work is to become Sufis, Muslims, mature human beings. It's not that exotic. It means having normal conversations and good communication. However, good communication is not common. Real conversations, in which both parties are present and there is a connection of the heart, are all too rare.

To be more conscious, we need to slow things down, become more aware, and become present in our hearts. Both head and heart are necessary. Some people are very emotional; they are emotionally available, but it is hard for them to respond with intellectual clarity. Others may be able to carry on a complex intellectual conversation but find it difficult to respond emotionally. We really need both thought and feeling; we need head *and* heart.

Heartfelt Service

According to an old Sufi saying, "A person who can properly serve a glass of tea can do anything." In other words, if we can serve someone really well, even in something as simple as pouring a glass of tea, we can accomplish whatever we set out to do. The simplest things in our everyday lives can be part of our spiritual discipline if we act with open, aware hearts.

Sufi teachers say, "Listen with the ears of the heart. See with the eyes of the heart." What does this mean? Working with the heart includes becoming aware of what is going on within us—our thoughts, our agendas, our worries—when we are with someone else. Ideally, we can reduce these inner distractions and become more present, more empathetic, and more connected in all our interactions. This in turn helps us become more present and heartfelt in our prayers and our *zikr*. We are building habits of the heart, habits of attention that form the foundation of the discipline of Sufism.

The secular and the sacred are not separate. There is no everyday life apart from our spiritual lives. They really are one and the same, and each builds upon the other. Unless our daily lives become an integral part of our spiritual practice, our growth on this path will be very slow. We are seeking to be more heedful and present to each other *and* to be heedful of and present to God in worship. If we are not present with a friend or a loved one, how can we be present when we worship God? It's that simple.

If our hearts are perfect mirrors, we will know what someone wants before they know themselves. We'll know what they need and can provide it—not after they ask us for it, but before they can even name it. That really is our goal. If we could be that way, we'd be real dervishes.

Then the whole quality of our being in the world, of our interacting with people, would be different. Everyone would say to us, "There is something special about you. Why do I feel so different around you?" Then we will know this path has worked. And more people will come to our center, and we'll be able to model for them this way of being. Ideally, that is how Sufism grows.

What is our experience of the heart? What does it mean when we say the heart "opens" or "closes"? What experiences open or close the heart? We must figure this out for ourselves. The wise words of those who know are merely hints and guides in our own self-exploration. As an old Zen master once said, "Teaching is but a finger pointing at the moon. Do not confuse the finger with the moon."[4]

The following section is taken from a question-and-answer session, which is often part of a sohbet. The interchanges between students and sheikh provide another perspective on the dynamics of Sufi teachings.

QUESTION:

Baba,[5] I'm trying to be genuine in my heart and loving, and I try so hard, but outside of the group of Sufis, how should I deal with negative energy? Because sometimes I feel people think that I'm stupid, or I can sometimes feel like people are thinking, "What's wrong with him?" How do I deal with society?

ANSWER:

First, let's look at how to deal with people saying you're stupid or you're different. We can say, "Yes, you are absolutely right. Honestly, I'm not as smart as I like to think I am. Yes, I really am different. Thank you for reminding me." Thank that person sincerely, because she or he is the enemy of your ego. My sheikhs say that praise feeds our ego and criticism weakens it. So we should be grateful to those who criticize us and suspicious of those who praise us.

According to an old Arab proverb, "The friend of my enemy is my enemy, and the enemy of my enemy is my friend." The friends of our egos are those who admire us, who ignore our faults and make us even more proud and arrogant. The enemies of our egos are those who criticize our mistakes, who keep us from becoming inflated with ourselves.

If people tell us we are stupid, they are right! We say and do stupid things. But our egos hypnotize us into thinking that we are not stupid, that we never make mistakes. Our ego gets us very upset if anybody dares to tell us we have so much as a smudge on our nose. Instead of looking at the mirror to see if there's a smudge, we become upset.

The old sheikhs used to say, "People will think you are peculiar when you follow this path." We have to get beyond caring. Old friends may find us boring or eccentric because we are no longer like them. It is like an ant moving into the wrong anthill; the other ants can sense the difference. People will feel that we are strange if we are no longer motivated by money, pleasure, or fame. Underneath their criticism may also be the thought, "I would like to be like you, but it scares me to death to change."

When others are critical of us, we can try to listen from our hearts and not become upset. The only thing that gets disturbed by criticism is our ego. However, to avoid becoming disturbed is not easy to do. I still get caught. We all do.

We have to expect criticism or even jealousy from time to time. The question is how to deal with it. It is a wonderful and demanding practice to keep on loving others when they are critical of us. That's a real challenge. Can we still keep our hearts open? Can we still feel connected to our critics? It is easy to feel a lovely heart connection when others are nice to us. It is a real test if they are angry or critical.

How sincere are we if we like others when they smile at us and reject them when they criticize us? Are we kind and caring only when we are rewarded by smiles and praise? That is not sincere love or compassion.

Learning to control our reactions to criticism is a real success, even if we still feel negative or defensive inside. We can say to ourselves, "Well, I wasn't perfect this time. I wish I had been, but I got caught by my ego." Developing such an attitude is difficult. It is very hard to accept being criticized. We really want to be loved and admired by everybody—or rather, our egos do. We think we deserve respect and love and admiration, regardless of our imperfections.

Tosun Efendi has said, "The person who is not intelligent is the one who always brags about their intelligence, and the person who is not particularly beautiful is the one who thinks they look like a movie star." If someone says to another person, "You're not very intelligent," an intelligent person will reply, "You're right. I'm not as intelligent as I'd like to be, but I'm working hard to improve." Or, "I know quite a bit about a few things, but there is so much more I don't know." Intelligent people are not that invested in their reputations for intelligence. But those who aren't very smart become upset if someone says, "You're not so clever."

Every interaction provides an opportunity to maintain an openhearted relationship. Having our hearts open does not mean we agree with everything others say. We can disagree with others and still love the Divine within them. Our egos almost always get upset when someone disagrees with us. When that happens, we can work on humility by reminding ourselves that we might be wrong, that we have made mistakes in the past and are likely to make more mistakes in the future.

We can remain present and not lose our connection with others, even when they are saying things that are unkind or untrue. Generally, our ego is responding to their ego. Those traits in us that upset somebody else are usually what they don't want to see in themselves.

We can keep asking ourselves, "Can I keep real presence of heart and not shut down and turn away from others?" If we keep turning our hearts away from others, we will become more and more closed-hearted.

The discipline of Sufism is really based on simple, fundamental things like this. Remember the old Sufi saying, "The dervish is the child of the moment." One of our most basic practices is to be present with our hearts open.

QUESTION:

I have a dear friend who is feeling very troubled, and I'm constantly struggling with this because I feel she is seeking negative attention. I very much want to be present with her, but I also want to establish some limits about how available I am. I am having a hard time deciding how to do that well.

ANSWER:

It is difficult to be with someone who wants negative attention. Perhaps they do so because they never got positive attention when they were younger and this behavior is all they know. But it doesn't matter what the cause is. Wanting negative attention is a habit. It is what they do. It's a good idea to set clear limits with them, because you want to help them but not feed their ego.

Some parents spoil their children and fail to set limits. Those of you who are teachers have had to work with unfortunate kids who suffer because their parents spoiled them. These children don't know limits; they also have little willpower because everything has always been done for them. It is very important to set limits in a loving way. This is true with adults as well as children.

We can also try to remember God in difficult interactions like this. We can attempt to keep the image of God in our hearts and trust that God will guide us. In truth, it is God who helps others, not us. At best we are God's instruments. God is the one who shows us truth because God *is* Truth.

Our ego, to the contrary, tells us that we can do everything all ourselves: "I'll say the right thing, and I will heal you!" Or, "I will do the right thing; I will show you the truth." There's a lot of *I* in these sentences. It is helpful to say, "I really don't know" and surrender to Truth. We can learn to say to ourselves, "I don't know, Lord. Guide me in this conversation, because I don't know what to say." We can say, "God, guide my tongue."

We can become better instruments of God if we slow down and become more heart-centered. If we slow down, our words will come from our hearts. Our words usually come straight from our heads. It takes more patience and greater awareness to speak from the heart.

To have heartfelt conversations is to be present and to connect with the other person's heart. It also helps to remember that all hearts mirror God's Truth. The heart is not just an instrument of good communication. (That reduces the heart to psychology.)

Fundamentally, we seek to establish a heart connection and to rely on God to guide our speech. One of my teachers advised, "Lean back on God." To lean back on God means to rely on the One who is far greater than we are instead of relying on solely on our minds and egos. That is everyday *zikr*: the practice of remembering God in daily life.

Remembering God is not simply manipulating our prayer beads and mechanically reciting words in Arabic. How much effect could that have? The kind of heart practice we have been talking about is a very profound form of *zikr*. We are seeking to remember God and to engage that remembrance in our daily lives. When someone speaks of constant, ongoing *zikr*, it doesn't mean saying the names of God throughout the day. It means leaning back on God and allowing God to speak and act through us. We can all learn to allow God's Truth and Wisdom to work through us.

This is a long-term project. We are going to struggle and fail at times, but everything valuable develops through trial and error. When we make mistakes, it is important to forgive ourselves and keep on trying. One of the great tricks of the ego is to say, "Oh, I am doing it badly. I am so terrible. I might as well give it up." This kind of self-criticism stops us from growing. It is much better to say, "Oh, I made a mistake. God, please help me to do better next time." In realizing that we acted badly, we become more aware of what we did; maybe we won't make that mistake in quite the same way again. If we do repeat the mistake, we can say to ourselves, "Oh, that's a habit I want to change. I really need to work on it," not "I'm so bad. I'll never change!" (which is a negative, self-fulfilling prophecy).

We all have bad habits. Simply realizing that truth doesn't make them go away. It takes time and effort to change a habit. An important part of this practice is being patient with ourselves. In

Arabic, the word *sabr* has two important connotations: "patience" and "perseverance." It means to remain calm and relaxed when events proceed slowly or badly. It also means to stick to our goals when progress is slow.

QUESTION:

Baba, how should I behave with someone who is in a position of power in relation to me? It is difficult for me. I was wondering if you had some thoughts about that.

ANSWER:

Most of us find that it is challenging to relate to someone in a position of power over us. In dealing with people who are in a position of authority, it is important to realize how much we project onto them. Start by acknowledging, "I do not see this person as they really are. I see my father or my mother in them, or an old teacher or boss." It is really helpful to do that. If we can't see another accurately, we can't relate to him or her very well.

Also, we want to look good to someone in authority. We should say to ourselves, "I want a relationship of honesty with this person. I will admit to my mistakes; I may even say critical things she or he may not want to hear. My goal is to have an honest relationship with this person, not merely to look good." We can try to be more honest with people in authority and take back some of our projections—to seek to overcome our need to look good to an authority figure. That is all hard, but rewarding, work.

We can take some of the pressure off a relationship with someone of authority if we realize that this relationship can be seen as a very valuable spiritual practice. Our relationship with authority is related to our relationship with God, the Authority upon which all authority rests.

Opening the Heart

The heart is a temple built by God to house the divine spark within each of us. In a saying much beloved by my teacher, God reveals, "I, who cannot fit into all the heavens and earths, fit into the heart of the sincere believer." My master explained that our heart temples are more precious than the holiest shrines and temples on earth. The earthly temples were built by great saints and prophets, but the temple of the heart was built by God to house God.

Many of us have neglected our heart temples. We have also allowed in our hearts the worship of idols, that is, the ephemeral things of this world. We have worshiped worldly success, fame, money, and power. Most of us have spent far more time on these worldly goals than we have in seeking God or in seeking spiritual development. We forget that one meaning of the sacred phrase *la ilaha illa Allah* is "there is nothing worthy of worship but God." Sufism includes cleansing our hearts of the idols we have enshrined there, making our hearts suitable temples for God's Presence

When I first met him, Muzaffer Efendi told me the goal of Sufism is to teach our hearts to pray. It is relatively easy to learn the outer form of prayer. Teaching our hearts to pray takes longer. The outside is always easier than the inside. For example, it is not difficult to make our outsides clean by bathing and putting on clean clothing, but it can be very difficult to cleanse our insides. Our hearts become cleansed through sincere worship, compassionate service, and Remembrance of God.

The heart is a mediator between the outer influences of the world and the spiritual influences within us. Our pride, greed, and negative habits generate fire and smoke that distract us and hide the spiritual light of our hearts. The more we open to our inner light, the more clearly we can see our own negative tendencies—and the more we strengthen our positive and spiritual tendencies.

The Need for Practice

One essential element in the knowledge of the heart is the practice of what we know. Heart knowledge is deepened by experience. Safer Efendi once said, with great humility, "I don't know a great deal about Sufism, but I have loved what I have learned, and I have lived it for over forty years." These are the words of a real Sufi, a real master. Sufism is a lived teaching. A little applied knowledge brings wisdom, whereas too much book learning results in mental and spiritual indigestion.

In the Middle East there are many stories of Nasruddin, a Sufi master who taught with a great deal of humor. Nasruddin clearly distinguishes between the abstract knowledge of the head and the experiential knowledge of the heart in the following story.

Nasruddin was serving as the local judge when a woman came to him with her son and complained that her son had an uncontrollable sweet tooth. She asked Nasruddin to tell the boy to stop eating sweets all the time. Nasruddin told her to bring her son back in four weeks. When they returned he simply said to the son, "Young man, I order you to stop eating sweets!"

The mother asked, "Why did you make us wait for four weeks? Couldn't you have said this to my son when we first came to you?"

Nasruddin answered, "No, I couldn't possibly have said that to your son two weeks ago."

"Why not?" asked the mother.

"You see, I love sweets myself. First I had to control my own love of sweets, and only then could I tell your son to stop." [6]

Our knowledge is not complete unless we act on what we know. Muzaffer Efendi taught that every action affects our hearts: a kind word or helpful act softens and opens our hearts, while a harsh word or harmful act hardens and closes our hearts. Muzaffer Efendi added that our actions also affect the world around us. He said that every kind word causes a rose to bloom, while every harmful word causes a thorn to grow. The more our hearts open, the more we become guided by our inner wisdom and intuition.

When our hearts begin to open, we have greater access to the wisdom of the heart. Then it is essential to *act* on our inner wisdom and insight. It is important that our outer actions are in harmony with the inner process of heart opening, and to achieve such harmony is often a struggle. Even though we know how we should behave, our old habits and tendencies still affect us.

If we could remember that our hearts are divine temples, we would be transformed. We would remember that we are not earthly creatures seeking the spiritual, but spiritual beings seeking to rediscover our own true nature. If we remember that everyone's heart is a divine temple, we can behave toward them with far greater love and caring. This is the foundation for the practice of service. In serving others, we are actually serving the Divine in them. When we remember that the human heart is a holy shrine, we become more compassionate and heedful in all our dealings with others. Honoring the heart in each person is a great spiritual discipline—and a challenge to remember.

Sufism gives us a spiritual context in which we can relate to others, a context based on the fundamental belief that God is within each of us. We can see our own and others' faults in this light. Some people are stingy; others don't keep their word; some have short tempers. But such characteristics do not define who we truly *are*. We all have good and bad habits, but we are not our faults. The habits are temporary; it is the Divine within each of us that is real and eternal. The deeper truth lies in whatever helps us come closer to God, whatever brings out the Divine within us.

Anything that obscures God is not the truth. From this perspective, the popular notion of "sharing" and telling others all our negative thoughts and feelings is absolutely wrong. If we speak about another's faults, we make those faults more real. This affects us as well as the person we are criticizing. It closes our hearts. But if we see the beauty in someone else, we do him or her—and ourselves—a service. For example, if someone has a bad temper and we criticize their temper and how they have hurt others, we harm them and we also harm ourselves. Focusing on their faults harms others because it strengthens those tendencies in them. And when we focus on the negative in others, we also strengthen our own negative tendencies.

Someone's temper may be a fact, but that is not who she or he truly is. The truth is that that person is a soul. The negative traits of the personality can be transformed, and the fundamental truth is that we all yearn for union with the infinite.

As Sufis, we should try not to let our egos get upset by someone else's ego. We have all done this often enough in the past. Sufism teaches us to change how we see ourselves and each other. We must first see the Divine in ourselves. Unless we view ourselves as having God in our own hearts, we will not be able to see others that way.

An Exercise for Opening the Heart

The more aware we are of our hearts, the more our hearts become open and energized. While we are going about our daily business, we can develop the habit of blessing everyone we meet and opening our hearts to everyone.

One of my teachers suggested that we think of our hearts as miniature suns radiating light to everyone and everything we encounter. We can send blessings to the trees and grass around us as well as the people we see. While our heads and our mouths are busy with conversation, we can let the light from our hearts touch and warm the hearts of others. It is as if there is a second, heart-centered interchange going on beneath the actual conversation.

Our heart-suns can touch the heart-suns of everyone we meet. No matter what the other person's personality is like, our hearts are alike. *All* hearts yearn for divine Light.

▸ 5 ◂

Reading God's Books

What was the first scripture God sent to us? What holy book came before the Torah, the Psalms, the Gospels and the Qur'an?

My Sufi teachers have said the first book is Creation, which is filled with God's signs and divine guidance. The Holy Qur'an is filled with spiritual lessons drawn from nature.

The second book is located in our own hearts. God breathed a "divine breath" into Adam and Eve. That is, a spark of the Divine has been given to all humanity, and this divine soul is housed in our heart of hearts. It is the source of divine wisdom within each of us.

Muzaffer Efendi used to say to us, "God placed a divine Book in your heart. Read your book. Look deeply within to understand your inner nature." This is one meaning of the famous *hadith*, "Those who know themselves know their Lord."

After these first two books come the revealed scriptures of all religions. The last of these is the Holy Qur'an. The Holy Qur'an has been called "God's Book" and "the Mother of All Books." In addition to reading the great scriptures, it is important to read the first two books—the book of Creation and the book of our own innermost nature.

It is spiritually nurturing to spend time in nature and open our hearts to the beauties of God's Creation. We cannot exhaust the meaning of a single tree, much less a forest. Nature is an endless source of inspiration and nourishment. But just going outside and walking around is not enough. We have to observe more deeply to read the Book of Creation.

Spend time in nature with the intention of encountering God's Presence, God's beauty in Creation. As God has taught in the Qur'an, "Wherever you turn, there you will see my Face."

I am reminded of the story of Brother Lawrence, a great Christian mystic.[1] He had been a soldier as a young man. After becoming injured in a battle, Lawrence left the army and was on his way home in wintertime. He saw a barren, leafless tree and suddenly realized that life was hidden in the tree, just waiting for God to bring it to life in the spring. He thought to himself, "If God can bring a barren tree to life each year, God can certainly bring *me* back to life as well." Instead of returning home, Lawrence entered a monastery.

Brother Lawrence did not have a living spiritual teacher. God guided him, because he had the capacity to see and hear. Seeing a tree and realizing the miracle of rebirth in the spring was enough to change his life.

Because he had no education, Lawrence could only become a lay brother. He worked all day washing pots and dishes in the monastery kitchen. The monks studied and chanted and prayed all day, while he worked hard in the kitchen. In spite of this—or perhaps because of it—Brother Lawrence developed a profound practice of remembering God's Presence throughout his daily life. Eventually, he found God was with him at all times, whether he was praying in the chapel or washing dishes.

As was true for Brother Lawrence, our lives can become completely transformed by the sight of any of God's signs in nature, or just a single verse from any of God's books. We can also adopt Brother Lawrence's spiritual practice by developing the habit of remembering

God throughout our daily lives. At first we may constantly forget, but slowly we can develop the habit of remembrance.

Because of the divine soul in our hearts, God made humanity God's *halife*, or deputies:

> When your Lord said to the angels, "I will place a deputy on earth," they [the angels] said, "Will You put there one who will cause trouble there, and shed blood? And this while we extol Your praise and we worship You?" God said, "I do know what you do not know." (2:30, Cleary)

And God taught the divine Names to Adam. That is, God taught Adam the essences of all things. As a result, we have the capacity to know both the *zahir* and the *batin*, the outer and inner truths in Creation. The angels did not know the Names, and God instructed them to bow to Adam, to honor him as their teacher because he knew what they did not.

The term *halife* literally means "vice-regent," one who rules in place of someone else. It means that human beings are given authority to serve and administer Creation, not in their own right, but as God's representatives. Similarly, ambassadors and generals have no power in themselves. Their positions give them power, because they act in the name of their nations, not in their own names. An ambassador enjoys tremendous status as the representative of her or his nation, but only as an ambassador, not as a private individual. Generals wield great military power, but only in their role as general. As God's *halife*, we have tremendous power and responsibility, but only if we act in God's name.

Every *sura* in the Qur'an except one begins with the phrase *Bismillah ir-rahman ir-rahim*, "In the Name of God, Most Merciful, Most Compassionate."[2] We have to keep remembering to act in God's name, not in our own name. It means one thing if an ambassador says, "In the name of my country . . ." It means much less if she says, "In my name, Jane Smith . . . " Few people care what Jane Smith has to say as an individual, but when she speaks as an ambassador, her words have great weight.

There once was a wife who was very devout and who always remembered to act in God's name. Before she did anything, she said, *Bismillah ir-rahman ir-rahim.* When she started preparing the food for a meal, she said, *Bismillah ir-rahman ir-rahim.* When she served the food, she said *Bismillah ir-rahman ir-rahim.* Whenever she left the house to go shopping or visiting, she said *Bismillah ir-rahman ir-rahim.*

Her husband got very tired of hearing this all the time. When you are in love with the world, you don't want to be reminded that God is the only Reality. The husband said to himself, "I've got to cure her of this stupid, annoying habit. It is not only annoying, it is primitive and superstitious."

The husband handed a bag of coins to his wife, "I need to invest some of our savings in a business venture. Please take this money and keep it safe; I will need it tomorrow morning." They had a locked strongbox at home, and the wife was in charge of it.

The wife went to the strongbox and said *Bismillah ir-rahman ir-rahim* as she took the key out from a chain around her neck.

With another *Bismillah ir-rahman ir-rahim,* she unlocked the strongbox.

Bismillah ir-rahman ir-rahim —she opened the chest.

Bismillah ir-rahman ir-rahim —she put the bag of coins in the strongbox.

Bismillah ir-rahman ir-rahim —she locked the box.

Bismillah ir-rahman ir-rahim —she replaced the key around her neck.

That night, while the wife was sleeping, the husband took the key from around her neck. He quietly went to the chest and unlocked it—no *Bismillah ir-rahman ir-rahim*, of course. He took out the bag of coins and went outside and dropped the bag down a well. He thought, "that is going to teach her! It is an expensive lesson, but if she finally stops saying *Bismillah ir-rahman ir-rahim* all the time, it will be worth it." Then the husband relocked the chest and put the key back around his wife's neck.

He did not realize that when we sincerely act in God's name, we are not acting in the name of our egos and not just calling on our own power. We make God our partner in any activity we begin by sincerely saying *Bismillah ir-rahman ir-rahim*.

The next morning the husband asked the wife for the money. He reminded her that it was her responsibility to keep it safe.

Bismillah ir-rahman ir-rahim—the wife took the key out from around her neck.

Bismillah ir-rahman ir-rahim—she unlocked the chest.

Bismillah ir-rahman ir-rahim—she lifted up the lid.

Bismillah ir-rahman ir-rahim—she reached in and took out a dripping wet bag of gold. The husband fainted.

Remembrance and Reality

Confronted so directly with the Reality of God, we might faint as well. A profound experience of God's Presence would probably completely disrupt our usual ways of thinking and being. This would happen if we ever entered into a state of real remembrance, which very few people can support. As Sufis we practice *zikrullah,* or Remembrance of God, by chanting God's Names. But experiencing the *Reality* of God is very different. Even the great prophets have fainted when struck with God's Presence because they were overcome by awe.

It is a good reminder. We don't know what real remembrance is. At best we have experienced "remembrance of remembrance." And most of the time, we forget to remember. At best, we see through a glass darkly. This is actually a blessing, because to see clearly would be overwhelming.

We have to work our way up to real remembrance. Our experience of partial remembrance is a way of accustoming ourselves to real mystical states. In a sense we are tuning our nervous systems, gradually developing our capacity to handle more powerful spiritual experiences. It is like strengthening our muscles with daily exercise, or like taking a 25-watt bulb and gradually increasing the current that passes through it, in a way that increases the bulb's capacity to handle higher wattage. Of course, a light bulb cannot develop in this way, but a human being can.

Ideally, as we practice *zikrullah*, we develop our capacity to remember more and more deeply. In some Orders, the dervishes push themselves to have an ecstatic experience in *zikrullah*, even to the point of passing out. In our Order, we do not seek to overload our nervous systems; we try to remain centered and aware of everyone around us, even as our awareness of God deepens.

▸ 6 ◂

Wherever We Turn, There Is God

One of my favorite passages from the Qur'an reads, "Wherever you turn, there is the Face of God." (2:115, Khalidi) God's Presence is everywhere, all around us and within us. The great Sufi sage Fakhruddin 'Iraqi comments that all of Creation mirrors God's infinite Presence. Wherever we turn there is a *reflection* of God. All of Creation is precious, because everything is a mirror that shows a different reflection of God, and these reflections are infinite in number. We can see many different reflections in a room full of mirrors, because the placement of each mirror is different. That is exactly what Creation is. There is one Reality; there is one God, but we keep seeing different reflections, different aspects of that Reality. Then we get confused, thinking the differences are real rather than different reflections of the same truth. Wherever we look, there is God's Face, but God's Presence is different in everything we see and in each person we meet. God is reflected in each sunset, each cloud, everything in Creation.

'Iraqi also writes that we ourselves are a *barzakh*, an isthmus, connecting heaven and earth. In geography, an isthmus is a narrow strip of land connecting two larger land areas, usually with a body of water on each side of it. If we stand on an isthmus, we can see what appear to be different bodies of water on each side of us, but there is really only one body of water. The separation is an illusion. In a similar sense *we* are not real. Our seeming existence divides the ocean, the Unity that is God. If we could dissolve the isthmus, we would realize there is only one ocean. If we could dissolve ourselves, we would realize that everything is God. That is the Unity we are all seeking.

God is Unity, but there is apparent multiplicity in Creation, because each aspect of Creation mirrors that divine Presence. Behind all the apparent differences, there is unity.

Love can separate or unite. We can love in a way that considers only one or two people as loveable and leads us to ignore or devalue everyone else. We can feel that we love a particular person so much that we don't care much for anyone else. In effect, we love one mirror of God, but we reject all the other mirrors. That won't bring us closer to God. Real love is different.

We can love in a way that our hearts become fuller and we become more loving of *everyone*. When we love in this way, the whole world becomes filled with love. Suddenly everybody around us becomes an embodiment of love. That is the love that brings us closer to God.

So loving alone is not enough. How does our love affect us? Does our love open our hearts or does it cause our hearts to close?

We can love in ways that are selfish, jealous, or separating. That kind of love causes us to reject other people. It causes us to try and control the one we love. We love them so much we want them to fit a certain mold. Of course that is not really love at all; it is control. Sometimes we do that with our spouses or children or with others.

On the other hand, there is the love that opens our hearts and leads us to love still more. My sheikhs have taught there is a still deeper kind of love that leads us to efface ourselves. At that level of love, our sense of separateness is in the way, and eventually there is only love. The lover is no longer separate from the Beloved.

'Iraqi describes this kind of love: "There is me and you. I am I and you are you. Then I am you and you are me. And finally I am I and you are you, but I am you." There is a sense of separation, and there is unity as well. We can begin to feel this in our relationship with all of God's Creation. Any loving relationship can lead us back to the Unity underlying Creation.

Unfortunately, our egos move us away from unity into multiplicity. In Latin the word *ego* means "I." This "I" is separate from everything else. It is actually *shirk,* or idolatry, when we assert that we are separate from Creation and exist independently of God. It implies that we don't need God to exist. But are we independent? Do we exist by ourselves in any way, shape, or form? We don't. Can we do anything by ourselves? No, we can't. We are not independent, but our ego says we are.

Caring in Community

In our community, one of our spiritual sisters recently passed away, and her family grieved deeply. They had suffered with her throughout her long struggle with cancer, and we suffered along with them. Tosun Efendi recently said the larger our community, the more we suffer, because the more tragedy there is. Of course, there are good things to celebrate as well, but the suffering stays with us longer. We all have challenges to cope with. We have family problems, job problems, health problems, and the like. It is extremely important to be loving, caring, and compassionate to one another during times of trial. And it is important to remember God in the midst of all this.

We can help and support each other during difficult times, but don't for a moment think that we are going to heal our brothers and sisters. Don't think that our kind words and loving presence will do anything without God's blessings. That is our egos talking. Our egos will say, "*I* will help. No one can help as well as *I* can. No one can say the wise words as well as *I* can say them." Notice the phrase "as well as *I* can." Our egos will make such boasts, but hopefully we don't listen.

When I hear that one of you has preached, "In Sufism you *have* to do this . . ." I get a little angry. It is a mistake to "play sheikh" with each other. Until you get your own *nafs* under control, you have no business giving others advice. Your egos want you to play sheikh. They will tell you it is a wonderful idea, and you will be so much more helpful to others if you take the position of sheikh. Please try not to. You don't *take* the job of sheikh. It is assigned to you.

Some of you love to give advice to your brothers and sisters. I suggest the less advice we give, the better. We have all heard the same talks, read the same books, and studied the same Qur'an. Instead, let's be good role models for each other.

When you are with others, try to remember God. Remember that you are with someone who is a mirror of God's Presence. When you are sitting with a brother or sister, remember there are three of you there—you, your brother or sister, and God. Your job is more to remember God than to do anything else. If you can sit with others remembering God and inviting God's Presence into your conversation, it is far more likely that God will guide you both. God may speak through you or through them; it doesn't matter. Actually, it is much better if God speaks through them and they hear advice in their own voice. That way they are more likely to listen. Or God may move you to say something, and you end up saying something you didn't intend. That is better than *trying* to help. Muzaffer Efendi used to say, "Don't listen to me if I am talking from myself. But if I'm not talking from myself, you definitely should listen."

We need to rely more on God, to have faith in God, and to be present to each other. It is wonderful when we meet with each other and are present as friends and provide a sympathetic ear. It is healing when we really listen to each other. The problem is, our egos don't want us to listen; they want us to talk. Generally, when we need to talk, it probably is not an impulse from God. However, I trust it more when we feel *moved* to speak than when we plan what to say.

The healer of hearts is God, the Guide who can direct our speech and actions is God. The One who give us patience, the Light in the darkness is God.

I am very grateful that we are together and have a real community. It is God's mercy and grace that we do, and it is in spite of our egos, not because of them.

Dark Night of the Soul

When our brothers and sisters are going through difficult times, we should gently reach out to them and let them know that we are available to be with them—to listen—without thinking that they are "projects" that we are going to fix. Sometimes others seem to be struggling. They may be going through a "dark night of the soul," as it is called in the Christian tradition.

In the natural course of our growth, we sometimes go through difficult transitions. Sometimes we need to relearn how to pray; after years of prayer, suddenly praying has become a struggle. We cannot keep our minds on our prayers, or we cannot pray at all. This may be due to our egos, but it may be that we are being called to a deeper understanding of worship, and our old approach to prayer is not enough: more is being asked of us. We don't need help getting out of this kind of struggle. Everything happens in God's time. We must be patient, do what we can, and trust in God's promise that we will not be given a burden greater than we can bear. Sometimes we grieve or go through a process of letting go, emotionally or spiritually. We have to empty ourselves so something new can come in, and emptying can be painful.

I have often told the classic story of the Zen master and the professor. A professor came to visit a Zen master and said, "I have read many books about Zen, and I have some theories about Buddhism and Zen that I want to share with you." The professor began talking about his own ideas regarding the philosophy of Zen, as professors often do. The Zen master poured tea for himself and his visitor.

As the professor continued to talk on and on, the Zen master picked up the teapot again and began pouring tea into the professor's cup, although the professor had not had a moment to drink anything during his monologue. The tea began to spill out onto the table and the professor shouted, "Stop. Stop. Don't you see the cup is full? Nothing more can go in." The Zen master smiled and replied, "It is true. The cup is full and nothing more can go in. You have to empty the cup so that something new can get in."

In our lives, we often have to empty ourselves. Sometimes God takes things away and empties us. This is often a painful experience for us because we are attached to our own habits and opinions. Our egos complain. But the emptying is natural. There has to be an emptying of the old so that we can grow. It is like a snake shedding the skin it has outgrown.

Listening

We all go through suffering and difficulty. I hope we can all be available for each other as sympathetic, loving listeners. I am very happy when I hear that we are doing so for each other. I am less happy when I hear that dervishes are talking more than listening. Tuğrul Efendi has said, "The beginning of the path is listening, and the end of the path is listening."

I strongly recommend that you not try to provide solutions for each other's problems. If a dervish asks you a question, our tradition is to tell him or her to ask the sheikh. Our egos love to "play sheikh," but that is not useful for us or for others.

Underneath all this is remembering God, remembering that God is the guide, the Source of all wisdom. It is also remembering that what we see or hear is just the tip of the iceberg; we don't know what is hidden. We need more humility and compassion and less judgment.

When listening to someone, I suggest we practice "three Ss." We should be *slow*, *silent*, and *simple*.

To be slow is to refrain from rushing to give an answer to another's problems—to wait without jumping to judgments or conclusions. Our egos will almost always come up with clever answers. It is a good practice to resist that and to say, "I don't know." Why do we think we can instantly come up with a brilliant solution to others' problems? We should be a little suspicious of that tendency. It is a sign of our arrogance.

To practice silence is to listen more and speak less. We can practice inner silence by listening deeply without engaging in internal analysis or judgment of what we are hearing.

To practice simplicity means remembering that we don't know all the answers. It means to reserve our judgment and remember that we can never completely know the truth. We may have opinions, but we don't *know* for sure. Instead of arguing for our opinions, we might say, "Have you thought about this? Have you considered other possibilities?"

Practicing simplicity also means praying for others, remembering that all solutions ultimately come from God. Too often we sit with someone, give them our opinions, and then forget to pray about their problems. We have forgotten that help comes from God, not from our advice. Often it is best just to say, "I do not know the answer, but I will pray for you." Our sincere prayers are of more use than our words. Sometimes God does move us to speak and give words of advice, but we should always try to make sure that the advice does not come from our egos. With practice we can learn to distinguish the two. When our ego moves us to speak, we generally feel proud of our understanding and also attached to our opinion. When we are inspired to speak, we are less attached and often surprised at what we have just said.

The love and friendship in our community is priceless. When I talk with our guests and hear their problems, I realize how wonderful it is to have the support of our community. We are very lucky to have one another.

Guarding Against Our Egos

In community we have to guard against the negative influence of our egos. We also have to do this in our prayers, in our relationships, and in everything we do. We can all remember to be slower, more silent, and simpler. We feed our egos when we think we know so much.

Let me give you a priceless spiritual practice. Keep repeating these words: "Only God knows." They contain a wonderful antidote to the arrogance of our egos. We see only the outer surface of things, not the inner nature of things—and we don't always perceive the outer that accurately, either: we see a piece of the outer and we take it for the whole. We are like the blind men and the elephant, making absurd conclusions based on limited experience.

By saying "Only God knows," we remind ourselves we know very little, and all too often we misunderstand the little bit we think we know. But we still fall in love with our own opinions.

Our task as dervishes is to spend time together and love and support one another through our trials and challenges. We can listen more, pray and care for each other, and judge each other less. For whatever we judge or criticize in someone else is in us. Whatever upsets us in someone else is within us. If it were not, we would not be so upset. When someone is arrogant or selfish, we become upset with that person, because we understand selfishness, arrogance, etc.—because those tendencies are in us.

Whenever we become upset by something, it is time to pay attention to ourselves. Our egos tell us to attend only to the faults of others, and we find it easy to become upset with others' shortcomings. But our criticism of others will not change them. It will only distract us from changing ourselves. As Muzaffer Efendi used to say, "Whenever you see dirt in someone else, wash your own glasses." We always see our faults in others.

If we can stop this cycle of projection and blame, we can begin to see each other as mirrors that reflect the Face of God. We can begin to experience the world as a place filled with mirrors that reflect God's Presence. Then everything and everyone around us will remind us of God. That is our work. As we grow on this path, more and more of the world will remind us of God.

Muzaffer Efendi taught that the world is only our spiritual enemy if *we* put it between God and ourselves. The world is our spiritual ally if we see God's Face wherever we turn. God's Face is everywhere; everything mirrors God's Presence, if only we could see it. Everything is beautiful if we have the eyes to see it. Everything is inspiring if our hearts are open and ready to be inspired.

Our Relationship with God

We can understand our relationship with God through the other relationships we have. My sheikhs have taught that everything in this world mirrors the hereafter. We have loving relationships here on earth, especially the relationships between spouses and between parents and children. Some of us also enjoy wonderful relationships with close friends. This should be particularly true in our relationships with our Sufi brothers and sisters. Ideally, these relationships should be as loving as the closest relationships between biological brothers and sisters.

Years ago, I mentioned to Safer Efendi that I would love to write a novel about dervishes. He suggested I write about the search for a true friend, a companion on the Path of Truth. In the old days, travelers needed trusted companions, because travel was very dangerous. There were wild animals, bandits, storms, and other perils of the road. Our journey on the Path of Truth also includes encounters with life-threatening obstacles.

I often thought about Safer Efendi's response: that a novel about Sufism should focus on friendship. True friendship is one of the foundations of Sufism, although it is rarely written about. Think of the famous friendship between Rumi and Shams of Tabriz. Before he met Shams, Rumi was a renowned scholar surrounded by devoted students. Through his friendship with Shams, Rumi became a great sage and a composer of some of the world's most inspiring works of spiritual wisdom and guidance.

We can attempt to practice this kind of friendship. We can be deeply compassionate and loving to our Sufi brothers and sisters, as well as to others. We can cultivate friendships that bring out the very best in ourselves and in our friends.

God is always present with us, but how often are we present with God? We often sandwich our prayers between phone calls and TV programs. The saints have the opposite priorities. They are jealous of the time the world takes from their worship. We can come to value our relationship with God enough that we feel the same.

When we are busy with something we enjoy and a phone call interrupts us, we resent it. We do have our duties in the world, but ideally we will put our relationship with God first. Unfortunately, we are still fascinated by the world. Spiritually, we are still in kindergarten. Sufism is supposed to be a little more advanced. We should be at least in high school, even college!

It helps to read about those who loved God more than anything on earth. I was recently reading about the life of Fakhruddin 'Iraqi, the great Sufi poet and author. He burned with the love of God, and he finally met a wonderful sheikh. His sheikh was very strict, but 'Iraqi was not. 'Iraqi was a poet and a bit of a wild man. The sheikh immediately recognized 'Iraqi's deep love of God. He said to 'Iraqi, "First, make a forty-day retreat. We will begin your dervish training with that." A forty-day retreat was not uncommon in those days. (Before Hazreti Nureddin al Jerrahi, the founder of our Order, began teaching, he made a forty-day retreat.)

A traditional Sufi retreat is done in silence. However, on the second or third day of 'Iraqi's retreat, some of the other dervishes heard him reciting poetry in the retreat room. They ran and told the sheikh that the crazy new dervish was chanting poetry instead of remaining in silence. The sheikh said, "Silence is for you, but not for him." After a few days of solitude, 'Iraqi's heart had begun to overflow. He did not choose to sing and recite poetry; he was unable to contain his love of God.

A week later, the dervishes begin hearing the townspeople singing 'Iraqi's poetry. The sheikh was disturbed by this and went to the retreat room. "My son," he said to 'Iraqi, "how did your poetry get out? Now the people of the town are reciting it."

'Iraqi replied, "I couldn't stop myself. I had to share it."

'Iraqi had left his retreat room, breaking all the rules. But he did it out of love of God. He was lucky enough to have a wise sheikh who understood the outer rules are not as important as love of God. The outer rules are a means to get us there. They are for those of us who don't love God enough. We need rules. 'Iraqi didn't.

It helps to read about the lives and works of people like 'Iraqi who devoted themselves to their relationship with God. Their love of God moved them in whatever they did. Those who truly love God are not afraid of anything in the world, because they only want God. Nothing in this world distracts them.

Here is another story that illustrates the importance of inner intention compared with outer action:

Once, two young men met in the marketplace. One said to the other, "Come with me. There is a Qur'an reading starting soon, and we can go and listen. It will be wonderfully inspiring." The other man said, "No, thank you. I am going to a brothel instead. I want to enjoy myself with the lovely ladies there."

After they went their separate ways, the man who was in the brothel began thinking, "I wish I had gone to the Qur'an recital." In spite of being surrounded by beautiful women, he was thinking of the Qur'an and of God.

At the same time, the other man was sitting at the Qur'an recital thinking, "Why didn't I go with my friend? He is probably having a great time now. I wish I were there sitting with all those lovely women instead of listening to this boring recitation."

Both men died at that moment. When they came to judgment the man who had been in the brothel was let into heaven, while the man who had been at the Qur'an recitation was sent to hell. Their thoughts and desires were more important than where they were or what they were doing. The desire of the one man to hear the Qur'an brought him to heaven. The desire of the other man for pleasure took him to hell.

Do we let our experiences deepen our relationship with God, or do we let our experiences distract us from God? Sufism stresses the goal of making our daily life an integral part of our spiritual practice. We don't have to go to a cave, an ashram, or a monastery. We have to learn to make whatever we are doing a part of our relationship with God.

We can seek God in our hearts and trust that our hearts will find a way to God. Muzaffer Efendi used to ask, "Of the positions of prayer, why does God most love *sajda* (kneeling and touching our foreheads to the ground)?" Maybe it is because our arrogant heads are touching the earth and we are in a position of humility. But my sheikh explained, "It is because it is the only time we put our hearts higher than our heads."

Sufism is about our hearts opening and leading us to God. Our souls are located in our heart of hearts. Our path is meant to lead us more deeply into our hearts. The outer forms of prayer or *zikr* cannot do it. We are easily distracted when we practice just the outer form. But if our hearts are alive with the love of God, we will not be distracted.

How can we spend quality time with God? We want quality time with our friends and family, but all too often we become busy instead of really paying attention to each other. Too many families spend every night in front of the TV. It is even worse today, because we have even more distractions—DVDs, computers, and so on.

We can spend quality time with our families and friends, and this will help us to learn to spend quality time with God. Our family and friends teach us about relationship. How can we apply what we have learned in these relationships to our relationship with our Creator?

Our relationship with God is an eternal one. It began with the covenant between God and every human soul, which occurred before physical Creation. God asked, "'*Am I not your Lord?*' They [the souls] said, 'Oh yes! We bear witness.'" (7:172, Cleary) This relationship will continue until the end of Creation, when we return to God.

If we have developed a beautiful relationship with God, all of our other relationships will be enhanced. Jesus‡ taught, "Love your neighbor as yourself," which means we have to love ourselves, to accept

79

ourselves as we are *even though we are imperfect*, before we can love someone else. Our personalities may be imperfect, but the pure, divine spark in us loves God. We have to develop a relationship with that part of us, the part that yearns for God. This is the foundation for love of ourselves, love of others, and love of God.

We are all lonely without our connection with God. And, in order to avoid our feelings of loneliness, we distract ourselves with TV, work, etc. We don't want to sit with our loneliness. But we have to sit with the loneliness that comes from our separation from God. As Rumi wrote, "The cure for pain is in the pain."[1] We will only overcome the pain of separation by feeling that pain and allowing it to move us closer to God. We have to keep our loneliness alive in us, not distract ourselves from it.

Unfortunately, most of our society is dedicated to distractions. There are the obvious distractions provided by the entertainment industry. But politics and economics are also distractions. We seek power or wealth instead of seeking God.

It is a challenge to remember God in our everyday lives, but we *can* do it. We can remember God while we are working. Each morning we might pray, "O God, please guide me at work today. Guide my hands; guide my tongue. Lord, please speak through me. May I serve your Creation today to the best of my ability."

Everything can be part of our relationship with God. As my sheikh said, don't blame the world. If we choose to allow the world to distract us, it is our own fault. We cannot overcome this distraction by ourselves, however. We need the guidance of teachers and a Sufi community. The outer world becomes our spiritual ally when it reminds us of God, and when we devote ourselves to service, love, and charity. We should not make our busyness an excuse. Muzaffer Efendi taught that if our hands are busy with our duties in the world, we can still keep our hearts busy with God.

God loves us more than anyone in this world can possibly love us. And God's mercy and compassion are infinitely stronger than the greatest love of a mother for her children. When I think of God's love and compassion, I am embarrassed that I forget God so often.

This sohbet *ended with the following question and answer session:*

QUESTION:

If we see someone hurting or criticizing someone else, what shall we do? Should we ignore it or should we intervene? Should we take care of the person whose feelings were hurt? Should we tell our sheikh?

ANSWER:

There is no simple answer to these questions. The issue is too complicated. Every individual is different, and the content of each criticism is different.

Once again, it is important to remember that we don't know, and yet we have to do our best for each other. We must use our judgment if we see someone behave in a way that seems hurtful to themselves or to others. We have to use our intelligence on this path. If any teacher tells you to park your mind and give up your intelligence, run from them.

First, we should pray for both people. We may feel tempted to pray only for the "victim." We feel righteous about criticizing the "wrongdoer" and supporting the underdog. Also, we can offer support for the one who was hurt—*without* saying "Oh, you poor victim." That language encourages others to think of themselves as victims. It does not really help, for it encourages the ego to say what it always wants to say: "I have been victimized."

It is difficult to be slow to judge. It is much easier to decide someone else is wrong. This pleases our egos. As I said earlier, I do not want us to give up our intelligence and judgment. At the same time, we *can* learn to be slow to judge. When we do make a judgment, we should temper it with the thought, "I might be wrong." We can also add, "Only God knows." I believe it is extremely valuable to repeat often, "I might be wrong." When asked for advice—a dervish gives advice only when asked for it—it is better to say, "My best opinion is such and such," and then add, "And only God knows for sure."

So, if there is conflict in our community, pray for those involved. Also, share the episode with your sheikh. And be sure to pray for the one you think is doing wrong and ask God to grant both of you guidance.

We should always take our opinions with a grain of salt. Tosun Efendi once commented, "People always say we should not be too attached to fame, money, or possessions. But that is not the deeper attachment. Our strongest attachments are to our own opinions." We rarely realize how attached we are to our opinions. The antidote is simple: remember God. We can remember God when our relationships are good *and* when they are difficult.

On the other hand, we *do* have to use the intelligence and judgment God gave us. There are some spiritual groups in which members refuse to look at the truth. They believe that everyone in the group is perfectly spiritual or that their teacher is perfect. This can be extremely damaging for everybody involved. I have known several groups in which the followers rationalized their teacher's serious failings. In one group everyone agreed, "Our teacher is only drinking alcohol to stay on the same plane as we are." They refused to admit their teacher was an alcoholic. One student later confessed, "Of course he was an alcoholic. How could I not have known? I lived with alcoholics in my own family, and I know what that looks like. I understand that disease, but I refused even to entertain the thought he was an alcoholic."

Of course, we should not be stupid in that way. If you see someone behaving badly, don't rationalize it or pretend it is not happening. Again, we must not leave our intelligence behind when we enter this path. At the same time, our path involves remembering God and learning to rely on God in all things. Not relying solely on ourselves, on our clever words or judgments.

Can we remember God in good times and in bad? Muzaffer Efendi used to say that God sends us two kinds of tests—success and failure.

Some people forget God when they are successful. They make a lot of money and accumulate expensive possessions, and then they start thinking they are better than everybody else. They think their success is due solely to their own efforts. They may even abandon their spiritual practice at this point. They think, "I don't need to rely on God. I have a good job and money in the bank. I have created a wonderful life, and I can rely on myself."

Loss is also a test. Some people forget God when they lose their jobs, become ill, or have other difficulties. They think, "I am too busy coping to remember God. I'll wait to do my spiritual practice when I feel more secure in the world." They question God. "Where was God when these bad things happened to me?" They forget that this world is filled with loss, pain, illness, and death. Their faith leaves when suffering comes.

When other people are tested, their faith deepens and their remembrance and worship improve. Some people become more generous when they are successful. Some become more compassionate when they suffer. All of our life changes are tests. When our lives change we can still remember God, and when our spiritual brothers and sisters go through crises we can still remember God. We can focus on our own practice of remembrance. Don't tell others to remember God. That is not your job.

The best thing we can do for others is to remember God. Our egos prefer *telling others to remember God* to remembering God ourselves. The ego loves that one. We lecture others on what to do, and we are so busy teaching we are not practicing what we preach. But we can feel so wonderful in thinking that we are spreading the truth.

As a sheikh, I have this problem all the time. I continually talk about what we should do, and I am always struggling to do it myself. I need to listen to my *sohbets* more than you do. If I begin to think I know what I am talking about, it is time for me to quit. Muzaffer Efendi used to say, "If what I am teaching comes from myself, don't trust it. I try to teach only what I have learned from my sheikh, the Qur'an, and the teachings of the saints." I don't trust my ego, and I hope you don't trust yours either.

It is all a wonderful struggle that God has given us. I have to call it a "wonderful struggle." What else can I say? This struggle comes from God. God gave us this inner *jihad.* We might as well embrace this struggle; if we do not we will be defeated and become the slaves of our egos. A sheikh once said, "It is as if we were parachuted into a battlefield. We are dropped into the middle of the battle, and we have to fight. We can't pretend there is no battle. If we do, we will get killed. If we are in the midst of a battle, we have to fight, or else we will lose."

However, it is misleading to call our inner work a battle. It is more an inner *struggle* than a battle. But we cannot pretend this struggle does not exist. We are parachuted down into the middle of this life-long conflict, and we cannot pretend it is not going on.

The struggle takes many forms. Some of us may manage our own inner challenges but become distracted by the challenges faced by others. We say to ourselves, "Oh, how she is suffering. Oh, look how badly he has behaved!" These judgments tend to distract us from our own struggles, and anything that makes us forget God is not good for us. It is that simple. It does not matter if we forget God because of a TV program or because of a real-life drama.

Even the terms *struggle* and *conflict* are misleading. Working with our egos is more a process of life-long inner education. When we hear the voice of our egos urging us to do something wrong, what should we do? In many ways, our narcissistic egos are like little devils in us. It is not a good idea to start an argument with the devil. The devil is a fascinating conversationalist, and the next thing we know we will be mesmerized. All traditions teach that fighting with the devil is a sure way to lose. Debating with the devil is like arguing with a champion debater. You can't win.

Instead, when we hear the voice of temptation, we can say to ourselves, "Oh, I know this voice. It has given me bad advice all my life. I won't listen to this voice in me." In the Jewish tradition, the voice of the ego is called "the evil urge." I really like this term, because it makes it clear that the voice is not *us*. It is an urge or impulse in us. In the Holy Qur'an, the narcissistic ego is called the *nafs ammaara bil su,* the self that urges or incites us toward evil. The term *ammaara* is often translated as "command," but it is really even stronger than that. It is an inner force that constantly urges us, nags us, and tries to compel us to do wrong.

It helps to refuse to identify with these impulses. We can say to ourselves, "I hear you, and I'm not going to follow you." It is not a good idea to ignore our egos altogether. If a child asks for something and we don't pay attention, she or he will just get louder and will eventually become extremely upset. We have to respond, "No, we cannot do that right now." In many ways, the ego is like a spoiled child, one who is impatient and self-centered and always wants its own way. And, as in dealing with a child, we have to discipline the ego kindly but firmly, with love and understanding. Unfortunately, our narcissistic egos are much cleverer than a child. Working with our egos is more challenging than dealing with a child.

Becoming aware of that compelling voice is the most important part. We can catch ourselves before the voice misleads us; we can say to ourselves, "That isn't me." We can't do that unless we are aware of our egos. Awareness always comes first; No growth happens without awareness.

Another way to react to these urges is to say to ourselves, "How would a dervish act in this situation?" We all understand how a dervish should behave, and asking this question can help us understand the situation differently. Even though we are not fully developed dervishes, we know what real dervishes are like. We have read about the dervishes and sheikhs of the past; we also spend time with each other and come to know others who are real dervishes, or who at least behave like real dervishes some of the time. They are wonderful role models for us.

We are here together to serve one another. That is what dervishes do. However, there is a fine line between listening to someone else's problems in order to serve one another and gossiping: If someone is sick or suffering emotionally, it is our duty to let one another know. Then we can all pray for, visit, bring food to, and otherwise comfort our fellow dervish. However, it is gossip when we talk about someone else, not out of a desire to help them, but because we are nosy or we like to feel superior to others. Many of us love to talk about the faults of others, but gossip never helps others. As one sheikh has commented, "Some people try to grow taller by cutting off other people's heads."

⟩ 7 ⟨

The Soul

Accordingto the great Sufi saint Ibrahim Hakki Erzurumi, when each soul descends from the world of souls to be born in a human body, the soul becomes covered with the elements of the material world.[1] First, the soul becomes covered with earth. Next it is covered by water, and the earth turns to mud. Then the air dries the mud. Finally, fire bakes it. It is as if the soul becomes enclosed by a clay pot. The soul becomes hidden in the material vessel of our bodies. It is our job to find the soul that is covered up within us.

The soul within us is like the air in a container. When a container is created, air is automatically enclosed in the container. No one has to put it there. As a result, the atmosphere becomes separated into the air inside that container and the air outside it. Our souls are similar. The development of a human fetus calls forth a soul to inhabit it. Our souls seem separate, but the truth is that there is only unity underlying this apparent separation.

If we put rose perfume in the container, the air in it will acquire the fragrance of rose. If we put something rotten in the container, the air in it will smell rotten. In both cases, the life-sustaining oxygen in the air remains. Similarly, our souls remain unchanged, although our actions and life experience may make our personalities more or less "fragrant." Our souls are not touched by the things that occur in our lives, just as the oxygen in the container is not changed by any perfume. Our souls are pure and perfect, sparks of God's infinite soul. The Qur'an says, "[God] gave him [humanity] shape and breathed into him of His spirit." (32:6, Khalidi)

If our soul is hidden, we cannot experience its beauty and light. Our job is to allow our soul's light to shine through us. When we perform our prayers and our *zikr*, it is like drilling through the "pot" covering our souls.

In the Sufi tradition, our soul is located in our hearts. The great sage Hakim Tirmidhi wrote that there are four levels of the heart. The first level is the breast, the *outermost heart*. It is the border of the heart, where we interact with the world. The next levels are the *heart proper*, the *inner heart*, and the *innermost heart*, or heart of hearts.

Tirmidhi explains these levels using the metaphor of a house. The outermost heart is like the land surrounding the house. Travelers and animals can enter easily, even though the land is fenced in. The heart proper is the house itself. Wild animals are kept out, and a visitor needs permission to enter. It is more secure and private than the outermost heart. The inner heart is a treasure room, or vault, at the center of the house. The family valuables are kept there, including the priceless heirlooms. The vault door is kept locked, and only the master and mistress of the house have the keys to it. The innermost heart is the precious contents of the treasure room. To enter the treasure room, one has to pass the gate of the outermost heart, the door of the heart proper, and the vault of the inner heart.

My sheikh used to say that the innermost heart is a temple built by God to house God. Our soul within it is a divine spark and it transcends the entire universe. This transcendent spark in us can ignite the universe in an instant. As dervishes, we should always remember that God has placed a divine soul within the hearts of every human being. If we remember this, we will treat everyone with respect and realize that we are honored to serve God through serving others.

If we dig a well and strike water, we can turn a desert into a lush oasis. When our souls are hidden, life is like a barren desert: love and compassion are absent. Instead, there is only narcissistic love of self.

Unfortunately, finding water once is not enough. We have all been inspired (or "irrigated") by *zikr*, prayer, and the presence of our spiritual teachers. However, these initial inspirations will gradually fade away if we do not continue to do our own work to uncover our souls. Steady spiritual practice serves to keep alive our connection to our souls and to widen and deepen that connection. But if we fail to live our daily lives in accord with that connection, each heedless or selfish action closes the openings we have created. Actions that harm others or ourselves will even thicken the covering around our souls.

The eminent psychologist Wilhelm Reich wrote that we armor ourselves to protect ourselves from the world, like a knight putting on armor to protect himself in battle.[2] We all develop unconscious, habitual defenses because we feel lonely and vulnerable. When people criticize or devalue us we feel hurt, and we defend ourselves against any more such feedback, which we fear will only cause us more pain.

According to Reich, we armor ourselves by constricting our throats and chests and inhibiting our breathing. By inhibiting our breathing, we diminish our ability to feel or express our feelings. In this process, we diminish all our feelings. We inhibit not only our ability to feel pain but also our ability to feel joy. When we armor our hearts, we lose touch with our souls.

Removing our armor is an essential part of our path. To use another metaphor, our armor is like a layer of rock over a pure aquifer, a vast underground lake filled with millions of gallons of water. The water is useless unless we can get to it.

We each have a life-giving body of water within us. We have to drill to reach it, through all the layers of armor that cover our souls. Then our souls will irrigate our lives and that priceless spiritual water will also nourish others. It will inspire others to drill for the water hidden within them.

Our souls can nourish us and those we love, but uncovering our souls is hard work, just like drilling a well. How much time do we put into this work? I am afraid we don't devote as much time to it as high-school athletes do practicing their favorite sports.

Spiritual progress is a function of the time and energy we put in. Most of us are not drilling deeply enough. A common mistake many people make is to start drilling with the expectation of immediate results. When no water gushes out immediately, they decide to drill somewhere else. Students go to a spiritual teacher and try a new discipline for a few weeks or months. Then they run to a new teacher and a new practice. We will never succeed by drilling dozens of holes only a foot deep each.

We need to be patient in our practice. We want to try something new instead of practicing more deeply what we have been given. For example, we don't need to seek out the latest books on Sufism (including this one). Instead, we can read our old books over again and *practice* what we have read. In fact, if we are growing on this path, I can almost guarantee we will find new depths in the books we have read before.

This work requires patience and perseverance. We need to keep drilling even though nothing seems to be happening, right up until we break through to the aquifer. Someone may have to drill for one hundred feet or more before they hit water. We may be tempted to drill for only a short time before resting. But if we rest for too long, the hole may fill up, and we'll have to start over again.

At the beginning of our path, God often gives us a taste of the goal to encourage us. It is a bit like a preview of coming attractions. We may feel more love and light when we begin to practice *zikr*, but later on it may seem as if nothing is happening. We need to keep drilling deeper, seeking the real, deep connection to our own souls.

What happens when the physical pot breaks? The air returns to the atmosphere, an atmosphere it has always been part of. This happens in death—we all return to God, as God says in the Holy Qur'an: "To Me is your final return." (31:15, Khalidi) Some people do live on after the pot is breached. They become saints. In Sufism we call this "dying before dying." By breaking the pot of individuality, the great saints attain *fana*, the state of the annihilation of the separate self.

Our apparent separation from God is actually an illusion. The air in the pot seems separate from the air outside, but it isn't really so. The pot isn't perfectly airtight. After all, if we were ever completely separated from God, we would instantly cease to exist.

We are constantly in God's Presence. God revealed, "We are closer to him [humanity] than his own jugular vein." (50:16, Khalidi) We ask, Where is God? when all the while we are *surrounded* by God.

We are not and never have been separate. Unfortunately, we live in the illusion of separateness. We know from the examples of many saints that it is possible to dig down and touch the soul. It is possible to make that connection with our own souls, and doing so will make our lives richer and greener.

In every generation some accomplish this, and we get a taste of God's Presence when we are in the presence of someone who has achieved this state. Their lives are enriched, illuminated, and irrigated by this living water, and their presence enriches our lives.

In the desert, water is life. Years ago, I camped for a week in the high desert. We hung a water skin in the middle of our campsite and the water skin dripped slightly. Within a week, green shoots began growing under the water skin. The land around me seemed lifeless, but a little bit of water brought this small piece of the desert to life. The seeds were everywhere, but it took water to bring them to life.

Similarly, the water of the soul within us nourishes our inner life. Farmers have turned deserts into lush farmlands through irrigation, and saints have turned the barren lives of their followers into spiritually rich, fruitful lives.

What is our own experience of opening up the connection to our souls? When did it happen? What did it feel like in our bodies? How can we recapture this feeling once again?

Reflected Light

To change metaphors once again, our souls are like the sun and our personalities are like the moon. Without the sun, the moon is dark. Only by virtue of the sun's light can we see the beauty of the moon. The moon's beauty comes from the reflected light of the sun, just as the beauty in our lives comes from the reflected light of our souls.

Our personalities reflect our souls as the moon reflects the sun. And yet that reflection is distorted, as are all reflections. As I mentioned earlier, the air in a container can be affected by what is placed in it, but something essential still remains unchanged. Our personalities are affected by the events of our lives, but our souls remain pure and untouched.

In a story from the Holy Qur'an, Moses‡ said to God, "My Lord, show me Yourself that I may look upon You." [God] said: "You shall not see Me, but look instead upon that mountain." . . . When the Presence of his Lord appeared upon the mountain, it leveled it to the ground. Moses fell down, unconscious. (7:143, Khalidi)

Even the sight of the *effects* of God's Presence was enough to strike Moses‡ unconscious.

Why did Moses‡ faint at this point? After all, he had already seen God up close in the fire of the burning bush. Why then did he faint on Mount Sinai? Tosun Efendi suggested Moses‡ was incapable of fully comprehending the Presence of God in the burning bush, but after he had become God's Messenger, his awareness of God's Presence in the mountain was too much for him.

God's pure Light is too strong for any of us, but we can experience divine Light though our own souls and as reflected in the rest of Creation. God manifests in Creation through each of us, and our destiny is to be like the moon, reflecting God's Light. As a single candle can light hundreds of other candles, a single believer can inspire hundreds of other souls.

We can understand the same principle through our water metaphor. We all have the capacity to water our own farmland and also the lands of others. We can bring to life that which is parched or dormant in others. If we open up our souls, we can serve as God's *halife*, God's representatives here on earth.

It is our duty to do our best to serve as God's instruments, because if God entered Creation directly, everything would crumble. God uses us to serve Creation. As human beings, we can reflect divine Light to others. The more we can reflect God's Light, the more we benefit Creation.

Many of us think of benefiting Creation through action, such as writing petitions or doing charity. These activities are certainly beneficial. It is far better to do good than to sit home and do nothing. However, it is easy to become distracted by activity when what we really need to do is to open our hearts. It is a good deed to go to the desert and pick up trash, but it is far better to dig a well and bring the desert to life. That is what we are being asked to do. Our greatest service to Creation is to pursue our own spiritual work. The greatest service we can do for our children is to model real spirituality and inspire them to faith and service.

Digging our well is a long-term project. As I have written earlier, it is like chewing an iron peanut, a seemingly endless process. Do not look for results too soon. Looking for results is a distraction from the real work of digging.

We should dig in the ways we have been taught by our sheikhs. They have taught us how to dig deeply through *zikr*, prayer, service, and other spiritual practices. This process is not a mystery. Many sincere seekers have accomplished it before us. Our efforts will be successful eventually—if we follow our tradition and do the work we have been given. Our souls are waiting to be uncovered.

This process involves developing more awareness and conscious-ness. It is important to work with a sense of optimism, knowing that God is closer to us than our own jugular vein. We are essentially con-tainers enclosing divine souls. Don't follow this path with the belief that it may take a very long time, because then that belief will become a self-fulfilling prophecy. Just as in drilling a well, success may hap-pen any moment. We don't know how close we are to success. We have no idea how long it will take to reach our goal.

It is important to remember the story of Hazreti Hajar‡. Hajar‡ (in English, Hagar) was the second wife of Hazreti Ibrahim‡ and the mother of his first son, Hazreti Ishmael‡. Her story illustrates the great principle that it is important to act in this world, and yet all help comes from God. God told Hazreti Ibrahim‡ to leave her and their baby alone in the desert.

Hazreti Hajar‡ began to look for help. God's aid generally comes through others, through other people, or through God's Creation. She ran to the hill of Safa to see if there might be a caravan in the area, but she saw nothing. She then ran to the hill of Marwa, a short distance away. She ran back and forth seven times between these two hills. We still commemorate her efforts in the *hajj* today. All *hajjis* make the same seven journeys between the two hills.

Hazreti Hajar‡ did all she could to look for help for herself and her baby, exhausting herself in the heat of the desert. When she could search no more, she set her baby down in the shade and rested.

Then Hazreti Ishmael‡ kicked his tiny feet, and, in doing so, his right heel made a small indentation in the sand. From that indentation, the angel Gabriel‡ opened the access to a great aquifer underneath the desert. So much water gushed up that Hazreti Hajar‡ exclaimed, "*Zamzam!*" (Stop!). It is said that if she had not cried out, there would be a great lake in that valley instead of the city of Mecca. The holy well of *Zamzam* has served humanity for thousands of years.

Hazreti Hajar‡ exhausted herself in seeking help for herself and her baby. She did the best she could. Then, through God's Mercy, a tiny indentation in the sand opened up a great well. This story reminds us we do not know how success will come. It reminds us our own efforts are not enough, but we still have to do the best we can. Nothing happens from us alone.

As you follow this path, remember: God can open our hearts fully at any moment and instantly unveil our inner source of happiness, joy, and inspiration. After this, darkness as we now know it will not exist for us. Our lives will be filled with light.

That heart opening can happen at any moment. It can happen during any prayer. It can happen when we recite a single verse from the Qur'an or when we touch our foreheads to the ground. Any act of worship could be the tiny indentation that God will use to open our hearts. In *zikr*, any single repetition of "Allah" may be enough to crack the clay covering our souls. We have to practice with that kind of optimism. That is faith.

We are following this path to come in touch with our souls, which have always been within us. We are not here to create something new, something we do not possess. Prayer and *zikr* are powerful tools in this process. The practice of *zikr* was designed by saints who broke through to their own divine nature. It worked for them, and it will also work to open our hearts. The elements of prayer were revealed to Hazreti Muhammad§. He engaged in prayer out of the fullness of his intimate connection with God.

Hazreti Muhammad§ often prayed for hours at night. One night, he was motionless in prostration for so long that his beloved wife, Hazreti Aysha∫, was afraid he had died. She was deeply relieved when she noticed a slight movement of his thumb.

Once she asked him, "Why do you pray for so long? Didn't God tell you your place in heaven is assured?" He replied, "Should I not be among the grateful ones?" He was not praying in order to achieve something. He was praying out of love and gratitude.

The forms of *zikr* were developed by those who knew. They are rooted in the saints' experience of connection to their souls. *Zikr* is also a celebration of that connection, a way of experiencing and enjoying the connection.

I have been talking about this process as one of striving, of seeking to open up a connection to our souls. We can also think of it as enjoying the connection that is already there. After prayer, we can sit still and enjoy the state we have experienced. Prayer and *zikr* can be thought of as processes of *enjoying* the gifts God has given us. What gift is greater than the gift of our souls, breathed into us from God's infinite soul? Shouldn't we celebrate this wonderful gift?

If we give someone an expensive stereo system and they never turn it on, we would probably feel they did not appreciate our gift—because they never bothered to enjoy the wonderful music it can produce. So it is with prayer and *zikr*. They are ways of enjoying the gifts God has given us.

Our path provides a practical technology for opening up the connection to our souls. It enables us to fulfill God's wish, expressed in the famous *hadith qudsi*, "I was a hidden treasure and I wished to be known, and so I created Creation." At the same time, it is a way of delighting in, appreciating, and taking the time to sit with, the gifts we are given.

These two approaches are two sides of the same coin, and both are important. One is to appreciate the light and love contained in our soul. The other is to deepen our connection. From one point of view we are moving along a path. From another point of view, we are as close to God as we ever will be. God has said, in another *hadith qudsi*, "There are 70,000 veils between you and Me, and there are no veils between Me and you."

Why are there obstacles on this path? Consider the *hadith qudsi* mentioned above, "I was a hidden treasure and I wished to be known, and I created Creation." If there were no obstacles between us and our Creator, there would be no *process* of knowing. It would be no different from the state before Creation, when only God existed.

God created the world so we might come to know God and achieve to a sense of unity. The process of knowing—of coming to know—is important. The very nature of Creation is that God is hidden. Our job is to seek the hidden treasure. If God wills it, we may be successful, at least a little.

The angels are in constant prayer and live in perfect harmony with God, but God was not satisfied with the angels. They do not have free will; they never change. As human beings we have free will, and we can use our wills to seek God. We can choose to come closer to God. There is great benefit in using our will to know God, to align ourselves with God's Will. God has given us free will, but unfortunately we can also use our will to harm ourselves and harm others.

This path of ours is not easy. The world is not easy either. There is a tremendous amount of pain and suffering in this world.

Some years ago, Rabbi Zalman Schachter-Shalomi came to visit Muzaffer Efendi. Rabbi Zalman loved Efendi, and Efendi had made him a *muhib* (literally "one who loves" or a "friend") in our Order, which is the first level of initiation. One of the Jewish students who came with Zalman asked Efendi to pray for peace in the Middle East. She said, "God wants us to work for peace. The Torah teaches that we should 'beat our swords into ploughshares.'"

Muzaffer Efendi drew himself up, and I suddenly saw him as the embodiment of the great Turkish warriors who were his ancestors. His voice boomed, "Beat your swords into ploughshares? Nonsense. If you do, your neighbors will come with their swords and take not only your ploughshares but your lands and possessions as well! God did not make this world as a place of peace and rest. We are meant to struggle here, to work hard and overcome obstacles in this world. That is how we will grow spiritually as well."

The natural world has always included loss and suffering, predators and prey. Certainly, God could have created this world with only lovely deer and gazelles and no lions or tigers. But then, these lovely herbivores eat vegetables, which are also alive. So the deer and gazelles still cause pain and death—to the vegetable kingdom. Who is to say that an animal's life is worth more than that of a vegetable?

The predators actually preserve their prey. If deer herds are not thinned, the deer will overgraze the land and eventually starve to death. This world is based on a cycle of birth and death, which comes to all creatures. Loss and death are painful and inevitable.

When we complain of life's tragedies, we generally complain of events that affect us directly. It is a tragedy if someone we love dies, but when thousands in Africa die of famine, most people don't feel it as a tragedy. We rarely think it is a tragedy when animals die, unless they are our pets. But, in God's eyes, are their lives any less than ours?

Death is an integral part of life. Our destiny is to be here for a few years, and our job is to do our best with the time God has given us.

It is a challenge to follow the Path of Truth. We may work hard for years and still not be successful. The joy is in the doing of it. We will be much happier if we enjoy this path, even with all our struggles. Success may come, or it may not. That is God's Will.

We cannot achieve anything by our own will alone. Whatever we experience on this path is a gift. We all seek God and we all have to deal with our obstacles and limitations. In the process, we learn how much we need God's blessings. That alone is a real achievement.

I have said before that Sufism is practice. It is not theory or philosophy. It is not having wonderful meals and a good time together. It is practice.

‣ 8 ‣

Ibrahim bin Adhem: A Sufi Saint

I have always loved the great Sufi saint Ibrahim bin Adhem, in part because my sheikh loved him and often told stories about him.[1] Ibrahim's father Adhem was a poor young dervish who had settled in Belkh, a cultural and economic center located along the Silk Road in what is now northern Afghanistan. Adhem lived in a cave with a friend who was a *hakim*, a doctor trained in traditional Islamic medicine.

One day, Adhem saw a young woman standing on a balcony in the palace. When his eyes met hers, Adhem was so struck that he fainted. Later he told his friend, "I don't know what happened. I saw a young woman and my senses left me. Now, I can't think of anything else. Her image is in front of me and nothing else in life has any meaning for me." Adhem's friend nursed him back to health in the cave.

The young woman also instantly fell in love with Adhem. She was a princess, the daughter of the Sultan and Sultana of Belkh. She sent servants out to find Adhem, but no one knew who he was. They searched for Adhem for days, but he was still recovering in his cave, and they couldn't find a young man matching his description.

As Adhem slowly recovered, the princess became worse. The palace physicians could do nothing for her, and the princess slipped into a coma. Everyone thought she had died.

Overcome with grief, her parents buried her in a royal crypt, which was located in a cave close to the cave of the young dervish. Somehow Adhem knew the princess had not died. His love for her was so profound that he knew he would have felt her death. Adhem told his friend he was sure the princess was not dead. The physician said that they should immediately examine her body, because if she was not dead she would not long survive her entombment.

The two men entered the tomb and removed her body. The physician examined her, crushed some herbs under her nose, and her consciousness returned. She and Adhem gazed into each other's eyes, completely in love with each other. Adhem had no money or position, and they were afraid her parents would not let her marry him, so they asked the physician to marry them and decided to remain together in the caves.

A year later the couple had a son, whom they named Ibrahim bin Adhem, or "Ibrahim son of Adhem." Ibrahim was kind, intelligent, and handsome. He loved to run around the city and play. One day, the Sultan and Sultana saw this charming young man who somehow reminded them of their daughter. They asked him about himself and he told them his name was Ibrahim and that he lived with his parents on the outskirts of the city.

The more the Sultan and Sultana saw Ibrahim, the more they came to love him. Finally they asked to meet his parents. They said they wanted to adopt him and his parents and make him their adopted grandson. Ibrahim told his parents about this kind couple who wanted to meet them and make him their adopted grandson, and they realized the time had come to leave their life of seclusion. When they came to the palace, the Sultan and Sultana were ecstatic to be reunited with their long lost daughter and to realize that the boy they had come to love actually was their grandson.

In time, Ibrahim became the sultan of Belkh. Ibrahim had two distinct sides to his nature. He was the son of a dervish and a princess, raised in a cave and in a palace. He was descended from a line of Sufis on his father's side and from a line of rulers on his mother's side.

When he became the sultan, Ibrahim bin Adhem vowed to serve his people. He became the best ruler he could be. At the same time, Ibrahim longed for God and wished for a life of quiet and seclusion. He wanted to devote his life to seeking God, and he felt trapped by his worldly duties and royal responsibilities.

The story of Ibrahim bin Adhem is reflected in each of us. We all have two sides to our nature. Our souls yearn for God, and our personalities yearn for the joys of the world. We all have embraced worldly responsibilities, yet we all yearn for something more.

There are many stories of Ibrahim bin Adhem's struggle to balance seeking God and performing his royal duties. One day, Ibrahim was lying in bed, resting after his morning prayers. He thought about how he wanted God more than anything else. Just then, he heard a noise on the roof over his head. He went out on his balcony and saw a man walking on the roof of the palace. He asked, "What are you doing up there?"

The man replied, "I'm looking for my camel."

Ibrahim said in amazement, "Are you crazy? How can you find a camel up there on the roof of the palace?"

The man answered, "It is just as likely that I can find a camel on the roof of your palace as you can find God lying in your fancy sultan's bed."

Even today there are guides who bring us spiritual messages when we least expect them. My old sheikh, Safer Efendi, told me of a strange encounter he had years ago. When he was a young dervish, he went to

Bursa with his sheikh, Fahridden Efendi, to make their Friday prayers at the main Bursa mosque, Ulu Jami. Safer Efendi was looking forward to the prayer, because it was said that great saints always came for Friday prayer at that mosque.

It was a long trip from Istanbul, and they barely arrived in time for the prayer. It was so crowded they had to sit in the back of the mosque. Throughout the prayers, Safer Efendi was upset that they were in the back, because it is said that those who come earliest receive the greatest benefits from prayer. Also, Safer Efendi was sure the saints were in the front row, while he was stuck in the back. When finished his prayers, the man sitting next to him turned to him and said, "We are not always in the front." And then the man got up and left.

Ibrahim bin Adhem received several messages like this. One day a caravan entered the palace grounds. The caravan guide led everyone inside the palace gate and told the caravan to set up their tents and make camp. Ibrahim exclaimed, "What are you doing?"

"We are setting up our tents so we can spend the night here."

"This isn't an inn. This is the palace, not a caravansary for transients."

"Really? Who are you?"

"I am the sultan. I live here."

"Who lived here before you?"

"My grandfather and grandmother."

"And who before them?"

"My great grandparents."

"And before them?"

"My great-great-grandparents."

"So what is the difference between this place and an inn? One comes and goes, another comes and goes. Same thing."

There are messenger and reminders everywhere, if we only pay attention.

Ibrahim bin Adhem struggled with these invitations to seek God. We have all had the experience of struggling, after we have had invitations to change. Ibrahim thought, "I really want to be a dervish. Maybe when I retire . . ."

We have all used this excuse: "I'll become serious about Sufism when I have more spare time," or, "Maybe when I retire," or, "When my children are grown," or "Sometime in the future I will devote myself to seeking God." We think we have a guarantee that we will live so long and continue to have the strength and vitality to pursue this path.

Ibrahim thought he had to serve his people, that they *needed* him. God taught him otherwise. One day he went out hunting with a group of companions. As they were eating lunch, a bird swooped down and grabbed a piece of bread from Ibrahim's plate. Ibrahim realized something strange was going on and he followed the bird. He came to a clearing and saw the bird drop the bread into the mouth of a man who was tied to a tree.

The man asked, "Would you please untie me? I've been here for days, hoping someone might come along and rescue me."

"What happened to you? How did you survive tied up for so long?"

"I was robbed by bandits, and they left me tied up here. Birds have brought food to me every day, and each day a few rain clouds came overhead and I opened my mouth and got some water."

At that moment, Ibrahim realized that God is constantly taking care of all of Creation. He understood that he was only God's instrument and that his people needed God's help, not his. Ibrahim finally decided to leave his kingdom and search for a teacher who would help him find God. He understood his kingdom would survive without him. He realized his search for God was more important than all his worldly duties.

When Ibrahim left his kingdom, he first stayed in seclusion, living in a cave and devoting himself to prayer and contemplation. He returned full circle, having been born and raised in a cave before he came to live in a palace. Then he went in search of a teacher.

Ibrahim bin Adhem found his Sufi master in Baghdad. He studied with his sheikh for several years; then his sheikh told him to travel, saying, "Travel is educational. Go back to your old kingdom and learn what you can. No one will notice you in your dervish robes. Don't tell anyone you were once the sultan of Belkh. When you return, I want to hear what you have learned."

Ibrahim bin Adhem returned to his old kingdom and nobody paid any attention to him. He was just another wandering dervish. Along the way, he met another penniless wanderer and jokingly said to the man, "I bet you got your homelessness for nothing."

The man replied, "What are you talking about? Of course I did."

Ibrahim exclaimed, "I paid the kingdom of Belkh for mine, and I think I got a good deal!"

Ibrahim arrived in Belkh at night. He went to the main mosque, which he had built when he was the sultan. After the night prayers, Ibrahim sat quietly, engaged in his personal recitations. The *muezzin* entered the mosque to make sure everything was okay, because someone had stolen one of the mosque's prayer carpets a few days earlier. In those days, wealthy people often donated expensive carpets to the mosque when they experienced good fortune.

The *muezzin* saw someone sitting in the shadows, and he immediately thought he had found the thief. He cried, "Aha, you won't get away with it this time." Ibrahim bin Adhem did not say anything. He just kept up his recitation of God's Names. The *muezzin* grabbed Ibrahim by the legs and pulled him out of the mosque. Then he pulled Ibrahim down the stone steps leading up to the mosque.

Ibrahim's head hit the first step, and he realized he had a choice. He could get angry or feel sorry for himself, or he could accept this experience, including the pain, as a gift from God. He said to himself, "As

God wills. I submit myself to God's Will." With Ibrahim's acceptance, his pain was transmuted into a kind of ecstasy. As his head hit each successive step, the ecstasy deepened. Finally, Ibrahim lay there, his head bruised, looking up with a smile on his face. He said to himself, "O God, if only I had built more steps!"

Later in his life, Ibrahim looked back on this experience as one of the finest spiritual moments of his life.

For a dervish, everything becomes part of their spiritual path—loss, death, joy, success. Many of Ibrahim's epiphanies arose out of painful experiences. In one extremely cold winter, someone gave him an old jacket. The sheepskin lining was teeming with fleas. Years later Ibrahim commented, "That night I could not sleep because the fleas continually bit me. That was a great spiritual moment."

Another time, Ibrahim was on a ship. He was wearing old, patched clothing, clearly a penniless traveler. The other people on the ship made fun of him, and one man would come by and kick and pinch him. It was a small ship, and there was nowhere Ibrahim could go to avoid this man. Then the weather got bad, and the ship was in danger of capsizing. The passengers decided to throw someone off, because they were sure someone had brought them this bad luck. Ibrahim was the obvious choice. Ibrahim recalled, "They grabbed me and threw me over the side into the freezing water. That was another wonderful spiritual moment."

Ibrahim's trials all somehow deepened his reliance on God, his connection with God, and his love of God.

We often talk about submission to God's will. We usually respond to pain and suffering with anger or self-pity. We *could* respond instead by saying simply, "As God wills." We don't, but it is nice to know it is possible. It is helpful to know there are human beings who are capable of submission. We all have the capacity to live in the world and constantly remember God. We can use all our experiences to bring us closer to God. That is what it is to be a real human being, a real dervish. (When I refer to "real" human beings or "real" dervishes, I mean those who use the capacities God has given them. Their hearts are open, and they are loving and compassionate. They have developed the intelligence God gave them. They have developed their faith, and their lives are filled with service and the Remembrance of God.)

Ibrahim eventually finished his traveling and returned to Baghdad. In those days, Baghdad was a walled city with four great gates. As Ibrahim approached the city, his teacher told the other dervishes he was returning. (Real sheikhs know the comings and goings of their dervishes. When I refer to "real" sheikhs, I mean those who have purified their *nafs* and who can access the wisdom and intuition of their hearts.) The sheikh said, "I want all of you to go to the gates of the city and prevent him from entering. Then come back and tell me what happened."

After all his trials and sufferings, Ibrahim was eager to see his beloved teacher, but when he came to the first gate, he encountered a group of dervishes barring his way. Ibrahim tried to get past them, but they formed a line and kept him out. Instead of fighting with his fellow dervishes, he went to the next gate and found another group blocking his way. He then went to the third gate and the fourth gate.

Seeing that all the gates to the city were blocked, Ibrahim began to push his way through the group of dervishes at the fourth gate, saying, "Excuse me, I have to see my teacher. It is my duty." As he forced his way through, one overenthusiastic young dervish kicked him in the back of the leg. The dervish's foot scraped along Ibrahim's Achilles tendon, causing bleeding and great pain, but Ibrahim did not get angry. He simply turned and said, "My brother, don't you know who I am? I am your brother dervish Ibrahim bin Adhem. I'm no longer the sultan of Belkh."

Everyone returned to the teacher, who asked Ibrahim to recount his travel experiences. At the end, Ibrahim described his attempts to enter Baghdad.

"The other dervishes were at all the gates of the city, and they refused to let me in. At the fourth gate, I realized that I would not be able to get in to see you unless I forced my way through them. I did apologize to them for doing that."

"What else happened?"

"That was all."

The sheikh asked the dervishes, "What else happened?"

The young dervish reluctantly admitted he had kicked Ibrahim. He said that Ibrahim did not even get angry at him, and that Ibrahim only commented that he was a brother dervish and no longer the sultan of Belkh.

The sheikh smiled slightly and turned to Ibrahim. "Ah, my son," he said, "you are not done yet. The taste of the sultanship is still in you."

We do not lose our past so easily. It is an excellent practice to ask ourselves who we think we are, and who we think we are not. I have always remembered that line, "I am *not* the sultan of Belkh" and also the sheikh's comment, "The taste of the sultanship is still in you." It is very important to notice our beliefs about who we are. Most of us are even more attached to our so-called "identity" than to our possessions.

Some years later, Ibrahim met a drunk who was lying unconscious in the street. His breath reeked of alcohol. Ibrahim thought to himself, "This man's mouth must have recited prayers. This mouth must have called out God's Names. It should be cleansed." Ibrahim immediately brought fresh water from a nearby well and washed the man's mouth. That night a voice came to Ibrahim in a dream, "You have cleansed a mouth for My sake, and I have cleansed your heart."

CHAPTER 8

Every moment is a moment for service. We say "Remember God
and serve others," but how often do we actually do it? Ibrahim's act is
a wonderful example of service. Service does not have to involve great
gestures. Sometimes the smallest things are the most important.

In the West, drunks are not that uncommon. In the Muslim world,
alcohol is forbidden, and drunkenness is tolerated far less than in the
West. However, one who has an awakened heart sees everything in
terms of God's Presence. Everything reminded Ibrahim bin Adhem
of God.

One day Ibrahim came to a public bath. These baths were extremely common in the Muslim world. They cost only a few small coins,
and dervishes and other poor travelers were generally admitted for
nothing. In this case, the bath-keeper insisted on the fee. He shouted
at Ibrahim, "You can't get in unless you have the fee."

Ibrahim began crying and fell to the ground. He kept weeping and
a crowd began to gather. People asked what the matter was. Someone
explained that the bath-keeper would not let Ibrahim in because he
did not have the bath fee. Several people offered to pay his fee, but
Ibrahim exclaimed, "No, it isn't that!" And he kept on crying.

Ibrahim explained, "They say everything here is a reflection of the
hereafter. When the bath-keeper said, 'You can't get in unless you have
the fee,' I asked myself, Will I have the fee to enter Paradise? How do I
know if I will have the fee? Will I be worthy of heaven?"

Ibrahim began crying again, and all those around him began crying
as well. All his listeners wondered if they would have the "fee" when
the Day of Judgment came.

One day Ibrahim spoke to a slave. He asked the slave, "What do
they call you?"

The slave replied, "My name is whatever my master says it is. Whatever my master calls me, that is my name."

"What do you eat?"

"I eat whatever my master gives me to eat."

"What do you wear?"

I wear whatever my master gives me to wear."

"What do you do?"

"Whatever my master tells me to do."

Ibrahim broke down crying again. He cried, "If only I could follow God the way he follows his master!"

When Ibrahim first went to Mecca, everyone heard the great saint was coming. The elders of the city prepared a feast for him and sent their servants to escort him into the city. The servants encountered a poor, dirty traveler. They asked him, "We have come to meet the saint Ibrahim bin Adhem. We were told he is coming today."

Ibrahim replied, "What do you care about Ibrahim bin Adhem? He is not really a man of faith. He is a hypocrite and an unbeliever."

The servants became angry at this and started beating Ibrahim. He kept insisting that Ibrahim bin Adhem was a hypocrite, that his reputation was false. After they finished beating him, Ibrahim lay there on the side of the road and said to his ego, "Ah, you were so happy the elders of Mecca were coming to greet you. See what you got."

Ibrahim settled in Mecca. He worked hard carrying heavy loads and never took a penny of charity from anyone.

God taught Ibrahim bin Adhem through his everyday life experiences. As he grew on the path, he realized that everything that happened to him was part of his spiritual journey. All his experiences reminded him of God and deepened his connection with God.

We are capable of the same. Whether we attain it or not is a matter of our own efforts and God's Grace. Ibrahim bin Adhem was not born a saint. He worked at it. He worked at his spiritual path his whole life. He was born the same as the rest of us. The only difference is, saints and prophets work hard and develop patience, remembrance, and love of God. They also generally undergo greater tests than we do.

We find it hard to give up even a little bit of the world; Ibrahim bin Adhem gave up his kingdom. We find it difficult to remember God in our comfortable daily lives. For Ibrahim, his trials deepened his remembrance.

The saints remember God at all times. Their lives are filled with worship and service. We generally see the world purely in terms of our own needs and desires. If someone cuts us off on the freeway, we get angry. We become deeply upset if someone criticizes us. We say to ourselves, "How dare they criticize me! Of course, I'm right and they are wrong. Besides, their motives in criticizing me are not pure."

When we are cut off on the freeway, we might respond, "Thank You, God, for reminding me to practice patience. If I slow down, I might even avoid an accident." When criticized we might respond, "O Lord, *You* have spoken through this person's mouth. What are You telling me? I need to listen, even though I don't want to hear it."

Imitation of Saints

We are not saints, but we can certainly imitate the saints. We can imitate our spiritual teachers, even imitate the great Messengers—Moses, David, Jesus, and Muhammad, God's peace and blessings upon them all.

In fact, what else can we do? Sincere imitation is what we are supposed to do. We should always remember the prayer of the great Sufi saint, Hazreti Rabia. She prayed, "Oh Lord, make my imitation real." We should not kid ourselves. Our prayers and our spiritual practices are at best imitations. In one *hadith*, Hazreti Muhammad§ said, "Pray as you see me pray." In other words, he told us to imitate his actions, the outer form of his prayer. He knew this is the best we can do. We should be grateful he did not say, "Pray as I pray." For how could we pray with the same profound faith and devotion as God's Messenger did? That level of prayer is impossible at our state.

Hazreti Muhammad§ never gave the call to prayer. He was afraid God might not forgive those Muslims who would have heard him calling them to prayer but failed to go to the mosque. Similarly, if he had commanded, "Pray as I pray," we would be sinning in every prayer, because we cannot pray with the same deep devotion. Luckily, we are only required to follow the outer form of prayer. That is, we are told to imitate.

When we perform *zikr*, we imitate the saints who were inspired to celebrate God in this particular form of worship. We imitate real remembrance. And, if God wills, God may to some extent make our imitation real. We continue to perform the outer forms of *zikr* in hopes that our remembrance will deepen and we will come to know God's Presence within and all around us. But we shouldn't fool ourselves and think what we do is the same as the *zikr* of the saints, whose spontaneous and inspired forms of worship are the models for our *zikr*. We can make intention to pray and to practice remembrance. If our intentions are sincere and we make sincere efforts, we can hope that God will reward our humble and limited attempts.

Our job is to follow this path, remembering we are imitating and hoping God will make it real. The little we do may be enough, if God wills. In a *hadith qudsi*, God says, "If you take one step toward Me, I will take ten steps toward you. If you walk toward Me, I will run toward you." So we can hope that our little faltering step toward God may actually bring us ten steps closer, through God's Grace. Intention is critical and must be followed by action.

The Bandit Who Repented

It is important to set clear intentions and then to act on those intentions. The rest is up to God. A wonderful old Turkish Sufi story that illustrates this beautifully:

There once was a bandit who decided to leave his life of crime and violence. He asked a well-known imam for advice. He told the imam, "I've killed ninety-nine people—men, women and children. Is there any way God might forgive me for this?"

"Was this in war?"

"No, I'm a bandit. I'm the well-known bandit, Mustafa the Terrible. I'm sure you have heard of me."

"How could God forgive you? You butchered innocent people. You are beyond redemption. You are certainly going to go to hell for what you have done."

The imam went on and on about Mustafa's horrible crimes, the suffering he caused to the families of those he had slain, and how he could never hope for any kind of salvation. Mustafa replied, "Well, if that's the case I might as well make it one hundred." He drew his sword and killed the imam.

The bandit was not satisfied, so he went to a Sufi sheikh. He said, "I've killed one hundred people; the last one was an imam. I've killed men, women and children. Could God ever forgive me for my life of crime?"

The sheikh replied, "God is All Merciful, All Forgiving. God has said that divine Mercy and Compassion are even greater than divine Justice and Wrath. To God, all things are possible, so there is certainly hope for you. But you must genuinely repent, and you must change your life. If you continue the way you have been, you will certainly go to hell, but if you repent and change your life, you can hope for God's Mercy and pray that God might accept your repentance."

The sheikh went on, "Where do you live?"

"I live in a bandit village in the hills, several miles from here. We are all bandits there."

"You have to leave that place. You have to vow sincerely to change your old life and leave the bad company you are in. Leave the village of the bandits and move to the closest village of God-fearing, honest people."

"Do you think that might work?"

"Given God's Mercy, it might. That is my advice to you. Follow it if you wish to be saved from hell."

Mustafa agreed. He went home, packed up his belongings, and set out for the nearest village of God-fearing people. His destiny was such that when he had gotten only a few steps away from the village of the bandits, he died.

As he fell, an army of implacable angels, the guardians of hell, appeared to take his soul. At the same time, an army of angels from heaven came and claimed *they* had the right to his soul. The angels of hell insisted that the bandit had no hope of going to heaven, for he was an evil man who killed one hundred people—innocent men, women and children, and even an imam.

The angels of heaven argued that he had repented. He sincerely decided to change, and he also acted on his intention. From the time he met the sheikh, he had done nothing wrong and he did everything he could to begin to change. He was clearly beginning a new life.

The angels of hell said, "A few steps in the right direction are not enough. That is nothing compared to his life of crime and murder. One hundred people killed—his soul is ours."

The two groups kept arguing; they eventually asked the archangel Gabriel‡ to mediate. After hearing the arguments on both sides, Gabriel‡ said he could not decide. He went to God and asked if the bandit should go to heaven or to hell. God replied, "Take my divine measuring rod. It will measure the distance between his body and the city of the bandits and the city of the righteous. Whichever city is closer will decide his fate. If he is closer to the city of the bandits, he will go to hell; if he is closer to the city of the righteous, he will go to heaven."

Gabriel brought down the measuring rod and told the assembled angels of God's command. The angels of hell were delighted. They were sure they were going to win the dispute. Gabriel laid the ruler between the body and the village of the bandits. The measuring rod instantly extended two feet, up to the walls of the village of the bandits. Then he laid the rod between the body and the distant village of the righteous. As the ruler began to lengthen, the walls of the city of the righteous moved to within one foot of the bandit's body.

This story is a wonderful reminder of God's Mercy. God may forgive us, no matter what terrible mistakes we may have made in the past. God's Mercy can and does work miracles every day.

The story is also a reminder of the importance of intention and acting on our intentions. Intention alone is cheap. Everyone has "good intentions." Everyone makes virtuous New Year's resolutions. Few act on their intentions with perseverance. Our actions make our intentions real.

These stories do not match our own experience. None of us have given up a kingdom as Ibrahim bin Adhem did; none of us are likely to become rapturous if our heads are banged on stone steps. However, these stories do remind us of our potential for a deeper spiritual life. They tell us what human beings are capable of attaining.

The example of saints like Ibrahim bin Adhem can change our conception of ourselves. We can remember that God has made us to be divine instruments to serve the universe. We can hold ourselves upright and proud as God's children. We each hold a spark of God within ourselves, and we are always in God's Presence.

It was said of Ibrahim bin Adhem that he always sat and stood erectly. He never slouched or leaned. When he sat, he always sat as if he were at prayer. When someone asked him why he always sat so perfectly upright, he said, "In my early years as a dervish, one day I was sitting informally and leaning on a pillow and a voice came to me,

'You would not sit this way in prayer. Are you less in the Presence of your Lord now?' I realized I am always in God's Presence, and since that time I feel I can never slouch or lean."

That was who he was, and that is who we can be also, God willing.

⟩9⟨

Inner Work

As Sufis, our spiritual practice is an integral part of our everyday lives. We do not spend our days solely in prayer and meditation. We work in the world, raise our families, and find ways to serve God's Creation in our daily lives. Ideally, every human interaction is an opportunity for service and a reminder of God.

Two Sides of Sufism

There are two aspects to Sufi practice. One is to develop love and faith, and the other is to become less self-centered, less narcissistic. Both aspects are necessary. They are like the two wings of a bird; both wings are needed for the bird to fly. One side is the deepening of our love of God, opening our hearts, learning to love, deepening our faith. The second side is becoming a more mature human being, less affected by our selfish egos.

This second process begins by acknowledging that we each have an ego. We are all proud, even arrogant. We become upset with anyone who says that we are arrogant, because we don't want to see ourselves as we are—which makes it hard to change.

On this path we are seeking to develop our character, or rather, to return to the character we were born with. I have never seen a baby with a bad character. We are all born in a natural, pure state. With good intentions, hard work, and God's blessings, we can return to our original state.

The Holy Qur'an praises Hazreti Muhammad§, saying he had the finest character. I would much rather be with someone with good character than with someone who is brilliant or successful but who has a bad character.

Outer observances alone—performing daily prayers, fasting in Ramadan, going on *hajj*—do not guarantee good character. Many Muslims practice the outer forms of Islam and remain very arrogant, convinced they are better than everyone else.

Good character means caring about others at least as much as we do for ourselves. In one famous *hadith*, the Prophet§ taught, "None of you truly believes until you love for others what you love for yourself."

One day the Sufi saint Hazreti Ibrahim bin Adhem was on the outskirts of a town, and a soldier came up to him and asked, "Where is the center of population here?" Ibrahim pointed to the cemetery. The soldier thought Ibrahim was making fun of him. He lost his temper and knocked Ibrahim so hard he became unconscious.

Someone told the soldier, "You hit the great saint Ibrahim bin Adhem. That was an awful thing to do." The soldier immediately ran to get some water and bathed Ibrahim's face. He apologized and begged the saint to forgive him.

Ibrahim said, "Of course I forgive you. In fact just before I became unconscious I prayed to God that you might go to heaven."

"Really?"

"Absolutely. Because I was so glad that God sent me a punishment that I am sure I deserved, and I didn't want to be the only one who benefited from the punishment. So of course I prayed for you."

This is a very demanding approach to daily life. When something painful happens to us we rarely remember our desire to come closer to God. If we did we would care more for others and less about ourselves.

A Sufi teacher was walking home when a man came up and began arguing with him. The man became loud and abusive, and the Sufi stopped walking and said, "Please let us stand here so you can finish whatever you would like to say. I don't want to keep on walking because we are coming close to my home. Some people in my neighborhood might become upset over what you are saying and harm you."

How different that is from the way we usually think! Instead of becoming angry the saint was concerned for the welfare of the man who was insulting him.

In all our encounters, can we try to do good to everyone we encounter, to be of service to others without expecting any service back? Can we seek to be of service whether they praise us or criticize us, whether they like us or not? It is easy to help someone who likes us. That is not much of an achievement. To be a dervish is to help those who do not act nicely to us.

One day a sheikh went to visit one of his acquaintances. The man he came to see said, "I'm sorry, but my house is not ready. Please come back another time." The sheikh returned some days later. Once again the man said, "I'm sorry. My house is still not ready to receive guests." This happened three or four times. Finally, the man admitted the sheikh. While they were sitting together over tea, the sheikh asked, "Your house seems just fine. What was the matter earlier?"

His host said, "I was testing your love. I wanted to see if you cared enough to keep coming after I sent you away a few times."

The sheikh said, "That is nothing. A dog will come back if you send it away. A Sufi should be better than a dog."

Developing good character reduces our egos. It is more effective to develop positive habits than to criticize ourselves constantly. We will change more through love and support than through criticism. Rather than seek to reduce our egos with the fire of criticism, it is better to develop positive habits and good character. If we develop good character, we will reduce our selfishness and arrogance. We will also begin to see how the negative traits of the ego are in the way of developing good character.

Instead of focusing on our self-centeredness, we can become more sensitive to others. We can listen to others more carefully and serve them better. Can we wish for the best for others, not just when they are nice to us but when they do something we don't like? Can we serve people who are selfish or unpleasant?

Service to others will transform us. I don't mean dramatic gestures like giving a poor person everything in your wallet. I mean *making a habit of service*. A kind word or compassionate glance may be worth more than money to someone in need of our kindness.

Practicing Kindness

I recently saw an inspiring movie, *The World's Fastest Indian*. It is based on the story of New Zealander Burt Munro. Munro had a 1920 Indian motorcycle that he had ridden and raced for years. He had set several records in New Zealand, and he wanted to go to the salt flats in Bonneville, Utah, where all the land-speed records have been set. In 1962, suffering from heart disease, Munro mortgaged his house, took a boat to Los Angeles, and headed for Utah.

Burt Munro is brilliantly played by actor Anthony Hopkins. When Munro's children came to the filming, they were moved to tears watching Hopkins play their father. They were touched that he captured their father's essential decency and honesty.

In the film, Munro is extraordinary in the way he treats everybody with kindness and respect. He acts like a true dervish. This is very different from the macho, violent, selfish roles we find in so many movies. Because Munro was honest and kind, everyone did his or her best to help him. Virtually everyone Munro met became a friend and assisted him in his journey.

Munro left New Zealand with very little money. When he arrived in Los Angeles, he bought an old car. The car-lot owner let Munro use his shop to build a trailer for his motorcycle. He and the owner spent all night welding the trailer. When the lot owner saw the way Munro tuned up his car, he said, "If you ever want a job, come back here. You are terrific with your hands." In gratitude for the use of the shop, Munro tuned some of the cars on the lot without payment. Munro was an honest, caring, and straightforward man—and everybody around him reflected those same attitudes back to him.

Munro had lived a quiet life in New Zealand. When he came to Los Angeles, he ended up in a hotel in Hollywood. The desk clerk was a transvestite, and Munro was naturally friendly to him, even though he had never seen a transvestite in his life. The clerk was taken with Munro's kindness and ended up taking him all over town. Munro never forgot that the desk clerk was a person. He didn't objectify or demean. He made real human contact with the clerk, as he did with everyone he met.

When Munro finally arrived in Bonneville, he was told he needed permission to race. (He didn't realize he needed to apply ahead of time.) The people in charge at Bonneville were shocked to find that his motorcycle had a partly handmade engine, makeshift tires, no brakes, and no chute to stop him at the end of the course. But some of the motorcycle lovers at the track sensed his sincerity and interceded for him, so he finally got to ride. That year, he set a small-motorcycle world-speed record of 178.9 mph, although his Indian motorcycle was originally built to attain a top speed of 55 mph. Munro later returned to Bonneville and set more world speed records.

Our words express our inner attitudes. Attitude and intention are critical. We can read each other's character and attitude through our words. Building character takes a lifetime, and one of the ways to develop our character is to be conscious of how we talk to people and treat them.

How many times have we heard the Sufi ideal, "Value the human heart; value the soul"? We respond, "Yes. Of course." It is easy if others are nice, well-dressed, middle-class people, but how do we relate to someone who is very different from us—poor or homeless, for example? Do we treat that person with respect and an open heart? Besides being a lovely movie, *The World's Fastest Indian* illustrates how a humble, sincere human being is a better dervish than most of us.

Silence and Solitude

Another fundamental Sufi practice is the practice of *halvet*, retreat. We can make a short retreat at home, even for a few hours. We don't have to spend months or years in a cave, but we do need some time for silence and solitude. Paradoxically, words are so important that silence is extremely valuable. We are surrounded by so much trivial language that we need to be deeply nourished by silence. We talk too much and enjoy silence too little. Through the practice of silence, we can come to value more the words we do speak. One of my teachers commented, "Words are bullets. Don't waste your ammunition."

I strongly suggest that everyone spend at least an hour or two a week in "retreat"—that is, in silence and solitude. We can all afford to reserve this time to enrich our spiritual lives. Retreat is time without phones, television or radio, computers, and so on. We are constantly engulfed by a torrent of words, so we don't value them. We are surrounded by so much information that we cannot absorb it. We get intellectual and spiritual "indigestion." To balance our lives, we need to take time for silence and solitude. We need to take time to study the Qur'an and read the inspiring writings of the great Sufi sheikhs.

Qur'anic Study

Hazreti Muhammad§ taught, "If one day is the same as the day before, that day is a loss." In other words, as Muslims we are instructed to learn and grow every day. If we are not growing we are stagnating. Hazreti Muhammad§ also taught, "Go even to China for knowledge." That is how important learning is for a Muslim. And the most important study for us is the study of the Holy Qur'an.

Let me suggest several basic practices for studying the Holy Qur'an. Safer Efendi, God rest his soul, taught me to look for those passages that have personal meaning for me. He advised, "Let your eyes skim over the Qur'an, and when something jumps out at you, write it down."

Read until you find a passage that touches you. Then spend time with those lines. If you can, read them first in Arabic, as there is benefit in hearing the original words of the Qur'an—after all, those are the words through which God's Truth was revealed to humanity. Then read these lines in English. Slow down and savor these holy words. Let them sink in.

Notice what touches you most in the passage. Is there a phrase or a single word that moves you? Write down that word or phrase. Describe how it touches you, what it means to you in that moment.

Later, you can review what you have written, and it will recall those feelings to you. You may also see something new when you go back to the passage. That is a sign that you have grown, and you have come to understand more.

We sometimes feel frustrated that we are not growing. Many dervishes have said that to me and I often feel that way, too. This practice provides useful feedback. We can go back to our selected passages and discover what they mean to us now. Ideally, we will be able to say, "Thank God, I now understand something I didn't understand before. Maybe God has opened the intelligence of my heart a little bit."

This is real study, not what passes for study in Western education. In this practice, we read, then take time to contemplate what we have read. The Prophet§ taught, "An hour of concentration is worth sixty years of prayer."

We can read over and over again what touches us. Read and let the meaning sink in; then reflect and write. Contemplate some of the different levels of meaning. Some have said that every line in the Qur'an has seven levels of meaning. Muzaffer Efendi used to say, "No, each of God's Words has *seventy thousand* levels of meaning!" In other words, the meanings of each word and each line are innumerable.

This kind of scriptural study can be found in many traditions. It's an old Christian practice, and many devout Christians read the Bible this way. In India, it is the way pious Hindus read their scriptures. And it is the way Muslim saints and scholars have read the Qur'an.

Every word, every verse, every *sura* of the Qur'an is a revelation. Because the Qur'an is revelation from God, we can never fully understand it. If we could understand with our limited intelligence, it wouldn't be revelation from the Infinite. Contemplation of these words will bring us closer to God.

The most sacred words cannot inspire us if we don't digest them. It's like putting food in your mouth and spitting it out, then saying, "This food is no good. I didn't get any nourishment from it." We have to digest what we take in. We have to "chew on it." So read, over and over again. Think about what you read, and *feel* it.

We can also draw images inspired by the words. We see powerful images in our dreams. Many dervishes have had wonderful teachings in dreams, and they are beautiful, profound teachings. The words are less important. It is the meanings that are important.

Give yourself at least an hour a week to sit and engage in this kind of contemplative study. Take a passage you know. The "light verses" of the Holy Qur'an, for example, are some of the world's most striking poetry. Consider this excerpt:

God is the light of the heavens and the earth.
His light is like a niche in which is a lantern,
The Lamp in a glass,
The Glass like a shimmering star,
Kindled from a blessed tree,
An olive neither of the East nor of the West,
Its oil almost aglow, though untouched by fire.
Light upon Light! (24:35, Khalidi)

Start with something easy, something you already love, and give it time so you can appreciate the beauty and deep levels of meaning of the words. Take time and read it over. If you can, read it in Arabic and write it out in Arabic. Then, write it in English and contemplate the meanings of this passage. Recite it several times, paying attention to what happens—mentally, physically, and emotionally—as you read the words aloud. It is important to read aloud as well as silently. We don't read aloud these days, except when reading to children. Reading aloud touches our hearts more deeply than reading silently, and the Qur'an is meant to be read aloud.

As I wrote earlier, Hazreti Muhammad§ taught that an hour of contemplation is worth as much as sixty years of prayer. How much clearer could he be? Could the Prophet§ have emphasized the importance of contemplation any more strongly?

What does contemplation mean? The basic practice is simple. Get in the habit of setting aside an hour or two a week. Begin at the beginning, with *Sura Fatiha*, and see what you can find in this short *sura*. It is said to be the essence of prayer, and the essence of the Qur'an is in the opening verse: *Bismillah ir-rahman ir-rahim*, "In the Name of God, Most Merciful, Most Compassionate." Only in this first *sura* is the *Bismillah* considered a part of the *sura* itself. In every other *sura*, it is considered an introduction to the *sura*.

The essence of this first verse is in the word "*Bismillah*"; the essence of *Bismillah* is in the first letter, the *beh*; and the essence of the *beh* is in the dot under the *beh*. (The letter *beh* is the second letter of the Arabic alphabet. It is a curved line with a dot underneath: ﺏ) This illustrates how much there is to contemplate in this *sura*.

Any part of the Qur'an can open our hearts and guide us—any *sura*, any verse, any word. We are not at the level where a letter or a dot is going to reveal great truths to us, but perhaps a particular verse will inspire us.

Language can transform us, and we should consider our everyday speech. The words we use should not be taken trivially, especially the words with which we pray, the words we chant in *zikrullah*. Every word in the Holy Qur'an is a divine messenger. God sent these words down to us to teach and inspire us. Each word in the Qur'an has so many levels of meaning that it is like a whole book in itself, if we could but read it.

A Good Beginning

There was a dervish who came from a very poor family and had never learned to read and write. He went to a teacher of Arabic who sat by one of the walls of the city. In the old days, many teachers did not have their own classrooms; they sat outside and taught whoever came to them. This teacher chalked his lessons on the stones of the city wall.

The dervish asked, "Teacher, I'd like to learn Arabic, so I can read the Holy Qur'an. I know I'm older than most students, but I have a great desire to learn."

The teacher replied, "If you want to learn to read the Qur'an, I will be happy to teach you free of charge. Let's start with the alphabet. The first letter is *alif*, and it is a simple vertical line written like this: ׀" The teacher explained. "The *alif* isn't pronounced; it holds the place for vowels."

The dervish bowed and said, "Thank you. Thank you, Master," and left.

The teacher thought to himself, "I usually get through the whole alphabet in the first lesson. This is going to go very slowly. Perhaps he will come back tomorrow, and we will study at least a few more letters."

The dervish did not come back the next day or the week after. Months went by, and finally the dervish returned. His eyes were shining, and his face was transformed. He bowed very deeply to the Arabic teacher and said, "Master, I am ready for my second letter now."

The teacher thought to himself, "It is going to take forever to teach this man Arabic." But all he said was, "Let's see you how you've done with the first letter. Please write the *alif* on the wall."

The dervish wrote the letter *alif*, and the wall crumbled.

What caused this? Perhaps it was the dervish's sincerity. Many people write *alif* thousands of times without anything happening. The dervish understood the *alif* far more deeply than the rest of us. For him, *alif* was the first letter of the language of God, the language in which the Qur'an was given. For the dervish, the *alif* was a miraculous letter, and he sincerely contemplated that letter for months.

The *alif* signifies unity, one of God's ninety-nine Names or Attributes, and the dervish came to understand unity through studying the *alif*. The letter was a window through which he understood God, and when he wrote the *alif*, the dervish invoked God's Presence—which was what had crushed the wall.

I wish I knew what kind of contemplation he did! At least we can take the first step in learning contemplation by sitting and spending an hour or two a week reading, thinking, writing, and reflecting deeply.

This story reminds us to be patient and go slowly in our spiritual practice. We always want to rush and do more, as quickly as possible. Going more slowly and deeply at the beginning will get us much farther. We want to jump to "advanced" practices without realizing what is contained in the most basic lessons.

Our bodies represent different Arabic letters in each of the postures of prayer. Standing upright forms the letter ا *alif*; bowing while standing forms the letter د *dal*; kneeling and touching our foreheads to the floor forms the letter م *mim*. Together these letters form ا د م, *Adam*, which means a "human being."

$$\text{آدَمْ}$$

The Practice of Zikr

In *zikr*, as in prayer, our movements are meant to bring God into our hearts. Muzaffer Efendi taught, "When we recite *la ilaha illa Allah*, 'there are no gods; there is God,' the *la* means 'no.' The word *la* is composed of *lam* and *alif*, and the two letters together look a little like a broom: لا. *La* is the broom that cleans our hearts. It sweeps the heart clean of the dust, the idols, and the worldly attachments we have allowed to accumulate there."

When we recite *la ilaha*, "no gods," we turn our heads to the right. Because most of us are right-handed, this means turning toward our active side. Our right hands grasp for things and try to control the world around us. This movement paired with reciting *la ilaha* symbolizes saying "no" to all that. We say "no" to our self-centered ambitions and to the ways we habitually interact with the world. We assert that God cannot be found in all our habitual, ego-based, willful activities.

Then we turn our heads to the left and downward toward our hearts and recite *illa Allah,* "there is God." *La ilaha* cleans the heart temple, and *illa Allah* places God on the altar of our hearts. We are putting God into our cleansed hearts. Remember the heart is a divine temple, built by God to house God within us.

In *zikr,* when we recite *Allah,* we turn our heads to the left and down. Again, we are placing God in our hearts. A single repetition of *Allah* or *"la ilaha illa Allah"* could take us into ecstasy. A single repetition of any one of God's Names could transform us.

After the formal sohbet *concluded, we had an informal question-and-answer session:*

QUESTION:

Reciting different Names makes me feel different. When I say *Hayy* [Life], I feel my whole being involved.

ANSWER:

Every cell in your body is alive, so every cell is continually vibrating with the divine Attribute *Hayy.* Everything in the universe exists through the Name *Hayy.*

In *zikr,* our breath is very important. The breaths of all the dervishes should become one, so that it is as if only one dervish is breathing and saying *Hayy.* Then we come to realize we are not separate; we are not performing *zikr* with the attitude, "I have my own rhythm. I am doing my own thing." There are some Sufi groups that do *zikr* that way. But for us, what is important is the sense of unity. The unity among us is like a magnet that draws to us the Unity of God.

Our group *zikr* is not an individual practice; it is the practice of our community. Our *zikr* is not based primarily on our individual efforts. We are always connecting ourselves with something greater. We seek to become a unified group in the *zikr*, and, in a deeper sense, we are seeking to connect with the unity of God, not just the unity of the group.

Sometimes *zikr* can feel overwhelming, as though our nervous systems are transforming. In time we become able to handle more energy and deeper inspiration.

One sheikh explained, "If you try to put too much current into a 25-watt light bulb, it will burn out. But a 100-watt bulb can handle the current that would burn out a 25-watt bulb." In *zikr* we keep increasing the current, so our subtle nervous system gets stronger over time. The light bulb cannot change, but we can. We can come to hold more energy for longer periods of time. A sheikh is someone who can maintain a "charge" strong enough to recharge others.

Once a sheikh and dervish went to the *zikr* of another Order. Afterwards, the dervish said, "My sheikh, did you see that young dervish? He was so devotional. His heart was so open!" The sheikh laughed and said, "You didn't see anything. You didn't notice the old dervish in the corner who was far more inspired. A pebble thrown into a cup of water makes a huge splash, but a boulder thrown into the ocean barely causes a ripple."

We are trying to become grounded so we won't become overwhelmed by the love of God. We are seeking to become like that ocean. Then we can live our lives remembering God *and* still do our jobs, pay our taxes, answer the phone, handle our email.

As *zikr* is Remembrance of God, so is prayer. Hazreti Muhammad§ said that prayer is the best *zikr*. Muzaffer Efendi once pointed out that prayer is difficult, but *zikr* is easy. In prayer, it is very challenging to keep our minds on God. Our minds wander. But *zikr* captures our minds and our hearts. The great saints have been inspired to express their love of God through movement, breath, and chanting divine names. That is the origin of the various forms of *zikr*.

QUESTION:

When we do *zikr*, I really enjoy it, but sometimes I can't chant loudly enough. I get mad at myself because I can't chant like everyone else. Is there anything that I can do?

ANSWER:

Don't try to be to be loud. God is not hard of hearing!

If we can't be "loud enough," that's okay. If loudness were important, only opera singers would be saints. It's not about the volume or the beauty of our chanting. It's about where our heart is.

Your voice is naturally quieter. Don't pull yourself out of *zikr* to make yourself do something special. Taking yourself out of *zikr* is always a mistake. Remember, someone quietly practicing *zikr* may be in an extraordinary inner state. Many times I saw Safer Efendi make the subtlest, most beautiful, and most profound movements and sounds in *zikr*, while some of the young dervishes were far louder and more active. In the Mevlevi tradition, the young dervishes turn actively, but the sheikh moves very differently—much more slowly and contemplatively. Don't worry. You're fine. Don't criticize yourself.

One of our greatest problems is criticizing ourselves. Let yourselves be. Feel the *zikr*, and let it flow through you as best you can.

Breathe with your brothers or sisters on each side of you. Remain in touch with them. Be with them. That is our practice. When we are standing shoulder to shoulder, if an older dervish is next to you, surrender to their movement as much as you can. An important part of *zikr* is to become one with the breath and the movement of the person next to you.

I have never forgotten one *zikr* in which I was standing next to one of the senior Turkish dervishes. It felt as if my shoulder was glued his shoulder. All I had to do was to stay with him. Of course, I thought I did it badly and he was almost perfect. It was an incredible experience, but I felt bad, because I thought I was interfering with his beautiful *zikr*. But that was just my ego judging and criticizing.

This was decades ago, but it feels like yesterday. I had a fever, so I didn't have much energy of my own, which was a blessing. I hadn't slept much the night before, and I had a powerful dream—or perhaps it was a vision—that night. I had gotten out of bed because I couldn't sleep, and I lay on the couch in the living room. I half-slept on the couch, and I saw our *Pir*, the Founder of our Order. I wasn't sure what I had seen, but Safer Efendi said I had seen our Pir.

I may have gotten sick because my wife and I had tried to stay up with Safer Efendi and we became exhausted. He would stay up until the morning prayer, making *sohbet* and counseling individuals. Then he would pray and then sleep for a few hours. We couldn't do it. After a couple of nights, we got sick. Many of the old dervishes need very little sleep, but we couldn't keep up.

We should prepare ourselves before each *zikr* and sit quietly and become more still. We should take our *zikr* seriously. One of the senior dervishes, Mustafa Baba, whom I dearly love, often came to the *dergah* without having shaved in several days; he shaved just before the *zikr*. He behaved as if preparing himself for an important meeting, which *zikr* is of course.

Also, after *zikr*, don't immediately leave the state you are in. Remain a little quiet and still. As one sheikh said, "Don't jump up after worship. If you milked a cow, you wouldn't leap up and kick the milk pail over afterward. We have done something in *zikr*, whether we know it or not. At the same time, don't try to hold on to your meditative state too tightly. We should neither break our state, nor try to hold on to it, because we can't.

The most important moment is the one after your formal practice is over. After we have finished our *zikr*, how much of that inner connection can we maintain? If we can't keep it for at least a little while, what have we accomplished?

Of course, there's a natural change in the state of consciousness of *zikr*. We are too hard on ourselves when we think, "Why am I not still in that inspired place?" But that's a part of any temporary state of consciousness. In the Sufi tradition, it is called a *hal*. It is temporary by definition. We don't ask ourselves, "Why am I not still in the dream I just had?" We can't remain in a dream. We wake up. Those states are like a dream state. They don't last. They are also previews of more stable states to come.

▶ 10 ◀

Adab: Sufi Manners

One of the fundamental practices of Sufism is *adab*. *Adab* might be translated as "manners," "respect," "etiquette," or "right action." Respect is the heart of *adab*, although no single word in English can capture the full meaning of the term. Years ago, every profession had its own *adab*, including Sufism. According to many sheikhs, it is the core of Sufism.

Spiritual *adab* is between us and God. It is the result of *ihsan*, developing a sense of the Presence of God. If we have *ihsan* and faith, we realize God is always present. Then, of course, we will automatically behave more consciously and respectfully..

Muzaffer Efendi used to say that every human heart is a divine temple, created by God to house the soul that God placed within each of us. If we remember that, we will respect everyone, honoring the divine spark in them. Remembering the divine nature in others is worship and Remembrance of God. If we fail to respect one another, we are insulting God within.

Adab has to come from the inside. Outer manners without inner respect are like the corpse of a movie star. It looks beautiful on the outside, but it has no life.

Besides knowing that God is present in each person, we have to learn how to express our understanding. First we have to know how to act, then we act, and then we will change. *Adab* is action. The more we act with *adab*, the more our behavior will reflect our being and the more it will transform our being. Sincere action will change us. How else are we going to change? We can wait for God to change us, but God is waiting for us to make an effort.

We can certainly improve our ability to pray, to perform *zikr*. But Sufism is not something to be practiced an hour a day or an evening a week. Sufism is something we must practice all the time. How can we do this? *Adab*.

There are many stories of the beautiful *adab* of the old dervishes. Their behavior reflected their inner understanding and their state of being. For example, the great saint Ibrahim bin Adhem never leaned when he sat. He explained, "I never lean on anything in this world. My only support is my Lord."

Muzaffer Efendi gave us an excellent guide to good *adab*. He used to say, "Respect everyone who is older than you. They have had more time to pray. Respect everyone who is younger than you. They have had less time to sin."

Adab is fighting our egos, because developing good *adab* requires us to reject the wishes of our egos. Our egos don't want us to practice respect for others. They just want everyone to respect us. They want everyone to serve us, but they don't want to serve others. That is how we are. In a sense, we are crazed egotists. I see it in myself, and I see it all around me.

We are here to practice respect for our brother and sister dervishes. Our old sheikh, Safer Efendi, was like a twin brother to Kemal Baba. They were the same age, and they had served together in the army. They were best friends. They came together to see Fahreddin Efendi, who was the Jerrahi sheikh years ago. They asked to become dervishes at the same time. Fahreddin Efendi first initiated Safer Efendi and then Kemal Baba immediately after.

Kemal Baba never forgot that Safer Efendi had become a dervish before he did. He always respected Safer Efendi as his senior, and years later we could still see this. When I first met them, Safer Efendi was the senior dervish in our Order, and Kemal Baba was the second in seniority. If Kemal Baba was teaching some of the younger dervishes, he would immediately stop when Safer Efendi entered the room and tell them to ask Safer Efendi. He would never turn his back on Safer Efendi and always insisted that Safer Efendi leave the room before him.

The two of them were like Siamese twins. They were always sitting together, shoulder to shoulder. It was as if they were joined together; it was strange to see one without the other beside him. Although the two men shared the deepest of friendships, Kemal Baba always behaved toward Safer Efendi with the greatest respect.

The difference in seniority was a few minutes, and we might think it is a small thing, but is it? It was God's choice that one was initiated as a dervish before the other. Did God make a mistake? Did Fahreddin Efendi make a mistake? We can trivialize the difference or we can take it seriously. Good *adab* means to take things like this seriously.

It was wonderful to learn *adab* from dervishes like these. *Adab* is not something we can learn from books.

We can all improve our practice of *adab*. We can respect each other more and show greater respect to our guests. In Islam, a guest is seen as having been sent by God. Sometimes I see guests in our center helping to set the table before dinner or cleaning up after dinner, while some dervishes are sitting and chatting. That is not good *adab*, not at all. I'm ashamed when I see it. Good *adab* requires the willingness to serve—and the awareness of when to serve. To sit and talk without noticing the table is being set by guests is either incredibly heedless or incredibly self-centered, or both. Neither one is acceptable. How can a dervish sit and let a guest serve them? We are here to serve our guests. You wouldn't allow guests in your house to serve you, would you?

Unfortunately, I have to remind us, because we forget. Every once in a while, some guests who have been coming here for a while do help out. That is fine. But work *with* them; don't sit and expect them to serve us. Why should they ever become dervishes if they are already working harder at serving than so-called dervishes?

We need to be more conscious. Our egos want to be served. Our egos think we *should* be served. All the more reason to pay attention, to become more conscious. This is where our practice starts. We have to become more respectful to each other, more respectful to our guests.

We also have to be more respectful to our sheikhs. For example one of the traditions of *adab* in Sufism is that we do not turn our backs on our sheikhs. Yet I still see dervishes turning their backs on me. As an individual, I don't care; I don't want other people treating me in any special ways. But as a sheikh, it bothers me that some of our dervishes behave so discourteously. Poor *adab* weakens the relationship between sheikh and dervish.

My relationship with the dervishes in our community is a gift given to us all. I have put up with all kinds of things over the years that I would never stand for in the rest of my life. God gives me far more patience with all of you than I usually have. But God can also take that away. It is something we should worry about. I worry about that with my sheikhs. But they are patient with me, thank God, even though they know my failings. But I worry about it, as I worry about the quality of my *adab* when I am with them.

It's crucial to take this matter of respecting the sheikh seriously—respect for the sheikh, not simply for an individual. Your sheikh is the link connecting you with hundreds of years of the history, wisdom, and blessings of your Order. Value that relationship if you value your relationship with your Order.

Our head sheikh, Tuğrul Efendi, once mentioned that a sheikh is like an electrical outlet. We have to plug ourselves into that outlet if we want to access the power that feeds into it. Ultimately, we are connecting with God's infinite power. There is no power within the outlet itself, but the outlet is essential in transmitting that divine power to you. It is a blessing given to the sheikhs that they can make this connection.

When Tuğrul Efendi became our head sheikh, he told the dervishes that some of them were senior to him and some knew more about Islam than he did. He said he did not want them to respect him personally, but he insisted they respect him as their sheikh. Shortly afterward, one of the old dervishes came up to him and said, "Let me kiss your hand." Tuğrul Efendi replied, "No. After all, you are my senior. I can't have you kiss my hand." The old dervish said, "It is not *your* hand I want to kiss. I want to kiss the hand of my sheikh." Tears came to my eyes when he told me that.

We all make mistakes. If some dervishes forget and turn their backs on me, I still love them. But it is not good. It is sloppy. We should be most concerned about the inner—our love and respect for each other. But we should be also be concerned with the ways we express this outwardly.

As I said earlier, how we act affects what we become. How else are we going to grow? It is not going to happen by magic. How we act will change us. If we act with respect and awareness, we will become more loving, more aware and more openhearted. If we act with *adab* toward each other, our connection with the Order will get stronger. Then there will be more blessing and more energy here to help us all change.

We can't change without God's blessing. How can we receive God's blessing? Through our sheikhs. Divine blessings do not come from the sheikh, but they flow *through* the sheikh. Good *adab* connects us

141

with the energy and blessing of the Order. This connection goes all the way back to Hazreti Muhammad§ and to God's infinite power and blessing. We are seeking to deepen our connection to something that will transform us. *Adab* is one of the things that hold our Sufi practice together.

Ideally, we will practice good *adab* in our community, with each other and with our guests—and outside our community as well. We can be role models of *adab* for each other, but we are only together for six or seven hours a week. How many hours are there in a week? One hundred and sixty eight. Our six or seven hours together represent a very small percentage of our time. Our center is a training ground for the rest of life.

The simplest actions can be demonstrations of good *adab*. A classic example in Sufism is the way we receive a cup of tea. Are we grateful for the tea? Are we grateful to the dervish who served us the tea? Or do we respond inwardly, "Thanks, but I wish you had served me sooner." With that kind of inner response, our outer behavior will be tainted by our lack of gratitude.

Our egos will always complain if we are not served first. Again, good *adab* always involves the struggle with ego. The ego always expects respect from everyone, but it tries to convince us we don't need to show respect to anyone else. Can we be truly grateful when we are served, and express that gratitude in the way we receive the tea? At the same time, the dervish who serves tea is grateful for the chance to serve. So when one real dervish serves another, it is a beautiful thing to behold. That moment of interaction is golden.

By expressing our gratitude, I don't mean effusive thanks. Some people think they are behaving like Sufis by kissing everybody's hands, bowing constantly, and using flowery expressions of gratitude for the smallest things. To me, this is almost as if they are making fun of Sufi *adab*. That behavior is really driven by the ego. They want everyone to notice them and to admire their overblown etiquette. The old dervishes behave far more subtly and less conspicuously.

Little things can express *adab* beautifully. Years ago, I was sitting with a group of senior dervishes. Someone turned on the television and we all turned to watch. The TV set was in back of me and so I turned around completely. A moment later, I realized that I might be blocking the view of one or two of the old dervishes. But by the time I realized that, they had already moved, so I didn't have to. It was that fast. It was an unbelievably embarrassing moment. Their *adab* was so much better than mine, and that showed me how I should have behaved.

Another time, I was sitting at lunch with the Turkish dervishes who were visiting New York with Muzaffer Efendi. The servers were all primarily focused on the head table with Muzaffer Efendi. I was sitting at a table with the senior dervishes and our table was served second. There was a group of young people at another table who had not been served because the servers were so busy with the "more important" tables. Without saying a word, Safer Efendi quietly got up and sat at the young people's table. The servers could not ignore that. After all Safer Efendi was the senior dervish in our Order. So they immediately begin to serve Safer Efendi and the young people seated next to him. Safer Efendi never said a word, never criticized or verbally instructed anyone. But he taught an important lesson for anyone with eyes to see.

If we remember that God is in everyone's heart, we will do whatever we can to avoid breaking someone else's heart. Good *adab* includes teaching by not breaking someone's heart. That is often a challenge.

After that same lunch, I sat with another member of our California Jerrahi community, a man who had just become a dervish the day before. I said to him, "Why don't we sit and wait for everyone else to leave? After all , you are the newest dervish in the room, and you should let everyone else go out before you. According to the *adab* of our Order, the sheikh and the senior dervishes go first. Guests should also go first, because we respect our guests and want to honor them. I'll sit here and keep you company as your brother from California, and we can leave last."

Everybody left the room except for Kemal Baba, who was senior to everyone but Muzaffer Efendi and Safer Efendi. He quietly let everybody go before him. He sat so quietly and unobtrusively that most people did not notice he was waiting for them to leave. I looked at him and he looked at me and he said to me, "Go ahead." He ordered me to go before him.

It was a deeply touching moment. I didn't have enough Turkish to argue with him. (And, of course, arguing with my senior would have been bad *adab*.) I hated to go in front of him, yet I could not ignore his request for me to go first. It seemed like a simple thing, but it was very powerful. Kemal Baba's humility was so strong and so palpable at that moment. It touched me deeply. He genuinely wanted everyone to go before him, even though he "should" have been the third person to leave the room.

That was real Sufism. Sufism is not singing and dancing or reading fancy books or spiritual poetry. Sufism is *adab*. It is how we act, backed up by sincere intention. We always have to check our intentions. Are we trying to show what good dervishes we are? Or are we acting from sincerity and a desire to serve?

The senior dervishes always served Muzaffer Efendi as best they could. When he was still smoking cigarettes, everyone wanted to light his cigarette. If I had my lighter out, the senior dervishes around Efendi would gesture to me to light his cigarette. If I was late getting my lighter out, they would light his cigarette immediately. Their goal was that he didn't have to wait, and they were happy to give me the opportunity to serve if I was ready to do so.

On the other hand, some foolish new dervishes would fight with each other for the "honor" of lighting his cigarette. It sometimes looked like a scrimmage under the basketball net, with people elbowing each other out of the way.

You see how easily our egos can distort *adab*. *Adab* can get hijacked. Saying to oneself, "*I* will light the sheikh's cigarette" does result in the sheikh being served; however, it easily becomes bad *adab* toward everyone else. The senior dervishes' attitudes were different. "All I care about is that Efendi's cigarette gets lighted and I'll be delighted if someone else gets the honor of serving him. But if they are not ready to serve him, I will." That is good *adab*.

The goal is that the sheikh or the guest is served, not that *I* do it. So we remember our goal and our intention, which is service. This includes struggling with our egos, which want us to be the one who serves. Our egos may lead us to be jealous of others because they are serving. We shouldn't; we should be happy if others get the blessings of service. Which reminds me of another story:

At the time of Muzaffer Efendi, many dervishes would gather at his bookstore on Fridays before the Friday prayer. Customers would come in and out, dervishes would come in and out. Sometimes people would ask questions. Efendi treated everybody with the same attitude they brought to him. To customers, he was a knowledgeable seller of religious books. To the dervishes, he was the most important person in the world. His *adab* was perfect in every case.

A young man would often come around with tea for everyone, and on one Friday an American dervish insisted on paying for the tea, wanting to serve his sheikh and his fellow dervishes. (It is traditional *adab* in our Order for one of the dervishes to pay for the others.)

After the Friday prayers, some of the dervishes returned to Muzaffer Efendi's bookstore. A waiter brought in food for everybody, and the American dervish immediately paid for the food. Then, after lunch, someone came with more tea. The American reached for his wallet and Muzaffer Efendi growled, "Stop! Enough. Do you want to take all the blessings today? Let someone else pay."

It was a lovely reminder. The American dervish sincerely wanted to serve, but he didn't understand that service is a privilege as well as an obligation. In addition to serving, we should let other people also have the blessings of service.

Recently, Tosun Efendi and I went to a fancy weekend brunch in Istanbul with a group of European dervishes who were visiting Turkey. Tosun Efendi paid by credit card, and afterward I paid a third of the bill and a third sheikh paid the other third. The visiting dervishes were not aware that the brunch cost hundreds of dollars, but they were aware that they were very well treated as our guests.

Service and good *adab* require consciousness. We have to be aware of what is around us. Most of the time, we don't know what is around us, because we are not looking. We have to learn to open our eyes. We also have to open the eyes of our hearts to see what is subtler. Muzaffer Efendi used to say that a dervish should be aware of what others need and provide it for them before they themselves are aware of their needs. If they have to ask, we have failed. That is *adab*.

▸ 11 ◂

The Importance of Action

Many people substitute words for action. We should all talk less and do more. In Islam and in Sufism, faith must be expressed in action. If our faith is not expressed in action, it will decay. Real knowledge is knowledge we put into action. And when we act on our knowledge, it can transform us.

According to a dervish saying, a camel does not become a *hajji* by carrying a pilgrim to Mecca, and a donkey does not become a scholar by carrying books to a library. The donkey can carry the most holy, inspiring books, but the donkey still remains a donkey. Some scholars carry wonderful books in their heads, but they are still "donkeys," because they refuse to act on their knowledge.

How can our knowledge transform us? Owning a large library of great books does not change us. We all know this, but we forget. We are proud of our collections of Sufi books, as if that matters. We are proud of our book collection even when we haven't read all those books, which is particularly foolish. Reading alone is not enough. We always need to ask ourselves, "How can I put these ideas into action?" We can learn and change by action—trying new things, making mistakes and getting feedback.

CHAPTER 11

Many students of Sufism prefer a dead sheikh to a living sheikh. It is wonderful to have a dead saint as sheikh—and also very convenient. They can never criticize us. We can ignore any of their teachings with which we disagree. They can't complain.

Many people prefer to listen to lectures, read books, and talk about Sufi ideas instead of acting on them. This doesn't do much. When we read inspiring poetry or prose, we must ask, "What do I do? How do I translate these ideas into action?"

We should always be learning, but it should not be mere book learning. According to a famous *hadith*, "If two days are the same, the second day is a loss." In other words, we should learn something new every day. If we don't keep learning, we become stagnant. The second day is a loss, because we are getting older and have less time left.

The *hadith* does not mean to read a lot and do nothing. That is not what Hazreti Muhammad§ meant. He meant that we should learn something concrete every day: how to boil an egg or how to hammer a nail into a piece of wood. These are simple things. There is nothing fancy about learning how to boil an egg or hammer a nail, but they are examples of real learning. The Prophet§ taught us to learn from everyone we meet. He said that even the simple shepherd knows something—how to herd and care for animals—that we don't know.

We are to act and to learn by doing. The Founder of our Order taught that all Jerrahi dervishes should learn how to earn a living with their own hands. In other words, we should develop skills. Islam teaches us to learn to care for our families and ourselves. Many of us can earn our living with our mouths. That is not a small thing. To be able to teach or supervise others is a real and very valuable skill. But we should also be able to earn our living with our hands. There is great wisdom in that. In Turkey, the sultans all developed these kinds of skills. Some were goldsmiths, while others were accomplished musicians or woodworkers.

Let us keep asking ourselves, "What have I learned today? What am I planning to learn tomorrow? How can I put my knowledge into practice?" It is too easy to become lost in words, to become fascinated by abstractions. The nice thing about action is we get to learn from feedback: our actions either work or they don't. The world is an excellent teacher. If we hammer a nail and it bends instead of going in straight, we have discovered that we don't yet know how to hammer a nail very well.

Learning does not have to be an individual activity. It is wonderful to learn together with friends or family. It is an excellent idea to practice new skills alongside our children. It is wonderful for them to see us putting new learning into practice.

In the old days, the dervishes lived together in their Sufi lodge until they got married. They learned and worked together. Most lodges were self-supporting. The lodge owned land, and the dervishes worked together planting, weeding and harvesting. Someone new would work beside a senior dervish, and in the natural course of working together, the novices learned how to be dervishes. In some cases, new dervishes would be sent to apprentice with a senior dervish to learn a trade, like pottery or silversmithing. In the course of their apprenticeship they also learned about themselves.

Even if our jobs involve speaking rather than working with our hands, we can keep learning if we look for feedback. If you are a teacher, pay attention to your students. What are they learning? How can you improve the learning process for them? I am amazed how many teachers don't really observe their students in order to get feedback on their teaching. Too many teachers blame their students if the students don't learn. As dervishes we should stop blaming others. We should always look at what we can improve in ourselves.

Blaming others takes us off the hook. We tell ourselves it was their fault and that they need to change. Or we can blame "the system" when things aren't going well. A teacher can blame the school system, a businessperson can blame his or her company's way of doing business, etc. Instead we should ask ourselves what we could do to make things better. We can always change and improve. The admonition to learn every day means we must become self-reflective, self-critical. We can always do our jobs better, become better spouses, better parents, better dervishes. This is not striving for better intellectual understanding. Mere abstract understanding is a booby prize. It doesn't change anything. Worse, it is distracting and does not lead to real change. Knowing "why" does not change us.

Old-fashioned psychotherapy was often stuck in clever mental models and sophisticated diagnoses. Years ago, one patient concluded, "I have spent years in therapy and now I know exactly *why* I'm neurotic." The patient did not experience real change. She was no less neurotic than she had been when she began therapy. Worse, she became *less* likely to change, because she had learned reasons to justify how she was. That kind of so-called knowledge is poison! It makes us become stuck in the habits we have developed.

I have been a university professor for over forty years, and I am shocked by the number of teachers who don't even try to improve. Many are complacent and self-satisfied. We have all had professors like that. They teach the same subjects in the same way year after year, using the same notes they wrote out years ago. The notes become yellowed, but they still use them.

A more modern version of this syndrome is exemplified by the lecturers who have PowerPoint presentations they use over and over again. Some even read from their PowerPoint slides. The students can read the slides for themselves or get the presentation electronically. They are wasting their time listening to canned lectures like that. Reading from a PowerPoint slide is not teaching.

This tendency exists in all of us. There is a lazy part of us that encourages us to repeat what we have learned years ago instead of spending time and energy improving our skills and understanding.

Our Sufi path is a path of action and service. Prayer and contemplation take up a small part of our days. The rest of our days involve action in the world. We can't avoid acting. The only way to avoid acting is by dying. If we are alive, we are acting all the time. We are breathing. Brain activity and other biological processes are constantly taking place within us. We can't avoid acting. Sitting still involves the inhibition of action, which itself is an action. In fact, all actions involve both inhibition and action. For example, if I want to move one finger, I have to inhibit all the other fingers of that hand from moving. It is much easier to move all five fingers. We are always acting, even when we think we are doing nothing.

We can develop the habit of remembering God in the midst of our activities. We begin by saying *bismillah* before acting. The Prophet§ taught this is the best form of remembrance. We can serve others and serve Creation in our actions. Then we are practicing Sufism all the time, not for the relatively few minutes a day we are praying. Every action can be worship, because every action is a chance to serve and to remember God.

Muzaffer Efendi used to say that we should remember God with every breath. He added that we really should remember God three times with every breath: when we breathe in, when we breathe out, and between each breath. A seemingly impossible task, but my sheikh said it is possible. At least we can try.

We can make every moment of our lives a part of this path of ours. Ideally, we can practice Sufism and Islam all the time. Every moment is a time to practice. God gave us our bodies and our capacity to breathe; shouldn't we be grateful all the time? God gave us the capacity to love others; shouldn't we exercise that capacity, ideally with everyone we meet?

This is all action. One way to minimize action is to sit with a book. Many of us have avoided our own personal and spiritual growth by reading and never getting our hands "dirty" with action. Serving others does not mean we have to dedicate our whole lives to serve like Mother Teresa, although she is a wonderful spiritual model. We can serve others by feeling compassion and praying for them. And when action is needed, we must act.

It is traditional to offer a silent prayer for the souls of the departed whenever we pass a graveyard. We can also inwardly bless whomever we see on the street. If we see someone who is homeless and we are unable to help them, for example, we should at least pray for them. Charity is important. If we cannot give someone what they physically need, a smile is a form of charity. We don't necessarily have to give them money, but they certainly need our prayers. Imagine how difficult their lives are. And we can be grateful that God did not put us in the same condition. We can say to ourselves, "There but for the grace of God go I." We can ask God to heal them, to make their lives easier. If we don't do that, what are we? Where is our compassion?

Muzaffer Efendi pointed out that if anyone asks us for something we should take his or her request seriously. He didn't tell us always to say yes, but he advised us to take the request seriously. If we see someone on the road who is trying to hitch a ride, we may decide not to pick her or him up, especially if we are alone in the car. We could speed by them without thinking, or we could automatically stop to pick them up without considering whether that is dangerous or not. I don't advocate either mechanical response. Instead, we could reflect that someone needs help and at least pray for them, "O Lord, I don't feel it is safe for me to stop. Please help this person." We could do that.

Muzaffer Efendi taught the more we develop on this path, the more responsibility we have to behave correctly. We don't expect as much from a one-year-old child as we do from a twenty-year-old. The more mature people are, the more we expect from them. (Of course, we should also expect more of ourselves as we grow more mature.)

My sheikh used to tell the story of a government official who brought his brand-new baby daughter to his sultan. The sultan said, "Oh, what a beautiful baby. Let me see her." The sultan took the infant on his lap. A few minutes later the sultan exclaimed, "Take her, she is wet!" The sultan's beautiful clothes had become wet as well. Muzaffer Efendi commented that the sultan would not get angry at the baby for wetting his clothing. However, if the official urinated on the sultan's clothing, the sultan would immediately have his head cut off. Then my sheikh pointed out that every time we pass by someone who needs help or fail to stop for a hitchhiker, we have wet the Sultan's pants. Luckily, God is merciful. God realizes that we are still spiritually immature.

Let me repeat, I am not suggesting we pick up every hitchhiker we pass. God gave us a brain, and we should use good judgment before we act. I *am* suggesting that we take seriously any request for help. If we decide not to comply, we can at least pray for the one who asks.

One of my colleagues is an Episcopal priest. One day she was riding on a subway in New York, wearing her clerical collar. A homeless woman sat down next to her. The woman began talking about God and asked the priest some questions about her spiritual life. The priest kept waiting to be asked for money and wondered how much she should give this woman. But the homeless woman kept on talking to her and didn't ask for anything. Finally the woman got up to leave and handed a subway token to the minister. She apologized for not having anything more to give and thanked the minister for such a wonderful and inspiring conversation. The minister sat there thinking, "I was worried that she was going to ask me for a few dollars, and this woman gave *me* something."

Every time we choose not to be generous, we are tyrannizing ourselves. We are hurting ourselves, hardening our hearts. That story reminds us to watch our assumptions. The minister was sure that the woman sat next to her in order to get some money from her. Instead the homeless woman gave something to her.

Our actions may not always turn out as we wish, but if we have the best intentions, I believe we will always benefit from those actions. It is an important Sufi practice to check our intentions, to ask ourselves what we really want to accomplish. We should consciously reflect on our goals before we begin to act. No spiritual path thrives on unconsciousness. Our path involves awareness put into action.

When Safer Efendi became our head sheikh, he gave a short talk to the Jerrahi dervishes. He began, "Sufism is not theory. It is practice." In this talk he discussed learning and teaching. He reminded us that the Prophet§ taught us to learn every day. Then he commented that we should not make too great a distinction between Sufi teachers and students. If we are always learning we will be students throughout our lives. And if people ask us about something we have learned, we should share our learning with them. Whenever we do that, we are acting as teachers. Being a life-long student entails becoming a life-long teacher as well. Of course, the opposite is also true—being a teacher means being a student as well.

Safer Efendi reminded us that we are *all* teachers and students, although some of us have been given the formal role of Sufi teacher. We should be learning and teaching all the time. If we become stuck in the role of teacher, we become stagnant and fail to learn from our students. If we become stuck in the role of student, we are failing in our obligation to serve others by teaching what we have learned. We shouldn't be stingy and keep our learning to ourselves.

The most profound way to teach Sufism is to be a role model of how a dervish behaves. As I have mentioned before, Safer Efendi once said to me, "I may not know much about Sufism, but what I know is what I have loved and practiced for over forty years." It is essential to love what we learn and love what we do. If we don't love what we are learning, we will not learn much.

Think of our experiences of education. We have all studied just to pass a class, not because we cared about the material. How much do we remember from this kind of learning? A day or two after their exams, most students have forgotten over half of what they have learned. A few weeks later they have forgotten over 90 percent. Why? The retention rate is so low because they didn't care about what they were learning and didn't put it into practice.

We can inspire each other to learn and to act on our learning. We can be role models for each other. In a *hadith qudsi*, God said, "If you learn something new and put it into practice, I will teach you another thing." With these words, God promises to teach us directly if we act on our learning. How could God have emphasized the importance of action more strongly than this? Think what a priceless blessing it is to have God as our teacher.

Unfortunately, we live in a culture in which words often substitute for action. Muzaffer Efendi used to say empty recitation is like someone in a jungle who sees a lion stalking him or her and reacts by saying, "I take refuge in this tree!" Those words won't help that person at all. She or he has to take refuge in the tree with action instead of words—by climbing.

Most people spend hours every day watching TV or movies. They constantly hear empty words, recited by actors playing a part. We are entertained at best. Every once in a while, the words of the actors do touch us. But how often does this happen?

The words we recite in prayer are incredibly rich and moving. But all too often we recite these words without even thinking about their meaning. We recite the words of the Qur'an without thinking that these are God's messages, words with limitless depth and meaning.

I recall a Sufi story about the power of words. Years ago, there was a Jerrahi sheikh who was known throughout Istanbul as a great healer. (Our Order has been given two gifts, the gifts of healing and of dream interpretation.) One night the sheikh was invited to a dinner party. One of the other guests was the Ottoman minister of health, who had studied Western medicine in Paris. The minister was very proud of his Western learning and looked down on "old fashioned" Muslims like the sheikh. The host's daughter had an epileptic fit that evening, and the host asked the sheikh if he would pray for her. The sheikh prayed for the daughter's healing and she began to recover.

The minister became extremely upset at this and declared, "We have to stop this kind of superstition and devote ourselves to modern, Western medicine. This old-fashioned nonsense is holding us back. We are in the modern world. We have modern medicines to use now instead of reciting this kind of mumbo-jumbo and pretending to heal somebody." The sheikh turned to the minister and said, "I didn't know they promoted jackasses to be ministers!" The minister turned bright red with anger. The sheikh continued, "How could someone with almost no intelligence at all serve our government?" The minister turned white, so furious he could hardly breathe.

Then the sheikh changed his tone completely. "My son, how upset you have become. Please sit down and calm yourself. This is not good for your health." The minister did not know what to say. The sheikh continued, "You see how a few words affected you. Your blood pressure has shot up. Your heart is pounding. If a few unkind words can affect you so negatively, then perhaps the recitation of the sacred words of the Holy Qur'an can affect someone positively."

▶ 12 ◀

Praying for One Another

There are two kinds of prayers in Islam. The first is formal prayer, or *salat*. In *salat*, the correct outer form is essential. We stand facing toward Mecca, we recite verses from the Holy Qur'an, we bow, etc. The other kind of prayer is personal prayer, or *dua*. These prayers are sometimes called prayers of supplication, in which we ask God for help.

We can make *dua* for others or ourselves. Many people pray for material things. They make prayers like, "O Lord, bring me a new Cadillac"—or, as Janis Joplin sang, "Oh Lord, won't You buy me a Mercedes Benz?" Today we are more likely to pray for a new TV or other electronic toys. Perhaps we don't often ask God formally for these things, but we do yearn for the things of this world.

It is better to make *dua* for our spiritual state—to ask God to open our hearts, help us become more honest, less selfish, more charitable, more mature. We can certainly ask God for those things as well as asking for others. Traditionally, Islamic prayers never use the words *I* or *me*. It is always *we* or *us*. We can also pray for others. We can pray for those we love, for family and friends, or for our brothers and

157

sisters on this path. We can also pray for those who are suffering. We should pray for those who are suffering or starving. Of course, we should not merely pray; we should also act to help them. But at a minimum, we should pray for them.

God says in the Holy Qur'an, "Pray to your Lord, humbly and secretly." (7:55, Khalidi) Our formal prayers are not secret. We pray in congregation, in the mosque, or alone at home, and our prayer is an outer act; it is not secret (although our formal prayers always include sentences we say silently). What does God mean by praying "in secret"? I believe that this means to make *dua*, to ask silently for help for ourselves and for others.

Outer prayer always becomes affected by our judgments and considerations of others' opinions. Our egos want us to look good, and we can't help hoping that others will notice how well we are praying, how spiritual we are.

Once, an imam remained in the mosque after night prayers to make his individual prayers. He said aloud, "O Lord, I am nothing." The *muezzin* came in, heard the imam, and said in his beautiful *muezzin's* voice, "O Lord, *I* am nothing." A poor beggar who had entered the mosque and heard the imam and the *muezzin* also said, "O Lord, I am nothing."

The imam angrily turned to the *muezzin* and said, "Who does he think he is, saying he is nothing?"

You see what so easily happens when we pray in public. Our egos get into the act. That is why God said we should pray humbly and secretly.

Why humbly? Who do we think we are? The most powerful, strongest, richest, most intelligent person will leave everything behind at death. We are beggars at God's door. God gives and God takes away. Also, if we are not humble, we can't ask properly. We tend to ask God as if we were ordering a meal in a restaurant: "Waiter, bring me a steak. I want it medium rare"—as if we were owed something. If we are humble, we realize we have no *right* to receive anything. We don't even have the right to ask. It is a blessing to be able to ask God for anything. Nothing is owed to us, and anything we might receive comes out of God's infinite generosity. That is the proper attitude in making *dua*. In addition, my sheikhs have said that in order to have our prayers answered, it is important to eat food that is *halal*, or lawful. We also have to make sure that our income is *halal* so that the food we buy with it is *halal*. Then what comes out of our mouths is not ruined by taking into our mouths something unlawful.

Remember, we are not owed anything. We don't understand God's Will, and we don't understand God's Creation. Our understanding is very superficial. God tells us to ask humbly. God will answer, but God does not always answer in the ways we expect or when we expect. In many ways, the act of making *dua* itself is more important than the answer. We focus on the goal—we want this or that—but it is our connection with God that is most important.

Hazreti Muhammad§ said, "Making *dua* is the essence of worship." What is the meaning of this *hadith*? Prayers are conversations with God. It is said that we are on one end of the prayer carpet and God is on the other end. The Qur'an teaches, "Prostrate thyself [before God] and draw close [unto God]." (96:19, Asad). But it is hard to remember that formal prayer is a conversation with God. We get wrapped up in the form and often pray mechanically, because we have made our formal prayers thousands of times. It is a struggle to remain conscious as we pray.

Making *dua* is clearly relating to God and having a conversation with God. If we are sincere in our *dua*, we are truly present with God in the moment of asking. We say to God, "God, I need You," or "Lord, bring health to my beloved friend who is ill." At these moments, we are truly present with God, and these times of being with God are the real reward. Don't think of *dua* only in terms of the desired results. Making *dua* itself is the real blessing.

There are some interesting questions about this that are often debated among scholars and sheikhs: Is it better to make *dua*, or to practice acceptance of whatever God brings us? Should we be patient and content with what we have, or should we ask God for what we want? These are not easy questions to answer. Should we pray, "I am sick; I want to be healthy"? "I want to grow on this spiritual path"? "I want the best for my children"? These are important prayers, but perhaps it is better to say, "O Lord, I trust You. I trust in Your wisdom, grace, and compassion, and I accept whatever You bring me." Safer Efendi recommended the *dua*, "Our Lord, grant us good in this world and good in the hereafter." (2:201, Khalidi) This is a way of praying "Oh God, I need You. You know best what is good for me." Aren't patience and acceptance important?

So what should we do? Why am I asking this question and confusing the issue when I began this chapter with the importance of making *dua*? Because we sometimes have to ask ourselves, "Is this a time to practice patience, or is this a time to try to change things?" How do we know? We can ask ourselves what is our heart telling us. Does our heart tell us to be patient, or does our heart tell us to ask God for help?

We must pay attention when we are making *dua*. As a general guideline, if our heart expands while we are praying, it is good for us. If our heart contracts in prayer, we probably need to practice patience.

Prayer is not meant to be practiced mechanically; Sufism is not a cookbook. Sufism and Islam are a way of life and not limited to rituals. The goal is to become a worthy servant of God, as God wishes us to be. There are all kinds of cookbooks and formulas available in some books about Sufism or other mystical traditions. There are books on dream interpretation that tell you what each dream image "means." Other books tell you that if you recite a certain formula so many times a day, it will have certain benefits. There is some truth to that, but always trying to change things can be a trap. Where is the faith and acceptance in that? We have to know when to practice patience and trust in God.

This path is a marathon, not a sprint. But it is a marathon for everyone, not just for athletes (or scholars). We have to ask ourselves what will help us grow in the long run. Does this pain or illness have something valuable to teach? Or is it better to ask for things to get better and move on—so we can experience new pains and new challenges.

Some sheikhs have taught that if we even *think* of making *dua* for our own benefit it is a sign we have not been doing our *zikr* properly. Because if we were remembering God deeply, we would not dream of asking for anything to change. There would be no room in us for anything but Remembrance of God.

Many Muslims make *dua* at the end of formal prayer. At times I don't feel I want anything for myself at that point. I take that as a great blessing. For a moment, I feel sane, content. I don't feel in need of anything. This is a very different state from the usual wanting, wanting, wanting of my ego. It is also a special time to pray for others.

In all our actions, we can benefit by asking ourselves if our behavior opens our hearts or not. "Does my *zikr* open my heart? Do my daily activities open my heart?" This can include reading books and watching films—and that doesn't apply only to books on Sufism. Our hearts can open from reading inspiring poetry or a great novel.

How can we nourish ourselves spiritually? How can we open our hearts? There is no simple answer. The hearts of most people open when they read a great spiritual author like Rumi, but this is not true of everyone, and it is not true all the time. Maybe we need to read Hafiz for a change. Or maybe we need to listen to inspiring music— for some that might be Sufi music, for others it might be Mozart.

It is very important to examine ourselves, to look at the inner effects of what we do. Sometimes we think we are becoming advanced on this path, but when we look inside we find we have been fooling ourselves. So we pick ourselves up and start over again—or, at least, that is what it feels like.

To return to the topic of making *dua*, I want to caution against making the *dua* of the ego. The ego always wants things, and we could spend all our time praying for worldly success, fame, wealth, etc. There is always something we want, but that does not mean we should have it. Just because we long for something, it doesn't mean we should pray for it.

This reminds me of the story of a wealthy man who came to a sheikh and said, "I lost my briefcase. It had a thousand gold coins in it. Please pray that I find it."

The sheikh did not say anything.

The next day the man returned and once more asked, "Please, sheikh, please pray that I might find my briefcase."

Again the sheikh did not reply.

The third day the man returned and pleaded, "Please pray that I might find my briefcase."

The sheikh raised up his hands and prayed, "O Lord, choose what is best for him."

That is an alternative our egos will never suggest to us. God tells us to pray humbly, and it is not humble to pray "God, I know what is best for me. This is what I need. And I would like it soon!" That is how we are. Instead, we might pray, "O Lord, I have these desires, but I trust that You will send what is best for me." What God chooses for us is always better than what we ask for ourselves.

And that reminds me of another story. A man felt he really needed a car, so he prayed, "O Lord, I really need a car. Please send me an old Nissan sedan." Every day for a week, the man prayed for a Nissan.

Nothing happened, so he prayed the same prayer for another week. Finally, he found a bargain on a used Nissan and he bought the car. That night he dreamed that he was complaining that it took so long for God to answer his prayers. A voice answered, "I had chosen a new Mercedes for you, but you kept insisting on an old Nissan and so I finally sent that to you instead." We do not know what is best for us.

The power of sincere prayer is very strong. A woman came to a sheikh and asked him to pray for her son. She said, "My son was sent to the army, and I have not heard from him. I'm afraid that he may get killed or captured. Please pray that he will come back to me."

The sheikh prayed for her son's return. Several weeks later, she returned along with her son. In tears she said, "My son was a prisoner, and he was kept in chains. Suddenly the chains fell from his body. He stood up and his captors immediately chained him up again. Once again the chains fell from his body. The jailers brought the prisoner to the warden of the prison. The warden said to him, 'You have a mother, don't you? Your mother has prayed for your freedom, and God heard her prayers. I have to let you go.'"

If we pray with the love and selfless devotion of a mother praying for her child, I believe God will answer. On the other hand, God does not always answer immediately. We always implicitly pray, "God, I want it now." God has said, "Call upon Me and I shall answer you." (40:60, Khalidi) But God does not promise to respond instantly. Those blessed lovers who continue to make *dua* will receive the blessings of making more prayers, and they will also receive the blessings of practicing patience. Rather than give them the lesser reward they are asking for, God makes them wait, so they may receive the greater reward of the intimacy of sincere prayer.

We want our rewards now; we want healing and relief now. But God may delay, so we may remain longer in the place of asking. That is why humility in prayer is important.

We hate to see the suffering of those we love, but that might be the best thing for them. Maybe there is a critical lesson they need to learn in their illness, loss, or suffering. The real reward may be growth in patience, and most of us have to be forced to be patient.

We need to remember that when we pray for something, we really don't know what is best for us or for those we love. There is an old story of three dervishes who were traveling together and saw some old bones by the road. The first dervish said, "I really wonder what kind of animal these bones come from. O Lord, please bring these bones together." And the bones began coming together.

The second dervish prayed, "O Lord, clothe these bones with flesh. Give life to these bones."

The third dervish quickly exclaimed, "O Lord, only if it is good for us."

And the lion that was almost formed in front of them went back to being just bones again.

We are like that. In our ignorance we may pray, "I would like such-and-such to happen." We think we are smarter than the first two dervishes, but we all have limited perspectives. What we pray for might not be good for us. It is important to pray from a place of humility, to always add to our prayers, "O Lord, if it is good for me."

In summary, I advise, "Yes, make *dua*. And, no, don't." I do think it is wonderful to make *dua*. We enjoy a wonderful relationship with God when we do, and God commands us to do so. But at the same time it should not be mechanical, or prayer that comes from a greedy or egotistical mindset.

It is good to reflect seriously on what we wish to pray for. What is worth praying for? Knowing that God loves sincere prayer, shouldn't we sit down and seriously contemplate questions like, "What *should* I pray for?" "What should I ask for myself? What should I pray for my loved ones?" "What should I pray for the world?" We can ask ourselves, "What does my heart want, not my head? What do I long for?" It is worth taking time to contemplate these questions.

In addition, let us make *dua* with a sense of God's Presence. If we can be present with God in those few prayerful moments, perhaps that is the greatest blessing of all. It is a blessing to be able to make *dua*. It is not merely a tool to get what we want. Look at it as a process of praying. How does the prayer affect us? In everything we do we can pay more attention to what is going on within us. The difference between Sufism and outer religious practice is, in Sufism we learn to pay attention to the inner effects of our actions.

One of the most important aspects of this path is to realize that we are in need. We are in profound need of God's Grace, blessings, and help. It is only our egos that say we do not need, that we can do it for ourselves, that we are self-sufficient. Only God is completely self-sufficient. Making *dua* is one way of saying "Lord, I am in need. I need You. I can't do it myself. I need Your blessings. I need Your help. I pray for Your help. And I don't even know enough to know what to ask for."

We always have to add, "...if it is good for me" or "...if that is what they need." We usually make the arrogant assumption that we know what is best for ourselves—or, worse, that we know what is best for others. Sometimes it may seem like common sense. If someone is sick, we pray for her or his health. But how do we know what will bring the greatest learning and the deepest blessings in the long run? Perhaps if the person is not healed right away, he or she will come to pray sincerely to God for healing, and that might be the greatest blessing of all.

Some people make *dua* in silence, and some pray aloud. I personally think it is better pray in silence, as God recommends in the Qur'an. People differ in how they pray and how they express themselves, in what touches their hearts. There are no hard and fast rules. As I said earlier, the most important thing is to pay attention to our hearts. If our hearts move us to speak aloud, or if we feel that our heart opens when we speak aloud, then we should do it. If it does not feel natural to pray aloud, then it is better to pray silently or privately.

My sheikhs have said that the best prayer is simply to be in God's Presence. That is where *dua* can lead us. It is wonderful to pray by simply sitting in silence, but true silence does not come easily. We can say inwardly, "God, You see what is in my heart. You know what I need better than I do." Then we can sit with God. That is a wonderful kind of prayer.

One of the most striking things I have ever experienced was hearing Muzaffer Efendi make *dua* publicly. I have not heard anything like it before or since. When Muzaffer Efendi first came to California, a young couple came and asked him to pray for them. They were among the twelve of us who became dervishes during his second trip to California a year later. They asked Muzaffer Efendi to pray for their marriage. He did not ask about their religion or anything about them. He simply turned his palms up, raised his hands, and raised his eyes to heaven. Then he made the deepest, most moving prayer I had ever heard. He prayed for their health and well-being, and he prayed for the health and strength of their relationship. He prayed that they might be spiritual partners to each other and lead each other on the Path of Truth.

It felt to me that Muzaffer Efendi went to another place, as if he brought the words of his prayer down from a heavenly place of prayer. He did not pray from his intellect, nor did he recite a memorized prayer. It was the first profound *dua* I ever heard.

After hearing him, I realized I had never heard real prayer before. All I had heard up to then was simply repetition of the words of others or superficial, intellectual compositions of words. Muzaffer Efendi's prayer was very different. There was a great power to this prayer.

If someone asks us to pray for them we can pray aloud or silently. It may ease someone's heart if we can pray aloud for her or him. If anyone has questions about how to make *dua*, ask your sheikh. Our egos may distort our efforts at prayer. In fact, our egos always get into the act. It is a question of how badly they affect us.

I cannot stress too much how important it is to pay attention to how our hearts respond to what we do. We can still fool ourselves. Our egos may tell us we are truly inspired when in fact we are not.

Muzaffer Efendi once told the story of a dervish who was very wealthy. His sheikh told him his money was an obstacle to his spiritual growth. The sheikh ordered, "Bring me all your money." The dervish immediately went home brought his money back to his sheikh, but he left a bag of coins at home for family expenses. The sheikh asked him, "Where is the rest of it?" The dervish admitted that he had left a bag of coins for his family. The sheikh exclaimed, "Take that bag of coins and throw it in the river! Where is your faith?"

The dervish brought his last bag of coins to the river. He recited, "*Bismillah ir-rahman ir-rahim*," and threw the first coin into the water. The dervish's heart expanded and he felt a burden had lifted within him. He did this with each remaining coin. By the end he felt that he had attained a higher state of consciousness.

He returned to his sheikh feeling this wonderful new inner state. The sheikh took one look at him and asked, "What did you do?" The dervish described throwing away the last of his wealth, coin by coin, each coin with a *bismillah*. The sheikh roared, "I told you to throw the bag of coins in the water. I didn't tell you to make a drama of this. Now get out of my sight!" The sheikh threw the dervish out.

The dervish had managed to put himself into a false state. At the river, he convinced himself, "With each coin I feel better. What a wonderful sacrifice I am making. How spiritual I am." His ego expanded, not his love of God. As I mentioned earlier, Tuğrul Efendi says that the beginning of the path is listening and the end of the path is listening. We should listen carefully to what our sheikhs tell us. This story illustrates that fundamental principle of Sufism.

I have been saying that we should follow our hearts, but it is not always easy. The poor dervish thought he was following his heart, but he was actually following his ego. It is always good to pay attention to our hearts, but we still have to use our judgment. Tuğrul Efendi has often said a bird needs two wings to fly, and for us to "fly," we have to use two wings as well. One is our intellect, the other is our heart. The intellect grows from inspired scholars. The heart grows by following the guidance of our sheikhs.

Our egos may tell us we are doing wonderfully spiritual things, and if we believe that, our hearts may seem to feel better. In truth, we imagine our hearts feel better, but they are really in pain. We all know our egos can do that. This path is not easy.

Real prayer is not just words. It is also actions. There is a fascinating collection of stories of the love the Prophet§ and the early Muslims had for animals. Some people felt sympathy for thirsty animals suffering in the desert heat. The sincere Muslims shared their limited water with the animals.

The *dua* of the average person is words. The *dua* of the Sufis is action. And the *dua* of the saints is their inner state. Ideally, these are all related, and our actions match our words and our inner state.

▸ 13 ◂

Hospitality

I t is our responsibility to be the most welcoming and hospitable hosts we can be, to everyone who comes to our center. If God wants people to come, they will come. And if God wishes, they will stay.

A dervish told me a story about Safer Efendi. One evening a visitor came to our center in Istanbul. The other dervishes did not like him for some reason and didn't treat him as a welcome guest. After the guest left, Safer Efendi addressed the dervishes in a very serious tone. "Every guest who comes here is to be treated as a personal guest of the Founder of our Order," he said. "No one can enter our Founder's home without his permission."

Every Jerrahi center is a branch of our Istanbul home, where our Founder taught and where he is buried. When we sit in our center in California, we are actually sitting in the corner of a room in our Founder's home. Safer Efendi also told me, "You are not my *halife* (representative). You and I are both representatives of our Founder." This definitely added to the weight of responsibility I felt as a sheikh.

We may think, "Wouldn't it be nice if we had more dervishes? I wish we had more people for *zikr*." However, when people come, we shouldn't treat them as customers to be sold on Sufism. We are like a large, happy family. We do not need more family members, as we are content with one another. But when our mother gives birth to a new baby, we are overjoyed. We don't just want more people; we want souls who yearn for God. We want more brothers and sisters who are on the Path of Truth and Reality. We must be happy and content with the blessings God showers on us, not wishing for more. And let us receive every visitor with respect and compassion, remembering that every visitor comes here as a guest of God. Material things diminish in importance for us when we give them away, but love is different. With love, the more we give the more we have.

When guests come, we should think, "Thank You God, You have given me the opportunity to serve as a host in this sacred space." In this meeting place and place of worship, our interactions with guests and with each other are sacred. Let's be with each other and with guests with the intention of service. I hope we all hold the intention of sincerely welcoming everyone who comes here, remembering that their hearts yearn for God just as our hearts do.

We all have personalities and personal quirks, and some of our guests may remind us of people from our past who behaved badly toward us, which may make us feel less than hospitable toward them. Just drop it. Let it go. It's important to try to remember that there is a soul behind everyone's personality. We are not the enemies of thieves; we are the enemies of thievery. We are not the enemies of liars, we are the enemies of lying. Our practice is to love the soul that loves God.

Of course, some of our guests are challenging. If everyone who came here were sweet and wonderful, well, they wouldn't need to come here. They wouldn't need this discipline. We are all here because we need to grow. We need to improve our own character, reduce our narcissism, and deepen our love of God; that's why we are here! Don't expect perfection in each other, and don't expect perfection in our guests. We are all seeking to become the kind of human being

God intends us to be. Every human being has a soul that yearns for God. The human heart is quite fragile, and it's our job to heal it, not damage it.

In the old days, the dervishes lived with their sheikh in a dervish community. That was how everyone learned Sufism. Recently, one of the old Turkish dervishes was talking about what extraordinarily gifted and inspired teachers were our old sheikhs Muzaffer Efendi and Safer Efendi. He said, "Even though I never met their sheikh Fahreddin Efendi, I am convinced it was their love of him that brought them everything." In addition to this love, our sheikhs constantly worked on acquiring knowledge and putting it into practice. They worked far harder than any of the rest of us.

The old dervishes spent all their spare time with their sheikh. Safer Efendi would work all day and then go to see his sheikh as soon as his work was over. He would stay with his sheikh all night until morning prayer. Then he would sleep for a few hours and go back to work. He kept that schedule for years.

That daily contact was a great blessing. We don't have those opportunities today. We don't live together, garden together, or work together. We have to find new ways of learning and practicing Sufism to make up for that. We have to develop a daily discipline that can transform our lives. We know how hard it is to transform our egos. We can't do that in one evening a week.

Safer Efendi once said, "If you don't have a family, you should have something to love. You should at least have a pet." That evening, one of the dervishes, an American who was living alone in Istanbul, found a half-wild street cat camped out in front of his apartment door. He took the cat in, and the cat was a wonderful companion for years.

It is easy to love a cat or a dog. They are bred to love us, and they rely on us for food, shelter, and almost everything else in their lives, just as we are dependent on people around us. Keeping a pet is

171

excellent practice in learning to love and serve God's Creation. Our goal is to serve all of Creation, including the earth, the water, and the atmosphere.

Once again, this sohbet *ended with an informal question-and-answer-session:*

QUESTION:

When I first came to this center, I expected perfection from everybody here, because this was God's place. Then I discovered that everybody here has problems too. So that was disappointing. I had expected to be around saints. So that was my lesson. I think it's really wrong to expect everyone in a spiritual community to be highly evolved, because we are all here for the same reasons.

ANSWER:

You're right. And it's important that we don't present ourselves in ways that would encourage our guests to think that we are special and they are not. Our guests may come in with that attitude, but we should be clear that we are just like everyone else. We are not special. We are no better than our guests. Our egos would like us to appear better than others. Our guests' egos also play comparison games, so they may see us as either better or worse than we are. We can sincerely do our best to welcome them, love them, and treat them as equals.

When anyone comes here, it will help if we say to ourselves, "Thank God for our honored guests." Why should anyone come to us? It's a wonderful gift when a visitor comes here. It's an honor for us. It is a gift to be able to serve them.

We don't know who comes here or why they come. Someone may visit us and not know how to do *zikr*. They may not understand much of what we do here. They may not know how to do prayers. They may not be Muslim. So what? Only God knows whose prayers are accepted. We don't know. I honestly believe that a naïve, sincere prayer from someone who has no idea how to do formal prayers might be more acceptable to God than ours.

Sincere Worship

Too much concern with the letter of the law often leads us to forget the spirit. In a well-known Sufi story, a scholar was rowing a boat on a large lake. He came close to a small island and heard a dervish reciting the traditional Islamic phrase "God is Greater." This phrase, *Allahu akbar*, is often mistranslated as "God is Great." However it literally means "God is Greater," that is, God is beyond everything that has existed or ever will exist. God is the only One who is truly transcendent.

However the dervish mispronounced the Arabic so badly that he actually said, *Allahu himar* —"God is a donkey"! The scholar was horrified, and he immediately rowed to the island to correct the man. After all, he was taught that this holy phrase could even bring a sincere believer the power to walk on water. The scholar corrected the dervish and rowed away, happy to have been of service to this poor, ignorant man.

A few minutes later, the scholar heard a voice in back of him. The dervish was running over the water and he called out, "Please recite the correct Arabic again. I'm afraid it is really difficult for me to get it right, because I have been pronouncing it wrong for so long." The surprised scholar humbly replied, "My friend, please stay with what you know. God surely accepts your worship as it is!"

The story makes me wonder about my own worship. We must all concern ourselves with improving our practice of worship. This also enhances our enjoyment of it. I still ask myself if am I too focused on the form and not focused enough on the spirit of my worship.

Muzaffer Efendi told the following story of Bilal al-Habashi, the first *muezzin*. Some of the early Muslims were upset with Bilal because he mispronounced the words of the call to prayer. Bilal's family was from Ethiopia, and he spoke Arabic with an accent. The Arab Muslims said, "He's reciting the call to prayer badly. The meaning is distorted. We need a *muezzin* who can pronounce the call to prayer properly."

The Prophet§ said, "You don't really know what you are saying." But they insisted that the call to prayer should be pronounced properly. So the Prophet§ finally acquiesced, "If that's what you want, have someone else give the call to prayer." The next day, one of the Arab Muslims gave the call to prayer.

That night everyone in Medina had the same dream. An angel came to them and said, "Why didn't you do your prayers yesterday?" They replied, "But we did." And the angel said, "We didn't hear the call to prayer, so we didn't think anyone prayed yesterday." Then the Prophet§ said, "You see. Let Bilal continue to give the call to prayer. God listens to the heart, not to the voice."

Remember this when visitors come. If our guests make mistakes, let them. If our guests don't know how to move during *zikr*, gently put your arm through their arm and guide them.

If someone cannot perform *zikr*, one of the senior dervishes should go and help that person. As a last resort, we may have to ask them to leave the *zikr* circle, but we should never make a guest feel badly. Once when Tosun Efendi was visiting, an older gentleman just couldn't move properly during the *zikr*, so Tosun Efendi brought him into the center of the circle. The man felt honored by being put in the center with the sheikhs. It helped the *zikr* and it did not break the heart of the person who couldn't do it properly.

It is not easy to be a gracious host. It is a good practice for us. Hospitality can be learned. Hotel employees, waiters, and waitresses receive training in how to serve. Why shouldn't we? Intention is what matters most. God judges us on the sincerity of our intentions, not by results. We are here to serve our guests and God's Creation, and one of the greatest services is to help others along the Path of Truth. That service begins with simple, everyday things.

We are all in this for the same reason. If anyone comes here and we can be companions together on the path, that's a wonderful blessing. It's really fulfilling who we are. That's who we are. We are all seekers. We are seeking Truth, that divine Truth which is another name for God.

Gluttony and Repentance

In his *Mathnawi*, Jelaluddin Rumi recounts an interesting story about hospitality. He introduces this story by reminding us of four negative traits we should transform in ourselves: gluttony, lust, ostentation, and worldly desires. Then Rumi tells the following story.

At the time of the Prophet§, some non-Muslim travelers came to Medina. In those days travelers stayed with local hosts, as there were no inns or hotels. The Prophet§ asked his companions to take each of the travelers to their homes and feed and lodge them. Each follower chose one of the travelers to take home.

However, there was one obese, crude man whom no one would take, and so the Prophet§ invited the man to his own home. His household kept seven goats and drank the goats' milk every day. The fat guest drank all the milk and ate all the food that had been prepared. There was nothing left for anybody else. The guest was fat to begin with, and after eating so much his belly became distended.

When the guest retired to his room, one of the maidservants was so angry at him for eating all their food that she locked him in. In the middle of the night, the man had to go to the bathroom. He tried to get out, but he couldn't leave the room.

The guest eventually managed to put himself back to sleep. While he was sleeping he dreamed that he went to a deserted spot and relieved himself. When he woke up the bed was covered with feces. He was incredibly embarrassed and didn't know what to do.

The Prophet§ realized what happened and opened the guest's door, then quickly slipped away so the man could leave without seeing him and becoming even more ashamed. A kind host will cover a visitor's faults.

One of the servants brought the visitor's bedding outside to where Muhammad§ was sitting. The servant exclaimed, "Look what this awful man did! His bedding is filthy!" The Prophet§ said, "Bring it here and bring me water. I'll wash the bedding myself." His companions were shocked at the thought of the Prophet§ soiling his hands with such filth. They tried to prevent him, but he insisted on cleaning the soiled bedding himself.

Meanwhile, the visitor had realized he had left a valuable amulet in the room and he came back to get it. When he returned he saw the Prophet§ cleaning his filthy bedding. The man burst into tears. He tore his shirt and banged his head on a pillar until his nose and his face became bloody. He cried, "Oh my God, what have I done?" He felt terribly ashamed.

The Prophet§ came to the man and consoled him saying that his weeping and repentance would cleanse him. Muhammad§ explained that outward acts of prayer and worship bear witness to the spiritual light within. He said, "Come with me. You are my guest. You be with me." The visitor became transformed in that moment and said, "I will be your guest for all the rest of my life. Wherever I'll be, I'll be under your roof. You are my host for the rest of my life." Then he recited "*La ilaha illa Allah, Muhammadan resulallah*" ("There is no god but Allah, and Muhammad is his prophet") and became a Muslim.

The Prophet§ invited the man to come back for dinner that night, and all he had was one cup of milk. He refused to eat anything more. Everybody was amazed. This man ate all the milk and all the food in the house the night before, and suddenly just a little bit of food was enough. The man said, "I'm full. I don't want anymore."

There are many levels to this powerful story. Who do we think we are in the story? Of course we would like to think we are the wonderful host. We think we are like the Prophet§ but are we? In truth, we are like the fat guest with the huge appetite.

The story is a graphic reminder that if we only think about this world, we will develop a huge appetite for the things of this world. We will want to swallow up everybody else's portion in order to stuff ourselves. We want to get as much as we can fit in our bellies, amass as much as we can put in our bank accounts, and so on. There's no end to what our egos desire. We want to stuff our lives with the things of this world.

When I look in my closet, I get embarrassed. My closet is full of clothing. At least half of it could go away. How many sweaters can I wear at a time? Or shirts? Or pants?

I was reading recently about a local businessman who wanted to build a huge house for himself and his family. The house would have been over 40,000 square feet and have nine bedrooms and eight bathrooms. What struck me was that he wanted to build *two* home theaters, with fancy chairs and expensive projection systems. What did he need two home theaters for? No one can watch two movies at the same time. This is a graphic reminder that the ego will never stop wanting more, no matter how much we have.

We are just like this man. For some of us, it may be a closet filled with dozens of shoes rather than a 40,000-square-foot house. But it's only a difference in scale. We all have shoes and clothing that we haven't worn in over a year. We should give those things away. We really should. There are people who truly need the clothing that is sitting in our homes unused.

We are hungry for the world, but what does this enormous hunger turn into? It turns into excrement. This story reminds us that all our love of the world turns into excrement. We spend our lives accumulating more and more things, but what are they worth? Less than nothing. That is why we are learning to love for God's sake, trying to serve for God's sake, trying to develop love of the transcendent. Only then might we get out of this awful state of stuffing ourselves with the material world, which then turns into feces.

In an old Sufi story, a sheikh said to the sultan, "What do you think your kingdom is worth? If you honestly consider this question, you will see it isn't worth very much." The sultan became insulted and angry and threw the sheikh out. As he left, the sheikh said, "You will see how little your kingdom is worth!"

From that day on, the sultan couldn't defecate. (This story is not that different from the first story. Whether it goes out or stays in, it's still excrement.) The sultan got worse and worse. He couldn't excrete anything, and the royal physicians were no help at all. Finally he remembered the sheikh's parting words. He cried out, "Oh my God, that sheikh does have occult powers."

So the sultan humbly invited the sheikh back to the palace. He told the sheikh, "After you left I became ill. You cursed me!"

The sheikh replied, "No, I didn't curse you, but perhaps you offended the One who owns me. He might have been the cause of this."

The sheikh went on, "What is it worth to be cured of your condition?"

The sultan groaned, "I would give half my kingdom to be cured."

Saying "In the name of God, Most Merciful, Most Compassionate," the sheikh passed his hand over the sultan's distended stomach, and the sultan suddenly passed an enormous amount of gas and then ran to the bathroom. When he returned the sheikh said, "You see what your kingdom is worth. Half your kingdom is only worth a fart."

It's true. That's what the world is worth. But it's hard to remember that. We all think the world is so wonderful. But when we truly see reality, we will say, like the Prophet's guest, "Oh my God, what have I done?"

The Prophet§ tried not to embarrass his guest. But God is the One who covers or uncovers our faults. We would like God to cover all our faults, but if we want to grow we should really pray that God *uncovers* our faults. That is more painful, but it is very effective in motivating us to change. Seeing himself so clearly, the guest became transformed.

Jelaluddin Rumi used to make the following prayer, "God, please make my inside like my outside. But if I cannot achieve that, Lord, please make my outside like my inside."

We can wash ourselves and put on nice clothes, and on the outside we will look clean and nice. That is relatively easy. It is not so easy to clean ourselves inside. Rumi was willing to appear to the world with all his inner faults and ugliness showing, because he knew this would be so painful that he would have to change.

That is exactly what happened with the Prophet's guest. Suddenly his ugliness was revealed to himself. He was a pig and a glutton, and as a result he soiled his bed. Then he saw his host, God's Messenger, cleaning that filth with his own hands. It was like shock therapy. It is similar to what the people in Alcoholics Anonymous call "bottoming out": at a certain point, we have no excuses or rationalization left. We have to admit, "My God, this is who I am—a big bag of shit."

The visitor was stuck with that incredibly humiliating image of himself. He became so embarrassed that he began smashing his head against the pillar, ripping his clothes. He knew he had to change. He couldn't live with who he was. This is exactly what Rumi meant when he prayed, "Make my outside like my inside." Do we have the courage to make this prayer?

God may uncover something ugly or painful in someone, but it is not our job to uncover it. Muhammad§ purposely slipped aside so that the man wouldn't realize that anyone knew what he had done. However, his fault was revealed in spite of the efforts of the Prophet§. And it transformed the man's life.

Reflect on the story of the Prophet's guest. It is a profound story as well as an extremely graphic one. The obese guest is a wonderful example of both extreme gluttony for the world and sincere repentance. After the man repented and embraced Islam, he was truly no longer able to eat as he had eaten before. His appetite for the world went away. Please God, may our appetite for the world be lessened as well.

The sign of real repentance is that we change. We know we've repented if we see something in ourselves and we become shocked and horrified. We don't have to hit our heads and get our noses bloody. (I know some of us would love to do that; it is so dramatic.) If we become so shocked and horrified that we automatically make profound and clear intention to change, we *will* change, God willing.

QUESTION:

When people do stay, is it also because our capacity to serve people has increased?

ANSWER:

Whether people come or go is not up to us. It is up to God. Also, it is said that the Founder of our Order is exclusive and accepts only a relatively few dervishes.

Please God, our capacity to be hosts will continue to increase. We have to develop our capacity to be good hosts when guests come. If we can do that, then we have to be able to sustain our love and hospitality. I think we can.

If we are not healing each other's hearts, what are we doing here? Of course, *we* are not healing each other's hearts. God is doing it. Our goal is good hospitality. That means making our guests feel at home, serving them, and making them feel comfortable.

I believe it is more likely that God will heal our hearts if our hearts are available. That is, if we are at ease we might begin to reduce the kind of armoring that we use to defend ourselves. When we are feeling safe, secure, and loving, we are more likely to open ourselves up and allow God in. We can do something invaluable for our guests by creating a loving, safe atmosphere in which people become open to receiving God's healing.

A spiritual companion is really like a midwife. The process of labor is a natural process. The doctors don't do much. They like to take a lot of credit, but fundamentally it's a natural process, built into a woman's body. Barring complications, a midwife basically has to be attentive and support the process of labor.

When we are good hosts who make their guests comfortable, we are like a midwife whose job it is to make women in labor feel relaxed and comfortable—because if they become tense birthing becomes more difficult. The midwife tells the mother to breathe and relax, and she gives the mother confidence in this natural process.

Becoming a dervish is like giving birth. My sheikh used that metaphor often. Every once in a while, we need the support of someone who understands the journey. That's where a compassionate companion is very helpful. The senior dervishes or the sheikh can help at critical times.

▸ 14 ◂

The Lessons of Ramadan

The following sohbets *were given before and during the month of Ramadan. They are meant to prepare the dervishes for a month of fasting and extra prayer.*

Thoughts before Ramadan

It is time to prepare ourselves for the holy month of Ramadan. Soon we will be spending our time and energy very differently from the rest of the year. Hazreti Muhammad§ said that the heavens and earths change with the arrival of Ramadan for those who are fasting. The gates of heaven open, and the gates of hell are closed during this month. While we are fasting, the angel who keeps track of our bad deeds stops writing, and only our good deeds are recorded. The angels come down this month and report back to God who is fasting. Each day of Ramadan, more and more who are fasting are given a place in heaven.

The time of breaking fast is a profound spiritual moment. We fast for God, not for any worldly reward. In a *hadith qudsi*, God says, "You have fasted for Me, and I am the reward of your fast." How is God the reward for our fast? My sheikhs have said that in the act of fasting or doing anything for God, we come closer to God and God comes closer to us.

Ramadan provides an opportunity to practice patience. According to one *hadith*, "Fasting is half of patience and patience is half of faith."

The Story of Hussain

One of the best Sufi teachings on patience is found in a story Muzaffer Efendi often told, about crazy Hussain, a farmer who lived in a village in central Turkey. When he married a young woman from his village, two traveling scholars attended the wedding, and the scholars were given a place of honor at the newlyweds' table. They began discussing interpretations of the Qur'an, fine points of theology, and Islamic history. They compared stories of their teachers and quoted from the writings of great Muslim scholars. Hussain was fascinated. He had never had any formal education, and suddenly he felt a burning desire to become a scholar.

Hussain spent his wedding night with his bride and when he arose the following morning, he told his wife that he wanted to go to Istanbul to become a scholar. He asked her to run their farm until he returned home. From that day on, he became known in the village as crazy Hussain, the man who left his beautiful bride to go far away to school.

No one knew what happened to Hussain. For years there was no further news about him, and his neighbors thought he might have been killed by bandits or wild animals. In fact, Hussain did make his way to Istanbul, where he devoted himself to his studies. Finally, twenty years later, he felt he had learned enough to leave, so he set off for home.

Hussain was looking forward to seeing his wife, old friends, and family. He eventually came to a village a day's journey from his home, and one of the local farmers offered to put him up for the night. After dinner, the farmer asked Hussain about his studies. Hussain asserted proudly that he had just finished twenty years of study with some of the greatest scholars in Istanbul.

The farmer asked, "Then perhaps you can tell me, what is the beginning of wisdom?"

Hussain replied, "The scholars say that the beginning of wisdom is trust in God."

The farmer said, "No, that isn't it."

Hussain gave many different answers from the teachings of famous scholars, but the farmer always responded, "No, that is not it either."

Hussain asked, "How do you know these answers are not correct?"

"I know."

"Please tell me then, what is the beginning of wisdom?"

"I will be happy to teach you the answer to this question, but you have just spent twenty years studying and you did not learn this. I can teach you the beginning of wisdom, but it will take a year."

Hussain felt the farmer truly did know the answer, and he agreed to spend a year studying with him. Early the next morning, the farmer said, "It is time to go and work in the fields."

"But I thought we were going to study."

"That is how we study."

They worked all morning, had lunch, and went back to the fields. That evening Hussain was so exhausted that he fell asleep right after dinner. This went on for days. Hussain had no time or energy to talk about philosophy or scholarship. Finally, he became used to the demanding routine, and one evening after dinner he asked the farmer about the beginning of wisdom. The farmer replied, "You spent twenty years and you still didn't learn the answer. You will need to take a year to learn this."

Month after month, they worked hard in the fields. One day, Hussain realized it had been a year since he came to the village. He said to the farmer, "I have worked day and night for you for a full year. Now, please tell me what is the beginning of wisdom." The farmer replied, "You will leave tomorrow. I'll tell you then."

The next morning the farmer and his wife packed a large lunch for Hussain and gave him many gifts. As he was about to set out, Hussain said, "Well, I am still waiting for the answer to the question you asked me a year ago. What is the beginning of wisdom?"

The farmer replied simply, "The beginning of wisdom is patience."

Hussain shouted. "What? You worked me like a slave for a year for that simple answer! What is the matter with you?"

The farmer said, "You see, you still haven't learned."

"You could have told me this a year ago."

"No, I could have given you those words, but all year you have had many opportunities to understand patience. Obviously you still haven't learned this lesson. But perhaps you have made a beginning."

Hussain didn't know quite what to make of this. Was the farmer a real teacher, or had he tricked Hussain into a full year's work for nothing?

At the end of the day, Hussain finally reached his home town. The sun had just gone down when he got to his old house. He looked in the window and saw his wife for the first time in twenty-one years. She was sitting on the couch caressing the head of a handsome young man. Hussain became furious at her infidelity. He had a pistol with him that he carried to protect himself while traveling. He pulled out the pistol, determined to avenge himself on both of them.

Then he remembered the year he had spent with the farmer. He thought to himself, "Patience. I've just spent a year learning about patience. Maybe I shouldn't react too quickly." He put the gun away.

Hussain went to the mosque for night prayer. No one recognized him. He asked, "Where is old Ahmed?"

"Oh, he passed on five years ago."

"What about the parents of Hussain?"

"You mean the parents of crazy Hussain, the man who disappeared years ago the day after his wedding? They died years ago."

Then one of the villagers said, "Just a moment. It is almost time for prayer, and our imam is coming."

The young man Hussain had seen in his house came toward the mosque. "Who is that man?" he asked.

"That is Jamal, the son of crazy Hussain," came the reply. "He was born nine months after Hussain left town. Because Hussain loved learning so much, his wife spent all the money she could save on Jamal's education. Whenever scholars came to town, she had them tutor her son. He became the most learned among us and is now our imam."

After night prayers, Hussain left the mosque and turned toward the village he had just left. He knelt and bowed in the direction of the farmer, and exclaimed, "Thank you, my master. You have saved my life and the lives of my family."

Patience

Ramadan provides a wonderful opportunity to practice patience. In the story, patience saved the lives of Hussain, his wife, and his son. Patience has that miraculous quality. In Ramadan we enjoy a God-given opportunity to practice patience for a month—and patience does have to be practiced. For the month of Ramadan, we have the honor and the blessing of practicing patience. That is why it is said that Ramadan is the month of the community of Islam.

Not everyone thinks of fasting as a gift. For some, it seems more like a trial. But it really is a gift. God rewards our fasting by strengthening our patience. One of the ninety-nine Attributes of God is *as Sabr,* the Most Patient. One famous *hadith* is, "Patience is beautiful." Another *hadith* is, "God is beautiful, and God loves beauty."

The Arabic word *sabr* means both "patience" and "perseverance." Steadfastness and sticking with our intentions are aspects of patience. Patience means refusing to quit, even if success or reward does not come immediately.

There are two aspects to patience. First, we need patience to avoid doing what we should not do. For example, it requires patience to refuse to rush into action when we have become upset. Patience means refusing to be dominated by our self-centered egos. Hussain exhibited patience by refusing to give in to his anger. In Ramadan, we exercise patience throughout each day when we refuse to give in to hunger, thirst, or tiredness.

The second kind of patience is to follow through on our good intentions. It means persevering with our spiritual practices to develop and maintain good habits. It means keeping on with our spiritual discipline even when we don't seem to be making any progress. Doing what is good and avoiding what is bad both require patience.

To pray, we need patience. First we make intention to pray, then we follow through on that intention. We try to stop our minds from wandering in order to make our prayers authentic.

One *hadith* teaches, "Without the presence of the heart, there is no prayer." Our hearts are not present in prayer when we become impatient. Instead of being in the present moment, we start thinking about the past or the future; we fantasize about our hopes and wishes. If we develop patience, we can be more fully present in our prayers.

Patience is an extraordinary quality. It is mentioned ninety times in the Qur'an and is one of the most oft-mentioned Attributes of God. God says in the Qur'an, "O believers, seek help with patience and prayer; for God is with the patient." (2:153, Cleary) Patience is among the central qualities of the believer. This month of Ramadan is a great gift to help us develop our patience.

Knowledge and Action

Islam requires both knowledge and action. We need to know right from wrong action—and act on our knowledge. During Ramadan, let us read about Ramadan in the Qur'an and in the writings of Sufi masters. Many have written about fasting. In addition to fasting, we should reflect on both the meaning of fasting and on our own experience of fasting.

Some so-called scholars today write about ideas and ideals without putting them into action. I've told you the following Nasruddin story before. Nasruddin was a Sufi master who taught with a great deal of humor; stories about him are famous throughout the Middle East. Muzaffer Efendi used to love to recount many of them.

In this story, Nasruddin was serving as a judge, and a mother came to see him with her child in tow. She said, "O *judge*, I just don't know what to do with my son. He has a terrible sweet tooth. Whenever I make dessert, he tries to eat it all. If I turn my back, the sweets in the kitchen are gone. I've told him over and over to control himself. I've lectured him and punished him, but nothing seems to work. Could you help me?"

Nasruddin replied, "Come back next month."

The woman went back home and next month she came again with her son. Nasruddin immediately knelt down and looked the son in the eyes. "Young man, be patient and wait until your mother gives you sweets. Use your will power and you can certainly succeed in overcoming your love of sweets."

The mother asked, "Nasruddin, I had to walk for hours to get here. Why didn't you say that to him last month?"

Nasruddin said, "No, I couldn't have said that last month. You see, I love sweets too, and I had to control myself for a month before I could honestly tell him it was possible."

We live in a world in which many people substitute knowledge for action. It is not at all uncommon for people to talk authoritatively about things they have never experienced. Words are empty unless they are backed by experience. Empty words have no substance; people are not touched by them. People will not change when they hear the words of those who have not lived what they are teaching.

Fasting during Ramadan is an easy practice in some ways. If our minds wander in prayer, that prayer may be worthless, but if our minds wander during Ramadan, it does not matter. In the beginning, all we need to do is cease eating and drinking during the day. Even if we are not highly developed spiritually, we can still practice this kind of fasting. We do have to exert our will and practice patience, but it is not nearly as demanding as prayer. If we are able to fast for God's sake, the fast of a sage is equal to the fast of the average man or woman.

Levels of Fasting

However, there are also higher levels of fasting. Ideally, we refrain from eating and drinking and also fast from doing or saying anything harmful. That is far more demanding than simply fasting physically. During Ramadan, we can try not to get angry and not to upset others. We can watch what comes *out* of our mouths as much as what goes *into* them. We can take a moment to reflect before speaking, to be careful of what we say.

In addition to abstaining from food, we should abstain from that which is harmful. We should watch our eyes during Ramadan. Too often, our gaze is arrogant and judgmental, or we look at others as sexual objects. We can look down more often. Ramadan is a time to be more careful and more conscious.

There is also a third level of fasting. It is the fasting of the saints, which is to fast from forgetting God. It is the fast of those who remain in constant prayer. Although we cannot accomplish this level of fasting, it is nice to know there are those who can. The saints never lose their sense of being in God's Presence.

We can certainly attempt the first level of fasting. The fasting of the body is relatively straightforward and not that difficult. However, even our ability to fast from food and drink during Ramadan is not really ours. It is a gift.

Rather than become proud of our fasting, we should be grateful that we *can* fast. There are many who are too ill to fast. It is a great blessing if our bodies are healthy enough to fast. There may well come a time when we will not be able to fast—when our doctors will tell us we have to take medication or we will wind up in the hospital. We should be very grateful every year we can fast. Fasting is a reminder of many blessings. We can digest food, and we can endure a little deprivation of food, water, and sleep.

A Month of Reflection and Retreat

In a sense, Ramadan is a month of retreat. Our energies are more limited during the day, so we waste less energy on trivia. Our daily rhythm revolves around prayer and fasting. Although we still work and carry out our worldly duties, they seem far less important this month. It is good to do less and spend more time reading Qur'an and the writings of the Sufi saints and poets.

Many Muslims read the entire Qur'an during the month of Ramadan, and I encourage you all to do so. When you read the Qur'an, I suggest you read quickly but slow down when you find verses that stand out for you. Copy those verses down so you can contemplate them at leisure. Develop your own notebooks made up of these verses. Each time you read the Qur'an, new verses will come to you.

One of the lessons of Ramadan is how quickly the days pass. We do not know whether we will be here next Ramadan. There are no guarantees. We do not even know if we will be here for our next prayer, but somehow we are certain we will be here next year. We are certain God will preserve us until tomorrow, even though hundreds of thousands die every day. We are confident we are not going to be one of them. We think we are somehow immune from death even though every day thousands of Muslims say their last prayers.

Even if we are still alive next year, we might not be able to fast. We might be lying in a hospital bed with an I.V. in our arm, unable to fast or even to swallow or digest food. We should be very grateful that we can fast. It is a wonderful gift.

Compassion and Gratitude

All the world's religions include some form of fasting. It seems that all the prophets God sent to this world taught their followers to fast.

Why is it important to fast? For one thing, it teaches compassion for those who are poor and are *forced* to fast, or for those in an area that suffers drought, famine, or the devastation of war. These conditions can be found all around the world.

We should be grateful we have food. Famine occurs all over the world. It is not limited to Africa or Asia. We have had terrible droughts in America in the past, and many Americans went hungry. Today many homeless Americans don't know where their next meal is coming from.

We think it cannot happen here, but the homeless and hungry are right next door to us. We don't see them because we do not look. They are invisible to us, because we do not want to see their suffering.

There are thousands living close to us without a home or steady income. They often fast, but not out of choice.

It is a great gift to be able to fast in order to please God, to do something God wishes us to do. God wishes us to do many things, but we do very few of them. At least, we can make sincere intention to fast in order to please God and follow God's commandments. Then, all day long we constantly "act" by declining to eat or drink. However, we can fast mechanically, out of duty, or fast in impatience, thinking of food all the time and waiting all day long for the moment of breaking fast. Or, we can fast with a sense of gratitude and patience. Then, each time we refuse to eat or drink, it becomes an act of worship.

When we feel hungry and thirsty during the day, we can feel grateful and say to ourselves, "Thank God I feel hungry and thirsty and I am able to choose to do something for God's sake. My hunger and thirst are a sign of my longing for God, my desire to please God. I am willing to suffer a little discomfort, and I am grateful that I can feel it. I hope that my small efforts bring me closer to God."

Why Do We Fast?

Why we are fasting during Ramadan? We should also ask ourselves why we pray, why we perform *zikrullah*. On my first *hajj*, Tosun Efendi asked everyone, "Why are you here? Why did you come here to Mecca?" He asked us to examine ourselves and our motives. We had to admit that we were motivated, in part, by a desire to be with close friends on a spiritual adventure, we were partly motivated by the prestige that comes from making the *hajj*, and we were fulfilling a religious obligation. We also hoped to gain something spiritual from the process.

So, why do we fast? The most obvious answer is that God commanded us to fast this month. But do we fast because we are afraid of punishment? Do we fast because other people are fasting?

We can also ask ourselves, "Who is fasting?" "Where in me is the desire to fast?" If we think of fasting as an obligation, fasting can easily become dutiful and perfunctory. This is one reason for the famous *hadith*, "One hour of contemplation is worth sixty years of conventional prayer." We have to consider what we are doing. Where in us is the desire to fast? What is our intention in fasting?

We can also ask ourselves, "Am I doing this out of love, rather than out of obedience?" We can explore our yearning to do something to please God. We have many different levels of motivation in this, as in all our activities.

While we fast, we can begin to examine these different motivations in ourselves. We can observe the part of us that wants to eat and drink instead of fasting, as well as the part of us that wants to be like everyone else. We want to do whatever it takes for our own comfort. We love sleep, and we do not want to get up early for a pre-dawn meal every day for a month.

But there is another part of us that *wants* to fast and enjoys this discipline. This part would feel badly if we could not fast. We can come to know this part of ourselves, the part that chooses to fast—not out of mechanical obedience, fear, or inertia.

We can engage in the same self-examination with prayer, *zikr*, and other practices. Which part of us remembers God? What happens as our remembrance deepens? *Zikr* begins mechanically. We begin with repetition, the *zikr* of the tongue. As the *zikr* deepens, it descends from the *zikr* of the tongue to the *zikr* of the heart. But what does that mean? What is our spiritual heart? Isn't descent really ascent? We can become aware of the place of remembrance in us. Where is the place in us that prays? Where is the place in us that longs for God? What part of us loves to fast?

We can also look at how this part sometimes becomes masked by other parts of ourselves. One part of us is impatient, incites our minds to wander, and distracts us from prayer. There is a part of us that does not want to fast. But we should not let ourselves forget the part that remembers and yearns for God. That is the part of us that chooses to fast, the part that loves fasting and other spiritual practices. That is the part that can truly pray. We have to look at ourselves and find this within us.

It is not enough to say, "*Zikr* descends from the tongue to the heart." The words alone don't mean anything. What is this heart? It is certainly not merely the muscle in the chest that pumps blood through the body. Throughout the world the great spiritual traditions and religions have regarded the heart as more than a physical organ. In Japanese and Chinese, the character for heart is the same. It is often translated as "mind" or "heart-mind." It is seen as a higher level of thinking and feeling than the work of the head. In Arabic, the word for heart is *qalb*, which refers both to the physical heart and also to the spiritual organ that is the seat of faith as well as intelligence.

We have to explore our own hearts. What is our experience of the heart? What does it mean when the heart opens or closes? What does this feel like? What behaviors open our hearts, and what actions close them? We have to figure this out for ourselves. The wise words of our teachers are merely hints, guides in our own self-exploration.

Why should we engage in any spiritual practices? Why fast, pray, go to Mecca? From the point of view of the ego, none of these practices make sense. The ego wants money, fame, and pleasure. But there is something else in us, and we have to understand it—the spiritual part of us. If we fail to understand our egos they are more likely to mislead us.

One of the blessings of Ramadan is that we engage in less busy work. We have less energy to spend, and we are a little tired and sleepy during the day. Because we are less energetic, we can be a more aware of ourselves. We can be more inwardly focused and less outwardly engaged. The good news is, if we are tired so are our egos. We can hope our self-centered egos are weaker this month.

When we are tired and hungry, we are often more quick-tempered and irritable, and if we pay attention we can see the operation of our egos in our irritability. We can hear an inner voice nagging us: "Feed me!" "Let's sleep now." "Let's have something to drink." We become more aware of the voice of the ego and its clever arguments.

Taking Responsibility for Our Spiritual Lives

In addition to investigating the operation of our egos, we can also observe the operation of our hearts. This is a good month to examine ourselves. It does not mean that our experience of our hearts will match descriptions we may have heard or read. It does not have to. There is a famous *hadith*, "There are as many paths to God as there are souls." If there are as many paths as there are souls, then certainly the experience of the heart will differ from person to person. It may also differ in each of us from time to time. Our understanding today may be different from our understanding tomorrow. Our own experience may not match what another person has written about his or her spiritual path.

Too often we blindly follow what we read in books or what we hear in talks. Of course, it is good to learn from others. But be careful. It is too easy to follow an authority instead of thinking for ourselves. We should not give anyone else responsibility for our own spiritual lives. Our sheikh can take responsibility to *guide* our spiritual lives, but we still have to make serious efforts to understand and to follow what we are taught. A teacher can only do so much. One of my teachers has said, "I can cook for you, but I cannot eat for you."

We have to eat for ourselves and digest our food ourselves; no one can do it for us. We have to breathe for ourselves. We have to pray for ourselves. And we have to understand our own spiritual lives. A teacher can guide us in our search, but do not forget that a finger pointing at truth is only a finger; it is not the truth. Each of us has to find our own way toward Truth. Ramadan is an excellent time to consider this.

The only one who can follow your spiritual path is you. And the things we encounter on our path are changing, from breath to breath. Ideally, our spiritual understanding grows day by day. It is not simple or static. What may have seemed true last month we might recognize today as false. Absolute Truth does not change, but the manifestations of truth change.

The term *sharia* refers to the principles and practices of religion. It means "road" in Arabic, a road that leads us through the desert. The *sharia* is like a clearly marked road that is relatively easy to follow. But the well-defined outer practices of the *sharia* are only one aspect of our practice.

Sufism focuses on the inner effects of our practice. The Sufi path, or *tariqa*, means, in Arabic, an unmarked route through the desert, where the sands shift and there are no clear markers. Following the *tariqa* requires judgment and sophistication. It also requires a guide who knows the way.

We have to think for ourselves, not mechanically follow others. That is taking responsibility for our physical and spiritual lives. What one moment requires of us may differ from what another moment requires of us. The *sharia* guides us in how to act. It provides a set of basic principles for action in a constantly changing world.

There is an old saying: we cannot step into the same river twice. We use the term "river" as if it is an object, but in reality a river is not a static thing. It is flowing, constantly changing water. The water we may step into in one moment is gone; the water we step into a second time is completely different. The same river may be a trickle during a drought and a flood in the rainy season.

Like a river, life is an ever-changing process. As life changes, one's path changes as well. Another person's spiritual journey is not—cannot possibly be—the same as ours. But it is still the same path. We must try our best to remain aware of ourselves and whatever we are doing—our worship, *zikr*, fasting, and everything else we do.

It is possible to follow only the outer rules of fasting without paying attention to the inner. That is explained in another famous *hadith*: "There are people who fast and get nothing from their fast except hunger, and there are those who pray late at night and get nothing from their prayer but a sleepless night." The outer form is no guarantee of inner results. But it all begins with the outer practice.

As Rumi has written, some people pray like a chicken pecking grain. The chicken bows down and touches the ground over and over again, just as we do in prayer. Does all that bowing nourish the chicken spiritually? Of course not. People who pray like chickens think they are gaining something, but they are only going through the motions. At least the chicken receives something—a piece of grain—when it bows and pecks. So chickens are smarter than many of us.

This is a good month to reflect on our Islam, to contemplate our relationship with God. It is a good time to remember that our understanding of Islam today should not be the same as our understanding tomorrow. If it is alive, our Islam will continue to grow and change. I do not mean the outer practice alone, or the label *Muslim*. The deeper meaning of Islam refers to our capacity to follow something greater than our ego's desires and needs.

During Ramadan, we are still in the world, engaged in all our duties and activities, yet we are somewhat divorced from our usual routine and concerns. We follow a different rhythm: our daily lives revolve around our practice of fasting and prayer. Normally, our daily rhythm is determined by our physical wants and the routines of society, and we organize our day around times for work, school, meals, etc. External demands structure most of our day. This month, our day is structured by the rhythms of Ramadan. We get up before dawn, we do not take lunch, and we spend our evenings together performing the Ramadan *terawih* prayers, the additional twenty *rakats* of prayer we perform together each night during Ramadan.

This month we are not as available to the demands of the world around us. We should enjoy our Ramadan routine. During the rest of the year, we collaborate with the world in keeping ourselves busy. It is hard for us to sit still. We work for a little bit, then we jump up for a coffee break. We begin a project, then we answer the phone. We make dozens of appointments and keep ourselves busy. We spend so much energy on worldly affairs during the rest of the year. All these things interfere with our going within. This month we can enjoy doing less and remembering God more.

Following God's Will

We recently read the following Qur'anic passage: "So if they dispute with you, say, 'I have surrendered my being to God, and so have those who follow me.'" (3:20, Cleary)

Some Muslims have done this, but very few. Only God's Grace enables us to fully surrender ourselves to God. We can say we wish to surrender our being to God; we intend to do this; we try to do this. We pray to be able to dedicate ourselves to God. We can wish to do this and ask for God's help, but we cannot do it all by ourselves.

During Ramadan, we practice, in small ways, following God's will. We oppose our bodies' desires for comfort and ease. We refuse to go along with these desires because we believe God commands us to fast. We exercise our wills over and over again every day, each time we feel thirsty and refuse to have a drink, each time we feel hungry and refuse to eat.

Anyone can perform this outward discipline. One sheikh pointed out that every poor person's donkey fasts. When their owner has no money, they have nothing to eat, but it does not make those donkeys into saints. Poor men and women fast as well, but the fasting they are forced to do does not transform them.

We can feel deeply grateful that we can exert our individual wills toward doing what we believe God wishes us to do. Every time we feel hunger or thirst, we should be grateful that we have a chance to worship God by actively submitting ourselves to something other than the desires of our bodies or egos. This month is a gift to us. We need to reflect on why we are fasting, how we are fasting, what part of us is fasting.

At the End of Ramadan

As we come to the end of Ramadan, let us reflect on what we learned this month. Hopefully, we have learned something about our egos. Throughout our fasting, our egos have fought us, demanding that we eat and drink. At one level, that is the simple-minded level of the ego, based on the animal soul. It is like a hungry puppy or child. A child will keep nagging, "I want to eat." Then, when we feed the child, it will say "Can I have some dessert?" If we serve dessert, the child will ask for whipped cream on top. This part of us is pretty simple and straightforward. If we refuse to eat, it will simply keep asking for food.

However, the narcissistic ego is subtler. It begins by saying "I want to eat" and when we refuse, it argues, "But you are tired and hungry, and it will be bad for your health if you don't eat." You reply, "I don't care; I am fasting. I am not going to eat." Then the ego argues, "You can't concentrate if you don't eat. You might lose your job." The ego comes up with all kinds of clever reasons not to fast. We have all heard this inner voice throughout Ramadan. It is part of the discipline and the blessing of this month that we get to hear this clearly. We begin to understand more clearly how our egos operate.

If we resist successfully and we do fast, the ego is likely to say, proudly, "I have been fasting. How wonderful I am. I'm better than everyone around me." That will take away the benefits of fasting, because then fasting has become a way of feeding the ego. The ego may also suggest, "We should tell people we are fasting, so they can appreciate how spiritual we are." Instead of fasting to please God, we end up fasting to impress others.

Our egos will always try to take away the benefits of our actions—by seeking praise for our actions or by finding selfish motives for our actions. Our egos will always seek approval and will try to feed our pride by telling us how much better we are than others. "How wonderful that I am fasting, what an incredible thing I have done." In fact, we probably eat more than usual during Ramadan. We have an early breakfast and a big dinner. All we have really done has been to skip lunch and between-meal snacks during the day. But our egos inflate our small efforts into something heroic.

Another trick of the ego is to tell us that we don't need to pay attention to other things because we are fasting. We can get away with less work at our jobs; we can rest and relax more, because we are fasting. The ego will always try to get us to do less.

What did we learn this month? What benefits did this practice bring us? What are the fruits of our actions? What did we learn, what benefits did we receive?

There are many things we can learn from Ramadan, and not all of them are obvious. We can learn how we became distracted this month. We wanted to devote this month to practicing Islam, but how much Islam did we practice apart from fasting? How did we benefit from this month? Did we become closer to God this month? As Hazreti

Muhammad§ said, "If one day is the same as the day before, that day is a loss." That is, if we have not learned every day, developed ourselves each day, then we have wasted our precious time. We should be growing in knowledge and experience every day. Did we learn from fasting or did our egos manage to distract us from learning anything significant during this holy month?

Zakat. The practice of giving *zakat* at the end of Ramadan is also a wonderful opportunity for learning. *Zakat* is one of the Five Pillars of Islam. It means to give one-fortieth of our accumulated wealth in charity before the end of Ramadan. Giving is not easy for some of us. My master used to say that many of us act as if our wallets are filled with nettles, and as soon as we touch our wallets to give charity our hands start stinging. Muzaffer Efendi also reminded us that God has promised a ten-fold return for charity.

How does it feel to give away our hard-earned money in charity? Does it hurt to give? Do we give a little less than we should? Or are we grateful that God has given us the capacity to help others and that we are able to give? God has given us enough that we can help others. Our egos will argue, "You shouldn't give away anything. You have to keep what you have." We forget that whatever we have is not ours but is from God. It is a great blessing to have the capacity to share with the needy. God has set up our lives so those who have can help those who do not have. Charity is an opportunity to serve God's Creation.

Safer Efendi taught us a great deal about charity. When he was a new dervish, just out of military service, he told his sheikh, happily, "I don't have to give charity this year. I don't have to go through all the complicated calculations for *zakat*, because I don't have anything." His sheikh scolded him severely. "How dare you think that way? You are a young, strong, healthy man. Many others are too old or too sick to work. Many are poor and needy. And you are saying you are happy you can't serve them!"

Then Safer Efendi vowed that every year he would give more *zakat* than the year before. His sheikh told him how to begin: "I am your bank. Bring a little of your weekly wages to me and I will keep it for you. At the end of the year, you will pay *zakat* on that." Safer Efendi said, "I followed my sheikh's advice, and that is how I became a wealthy man." He resolved to work hard, so he could give more each year. In time, he started five businesses, including a hotel and a catering service, and he became very wealthy indeed. And he did manage to give more each year than the year before.

We can learn from his example. For some of us, giving charity is a greater discipline than fasting. Someone who is miserly finds it is a lot easier to fast. Stingy people come up with all kinds of rationalizations not to give. They say to themselves, "The poor will use the money for drugs or alcohol," or "They need to learn to earn their own way," or "We shouldn't make them dependent on charity." It is hard for some of us to be generous.

Do not neglect this practice. There is a lot to learn from *zakat*. Sit down and reflect on all the reasons for giving charity, and reflect on the blessings you have enjoyed, blessings that enable you to have the abundance to be able to give.

By the end of Ramadan, we have fasted for a month. Imagine the fasting of those who do not fast by choice. We fast with full refrigerators in our homes. How much more difficult is the fasting of those who have nothing in their refrigerators or no refrigerators! Many people try to find work each day just to make enough money to purchase food for their evening dinner. Their children may suffer physically and mentally from lack of nourishment. Incredible as it seems, people still suffer this kind of hunger in many areas of the world.

Muzaffer Efendi said that when Moses‡ was speaking to God on Mount Sinai, God asked him, "What have you done for Me? What have you done for My sake?" Moses‡ replied, "I prayed for You." God said, "No, your prayers are not for Me, they are for the sake of your own soul." Then Moses‡ said, "I have given charity for You." God answered, "Whose goods did you give to whom?" Moses‡ gave up and God told him, "When you feed one of my hungry servants, you feed Me. When you give shelter to one of my homeless servants, you give shelter to Me." Let us give *zakat* with the sincere desire to help the hungry and the homeless, not merely as an obligation.

Muzaffer Efendi used to warn us that if we do not give generously from what God has given to us, God may take our savings anyway—in doctor bills, for medicines, or for surgery, for example. It is far better to spend that money generously to help others. It is better for us to give than to have God take from us. God teaches.

Thank God we have the capacity to give *zakat*, to help the hungry and their families. One of the goals of fasting is to make us more compassionate toward the poor and hungry. I hope Ramadan opens all our hearts each year.

▸ 15 ◂

The Night of Power

God's blessings are constantly with us, but Muzaffer Efendi used to say these blessings are more available at certain times and places. One such time is the Night of Power, which we celebrate on the eve of the twenty-seventh day of Ramadan. The veils between heaven and earth are thinnest on this night.

The divine Name *al Wahhab*, the Bestower, refers to the quality of divine blessings that fall like rain on everyone and everything without exception. Muzaffer Efendi used to remind us that God's Mercy constantly showers on us, but we need to employ another divine Attribute, *al Fattah*, the Opener, to receive it. When we complain that we do not experience God's Mercy, it is like going to Niagara Falls with our fists tightly clenched and blaming the Falls because we have not received any water. If we just opened our hands, they would instantly overflow with water.

These two divine qualities, *al Wahhab* and *al Fattah*, are closely linked. God's blessings flow constantly, and we have the capacity to receive them. It may be that the blessing of the Night of Power is that we are more open on that night than at other times. Perhaps on the Night of Power *we* are more open to heaven, rather than heaven being more open to us.

This night is the night the Holy Qur'an was sent down from God to the lowest heaven—that is, to the place of interface between heaven and earth. On this night the first revelation of the Qur'an was given to the Prophet Muhammad§. Then, the rest of the Qur'an was revealed, verse by verse, over a period of twenty-three years. Why did this revelation occur in this way? God could certainly have revealed the Qur'an all at once. Had God willed, Hazreti Muhammad§ could have instantly become a *hafiz*, one who has memorized the entire Qur'an.

According to one interpretation, there needed to be a continual flow of revelation is in order to nurture the fledgling Muslim community. Every revelation was in response to a particular problem or issue during that time. Each verse of the Qur'an is a miracle. Like a hologram, each verse reflects the Truth of the entire Qur'an. As each verse was revealed, those who listened were inspired, and their Islam was deepened.

On this night, the Qur'an descended from the eternal Tablet, on which all things are written, to the lowest of the heavens; from there, it flowed down to this world for twenty-three years, to enhance Islam, teach the new Muslims, and guide Muhammad§. The Prophet§ was the guide for the community of Islam, but he was also guided himself. He could not have been a guide unless he had been guided.

So, on this night, we celebrate this time of descent, this time in which God sent Truth down to earth. It is as if God seeded the clouds with Truth, and, from that point, the Truth rained down for twenty-three years and soaked into Creation. Remember, the Qur'an was sent down for everyone, not only for Muslims. It was sent down to all humanity and all Creation.

The Truth that God revealed through so many Prophets is a Truth for everyone. It came from the heavens to the material world. Just as the Qur'an flowed down to earth for twenty-three years, the Truth of the Qur'an is still flowing, still blessing Creation. As we live according to Truth, we touch others and inspire them to faith. Doing our best to live according to Truth *is* Islam. Living the Truth touches all of Creation—humanity, other living things, the earth, the water, the air. God said that Hazreti Muhammad§ was sent here not only for the community of Islam, but also as a mercy to the whole of Creation: "And [thus, O Prophet,] We have sent thee as [an evidence of Our] grace towards all the worlds." (21:106-107, Asad)

We think the Qur'an is just a book, a collection of pages contained between two covers. But the Qur'an cannot be captured on paper. The words of the Qur'an are like fingers pointing toward the Truth. The Qur'an is not writing on a page, nor is it words that can be recited. There is a hidden miracle that occurs when anyone recites the words of the Qur'an. As human beings, we cannot recite words of infinite Truth. Each verse of the Qur'an is beyond what a human mouth can utter.

Each Qur'anic verse is a sign of God. The word for verse, *ayet*, also means "sign." Each verse is an *ayet ullah*, a sign of God. Each is a spark of the Infinite, greater than the universe. How can a human tongue and human lips recite that which is infinite? So each recitation of the Qur'an is a miracle.

The outer form of the Qur'an seems to be words and sentences, written on paper, recited, limited in time and space. But these holy words are not limited in time and space. As it says in the Holy Qur'an, "Even if the ocean were ink for the words of my Lord, the ocean would be exhausted before the words of my Lord were exhausted." (18:109, Cleary). That is what the Qur'an is. It is not a finite book. It is inexhaustible, living Truth come down to this world.

What descended on this night is far greater than we can imagine. We are blessed to celebrate the anniversary of this event. It is an event infinite in meaning and blessings, touching all time and space. It contains everything. The Qur'an teaches, "The Night of Power is better than a thousand months." (97:3, Khalidi)

Muzaffer Efendi told a story of the great Sufi sage Hazreti Ibn 'Arabi◊. One day Ibn 'Arabi was out riding and fell from his horse. He lay on the ground, lost in thought. When his companions rushed back to him, they thought he was badly hurt. But he reassured them: "I am fine. When I fell, I remembered that everything is in the Qur'an, so I asked myself, 'Where is this? Where is my falling off my horse referred to in the Qur'an?' I lay there thinking about this until I realized it is in the *Sura Fatiha.*"

Sura Fatiha is the opening *sura* of the Qur'an. It is a short *sura*, only seven lines. A great sage like Ibn 'Arabi can find such things in the Qur'an. We are not great sages, but as we continue to study the Qur'an and grow closer to the Qur'an, its depths of meaning will begin to open to us. Every sacred phrase in the Qur'an has incredible power. We are told that even a single sincere recitation of *la ilaha illa Allah*, "There are no gods; there is God," would transform our lives if we could understand it—as the following story illustrates.

According to a well-known *hadith*, at the time of the Prophet§, a Bedouin sheikh came to Medina to become a Muslim. He was a handsome and charismatic man, the leader of a large and powerful tribe. The sheikh came to the Medina mosque, and the Prophet§ welcomed him and spread out his own cloak in front of the sheikh so he could do his prayers on the earthen floor. The other Muslims became a little jealous. This man was not even a Muslim, yet he was praying on the Prophet's cloak. This was an honor none of them had been given.

When the sheikh finished his prayer, the Prophet§ invited him to become a Muslim. He recited *eshedu en la ilaha illa Allah*, "I bear witness [or, I believe beyond a shadow of a doubt] that there are no gods; there is God," and burst into tears. Some of the companions of the Prophet§ felt that the man was already regretting becoming a Muslim. So the Prophet§ asked him, "Why are you crying? Do you regret becoming a Muslim?"

The sheikh exclaimed, "No, not at all. My heart began to open, and I began to see my life with fresh eyes. I realized that I have committed many sins in my life. I have killed innocent people; I have permitted my tribe to do great harm to others. I cried because I deeply regret all these things I have done."

The Prophet§ replied, "My son, sincerely saying *la ilaha illa Allah* has cleansed you, as if you are newborn. Now your life is fresh. You can go on without regret."

This was the result of a single sincere repetition of *la ilaha illa Allah*. Do we understand *la ilaha illa Allah*? Do we understand the potential of this phrase to transform our lives? We should feel a sense of awe whenever we recite this holy phrase, or any other line from the Qur'an. Some believers, when they say "Allah," the hairs on their heads stand up. Some saints have said "Allah" and fallen over, unconscious.

If one word or one phrase from the Qur'an has such power, what a great blessing is its entire revelation! Each word, each verse, each chapter of the Qur'an is a miracle. On this Night of Power, this entire revelation was sent down to the lowest heavens, a place of access to Creation. And on this night we celebrate the descent of all the scriptures. Truth was sent down for all Creation, not just for Arabs, or Muslims, or humanity. That is how extraordinary this night is. This is one of great events that ever happened in history, one of the greatest blessings in all Creation: the sending down of Truth and Mercy to the universe.

The blessings of this night are immense. The reverberation of that event, the descent of Truth, is here this night; it is timeless. Muzaffer Efendi taught that every sincere prayer is answered on this night. Truth is being sent down to us even now, at this moment.

Muzaffer Efendi has said there are many holy places on earth. These are places where a prophet or great saint has lived and worshiped God. There are very special places in which the greatest of prophets spoke to God, and God spoke to them. Because of those events the veils between heaven and earth are thinner, and our prayers are deeper and more powerful, in such places.

There are also holy times as well as holy places; at such times, the veils between heaven and earth are likewise thinner. The Night of Power is the holiest night of the year. We are in the Presence of God as if we were in Mecca, Medina, or one of the other holy places on earth. Heaven and earth are closer than at any other time. Our sincere prayers are accepted, because the flowing down of Truth from heaven to earth is accompanied by the rising up of our prayers and worship.

This is a night to open our hearts to God and to pray for those we love, for our departed loved ones, for our brothers and sisters on the Path of Truth, and for our own souls. It is a night to pray for our own spiritual growth, to pray for those who are suffering, and to pray for all of God's Creation. The gates of heaven are wide open. The angels are with us, and as soon as a prayer comes out of our mouths, they bring it straight to God.

Years ago, I fell in love with a wonderful imam in Turkey. He led prayers at the Dolmabahçe mosque in Istanbul. I have never heard the Qur'an recited with such depth of meaning. Everyone who was there felt the same. He was a friend of Safer Efendi, and after the prayers we sat down and talked over tea. When he heard I was a sheikh from California, he said, "When you return home, tell all the dervishes to make *dua* [to pray for others]. Tell them to make *dua*; you cannot make *dua* enough."

When we make *dua*, we have a special relationship with God. We are fulfilling our nature, because we were made to pray to God and rely on God. Think of the ninety-nine Attributes of God. Each Attribute is an answer to our prayers. We are all seeking Truth, Love, Mercy, Justice, Light, Guidance, etc. When we make *dua*, we try to connect with God in these various Attributes. If we ask for ourselves, we connect in a certain way. If we ask for others, it is a special form of worship, because we are trying to serve them.

This is a wonderful night for this kind of prayer. Ask God for help. God wants us to ask. God tells us, "Ask that I may give." By asking, we develop a special relationship with God. We realize how much we need God, and we become more conscious and more grateful for what we have been constantly receiving from God.

We do not know what our hearts really want and need, because we are so involved in the world. Like children, we have become involved with plastic toys and childish games. That is OK for a child, but we are trying to become mature human beings. Mature human beings seek God and seek to please God. They have given up their attachment to childish, worldly pastimes.

We need to take time, become still, and contemplate deeply in order to discover what our hearts want. If we ask superficially for what we want, we will only discover what our egos want. Our egos always want more *things*—a new car, more money, a fancy house. Our egos also want fame and praise. We know what that brings us—nothing that is valuable or important in the long run. A new car or some other new toy is nice for a week or two. Then it becomes old. When we are run by our egos, we cannot see beyond these trivial desires.

When most of us make *dua*, we imitate the prayers of others, because we do not know what is in our hearts. We need to pray out of a deeper sense of what we truly want and need. Can we find the words of our hearts, the longing of our hearts, and make *dua* from that place?

Let us not be satisfied with the prayers that come from the top of our heads. Let us not be satisfied with the prayers we have read or heard. Instead, let us look for the prayers that come from deep within us. Let us seek the words of our hearts. The yearning of our hearts goes beyond our everyday desires. We are usually so focused on the

outer events of our daily lives, we do not go deeply within. We become occupied with work, cooking, raising our children, etc. We need
to make time to look more deeply. We are so busy living that we forget God, the Source of all life. We are so busy with what is transient
that we forget what is eternal.

The Night of Power is a good time to step back from our daily lives,
go within, and ask ourselves, "What are the yearnings of *my* heart?"
Not what we have read in books. In fact, the words of the saints and
prophets are only the shadows of their actual experiences. They have
tried to convey their experience through these words. But spiritual
experience goes beyond words. Let us be inspired by the saints and
lovers of God to try to experience God as *they* experienced God. Let
us go within and discover the yearning of our hearts, and then go
still deeper. What is in our heart of hearts? Some of this may even be
wordless. Not everything can be captured by language. To do this, we
have to become still. We have to listen with love, because love is the
key to deeper understanding. The quieter we become, the more sensitive we are.

Psychologists discovered this phenomenon years ago. There is an
old law in psychology called the Weber-Fechner Law. It was developed
after years of research on perception—hearing, sight, and touch. The
Weber-Fechner Law states that the more stimulation there is, the less
we perceive. The busier and more active we are, the less sensitive we
are. In order to become sensitive, we have to become still and quiet.

One of the clearest examples comes from research on the perception
of weight. If we add weight to what someone is holding, how much
additional weight does it take to notice the change? For example, if
you are holding a piece of paper in your hand, you can easily feel
the weight of a quarter placed on top of the paper. If you are holding
one or two quarters, you can feel the weight of an additional quarter.
However, if you are holding a brick, you will not feel the weight of a

quarter added to that brick. The weight of the brick will completely mask the additional weight.

On the Night of Power, we can drop the brick. We can calm down and become more still and sensitive, so we can hear the quiet voice of our heart of hearts. The inner voice is quiet. The ego is much louder, more insistent. Perhaps that is why it seems to win a lot of inner battles. Stillness is one of our great allies on the Path of Truth.

ᐧ 16 ᐧ

Reflections on New Year's Eve

for almost thirty years, we have practiced *zikr* from 11:30 p.m. on New Year's Eve until 12:30 a.m. on New Year's Day. It is a wonderful blessing to end each year and begin each new year practicing Remembrance of God.

When we finish that *zikr*, we are at the beginning of a new year. Of course, we are always at the beginning of something. This moment is really no different from any other moment. Every moment begins the rest of our lives. But there's an advantage to the delusion that this time is something special, a time of beginning. At the turn of the year, we are in a time of *barzakh*, a threshold between one year and the next.

To be at a threshold is to be between two different things. The old year is just over, and the new year has barely begun. Hopefully we are a little more conscious at this time. We can be a little more aware, because we are in between two different times. In a threshold we are generally a little more aware than we usually are. When we are in the middle of our daily routine, the days, weeks, and months of the year rush by. It is easy to become unconscious, because our daily routine has become habitual. We spend too many days filled with too much habitual acting and too little thinking.

215

A threshold, or space between time periods, can help us become a little more conscious. We can reflect more at such times. So let us all sincerely intend to make good use of this time and reflect that we are at the beginning of a new year. Something has ended—a year we can look back on and learn from. And, we can make a conscious beginning of this new year and set our intention to achieve something in this year.

Of course, we could do that *every* day. It would be a wonderful practice to treat every day as the first day of the rest of our lives. At least let us start by doing this for the new year. And, if we get good at it, we can do it more often. In Zen Buddhism, every morning the monks take off their *kesa*, or meditation robe. Then they pray, "For this one day may I be a true Zen monk. May I do this for today." After the prayer they put their *kesa* back on. It's a very intelligent ritual, a conscious beginning for each day.

We might say at this time, "During this new year, may I behave as a dervish." We could do this every day. Or, just before going to work, we could say, "May I work today like a real dervish." I could pray before going to teach, "May I teach like a dervish would teach." If I can't truly be a dervish, maybe I can imitate one. Maybe I can behave *like* one, which might be good enough.

In a *hadith*, Hazreti Muhammad§ said, "Pray as you see me pray." He did not say "Pray as I pray," because who could pray like one of God's Messengers? Instead, he told us to follow his outer practice.

We can have the intention of doing our best to serve in our jobs, to work as real dervishes might work, to act as best we can. Even if we can't get the inner practice perfect, at least we can try to imitate the outer behavior of a dervish.

In our Sufi practice, we're always imitating. Hazreti Rabiaʃ, a Sufi saint, used to pray, "Lord, make my imitation real." In 1978, Muzaffer Efendi and the Turkish dervishes performed our traditional *zikr* at a music festival in France. The entire audience was very deeply touched. They had never heard anything like it before. When the *zikr* was over, Muzaffer Efendi said to the audience, "Thank you for listening. This was an imitation of a real *zikr*. We have learned the traditional form, and we are imitating the real *zikrs* of the past."

Let us all intend to behave like dervishes throughout the new year. That is, to be more conscious and more compassionate, to serve others without any desire for praise or reward. Most people often behave like animals—slaves to their greed, lust, and anger. Throughout the new year, let us try to remember after morning prayer to ask God that for this one day we might behave well, that we might behave as dervishes, as Muslims, as human beings. (They are all the same.)

Our battle with our egos requires that kind of daily attention and effort. We need all the help we can get with this struggle. As one of my old teachers said, "It's as if you've been parachuted down into the middle of a battlefield. You can't say, 'I see no battle,' or 'I won't defend myself.' Those who do are going to lose, because there *is* a major struggle going on. It is a struggle between what is best and what is worst in us."

Although I don't like the metaphor of battle, it is a good reminder of the seriousness of our inner struggle. As I have said earlier, the literal meaning of the word *jihad* is "struggle." And if we don't struggle we will certainly lose, because our egos are not pacifists. Perhaps we should all use the bumper sticker: "My ego is a terrorist." (Unfortunately, I could just imagine what would happen if we did. We would get pulled over by the police, and then they would find out we are Muslims!)

Our egos *are* terrorists. They terrorize us, those we love, and everyone we come in contact with. This is true of everyone—Jews, Christians, Buddhists, Hindus, and Muslims alike. Our egos are terrorists. And the worst among us are those who claim that they don't have any ego or any violence in them. Those who are unconscious of their egos are those who are most easily led by their egos.

In the next few days, let us take time to reflect on the past year. What did we learn? What mistakes did we make? In what ways did we grow as human beings and as dervishes? After we have done this, let us make intentions about the new year. How do we want to change and grow? What do we wish to accomplish in our lives, in our families, our jobs, and our spiritual lives? Reflections of this type can be surprisingly effective in guiding us through the coming year.

▸ 17 ◂

On Marriage

I am always delighted whenever we celebrate a wedding. It is wonderful to celebrate such a loving event. In Islam, we do not perform a wedding, we *witness* a marriage. The essence of a marriage lies in the love for each other that God has put in two people's hearts. God makes the marriage, not us.

There is an inner and an outer aspect to marriage. In the outer form, the bride and groom sign a marriage contract, put on wedding rings, and register the marriage to become a legally married couple. But the outer form is meaningless without the inner. The inner is God's blessing of mutual love. Of course, God's blessing is in everything, but we so often forget. When we celebrate a marriage, it is particularly important to remember that it is God who opens our hearts and enables us to love each other. Marriage is a divine blessing.

I believe God created marriage to open our hearts. As dervishes, we believe love is the most important part of our practice.

Children are naturally loving and they are manifestations of God's Light. Unfortunately, this light often diminishes as we grow older. Marriage brings back this kind of love. Marriage means loving and serving each other. The bride and groom are God's gift to each other.

Sheikh Tuğrul has often said to new couples, "Until now in your lives, you have walked with two legs. Now you must walk with four.

You are no longer two separate individuals. You are partners in a life-long relationship. Be very careful not to break your partner's heart. Over time, the body will heal from an injury, but a broken heart never heals."

It is very important to remain respectful to each other, even while having a disagreement. Arguments are inevitable. Safer Efendi used to say, "A home without an occasional quarrel is like a marriage celebration without music."

The opening of our hearts is the most important thing that happens to us in our lives. If our hearts are closed, nothing matters. We can have all the money and fame in the world, but if our hearts are closed we will not enjoy it. We can have a fancy job, impressive sounding titles, and an expensive house, but if we cannot love we have nothing.

Muzaffer Efendi was a bookseller whose bookstore was next to the great Beyazid mosque in Istanbul. He used to tell the following story about the opening of that mosque.

The sultan asked a well-known Sufi sheikh to preach the first sermon during the Friday prayers in the mosque. The sultan came with his court, and a huge crowd came to the mosque that day. The mosque was so full that many had to pray outside. When the time came for the sermon, the sheikh got up to speak. A poor, simple water seller grabbed him by the sleeve and asked, "O sheikh. Would you please do me a favor? I lost my donkey. I am a water seller, and I make my living bringing water to people who live far from a well. I need my donkey to carry the water. My donkey is my livelihood. And almost everybody in Istanbul is here. Would you please ask if anyone has seen my donkey."

The sheikh smiled and replied, "Yes, my son." Then the sheikh began his sermon on the subject of love. He asked the congregation, "Are there any of you who have never experienced love, who have never loved anyone or anything?"

No one said anything. No one was willing to admit they might not know love.

The sheikh went on, "Do not be embarrassed. Be honest. We are here together in God's house. Be honest here. Do any of you not know what love is? Stand up if that is true for you."

Finally, one man was brave enough to stand up. The sheikh asked, "Is it true that you have never known love?" The man replied, "Yes, I have never felt love in my heart. My heart has always been closed."

Seeing this man's example, two other men got up. They also admitted they did not know love.

The sheikh looked down at the simple water seller and said, "You lost one donkey. I found three for you."

After telling this story, my sheikh would comment, "Actually, a human being who does not know love is even lower than a donkey. A donkey at least loves fresh grain. A human being who loves can rise higher than the angels, but someone who cannot love has become lower than the animals."

That is how important love is. Love makes us human. Someone who does not love may look human. They may have a human form, but they are not truly human unless they can love. How many of us are "donkeys" pretending to be human?

For those of you who are not married, let me suggest that you keep a pet. Everyone should have someone or something to love. Years ago, sheikh Safer Efendi was talking about the importance of love, and he told the dervishes to keep a pet if they had no family. An American dervish who was living in Istanbul went home that night and found a half-wild street cat curled up in front of the door to his apartment. He took the cat in, and it was a wonderful companion to him for many years.

So love is the inner and marriage is the outer. In addition there is service to each other, and showing one's love to the beloved. My sheikh used to teach that if we love, we need to practice it. We should express our love. We should say "I love you" more often. This is especially true of most men.

Love is also expressed in service. One sure sign of our love is that we prefer to serve the beloved to being served. It is a good sign if we get more pleasure from bringing a glass of tea to our spouse than from receiving a glass of tea from her or him. I pray we all get more pleasure from giving to our spouse than from receiving. Ideally, we can look with the eyes of our heart and see what they need, so they don't even have to ask. My sheikh used to say that if someone has to ask us for help we have already failed; we have not truly been paying attention to them.

In a real marriage, we don't serve with the idea of getting something back. We serve because it gives us pleasure to do something for our beloved. For example, on a Friday evening a husband says to his wife, "I know you love the movies. Let's go to a movie tonight." The wife says, "I know you prefer to stay home and there is something on TV tonight I'm sure you would like to watch, so let's stay home and watch that program." Then the two argue about what to do. One says, "Let's do this because you want it," and the other says "No, let's do *that*, because *you* want it." That is the perfect argument!

This is the ideal attitude to bring to our marriages. We serve not because we think we should, not for any reward or to look good. We serve because we honestly want to serve our beloved.

Marriage is a challenge. It is a long-term, spiritual partnership, a partnership in the journey we are taking back to God. Ideally, we can support each other in giving charity, in prayer, in being Muslims, and in being kind, compassionate human beings. Each spouse supports these things in the marriage relationship.

We all fall asleep sometimes. Our egos try to convince us to be selfish at times. Ideally our spouses are awake when we are asleep.

They will say, "That doesn't sound quite right to me." If we listen and reflect, we may wake up. We all fall asleep. In a famous *hadith*, the Prophet§ said, "O humankind, will you wake before you die?" Our egos are like master hypnotists who put us into a trance. This is true of every one of us.

Everyone is in danger of succumbing to this hypnotic trance—not just in danger. It happens to every one of us, and it happens very quickly. We can be driving on a sunny day, in a beautiful mood, then someone cuts us off on the freeway. In that moment, the ego will take over. We don't say to the other driver, "Blessings on you. You are in such a hurry. I hope you get there safely and on time." That is not what we usually say at such times, is it?

We need to recognize that our pride and our egos are strong. When we get challenged in our lives, our spouses can remind us to be better human beings. Ideally we will listen to them. Our spouses are our partners in our struggle with our egos.

Loving someone and being with them for years is an opportunity to grow together, to travel together. We are all travelers on the Path of Truth. Years ago travel was far more dangerous than it is today. Travel in the desert, where Islam began, was especially hazardous. There were bandits and wild sandstorms, and it was worth one's life to choose the right traveling companion.

In a marriage, it is important to maintain our love and mutual support. Just like traveling in the desert, we get to serve each other and to save each other from the dangers around us. The dangers in our lives today are not as dramatic as sandstorms or bandits or running out of water, but they are real. There are emotional and spiritual dangers. We live in a culture that focuses on materialism and rarely recognizes real human values. We need to support each other. Our homes should be places of light, and two hearts filled with light are far better than one.

Spouses should remind each other of the truth, and teach each other by example. Example works far better than words. After one hundred years of psychotherapy, we have finally realized that words alone do not matter that much. As we know, words can be cheap.

Of course, words that are sincere and come from the heart *do* have real weight. We should speak loving words to each other and include loving action with our words.

We can all practice loving more. We can love our families, love God's Creation and love as much as we can. It really is important. There are always those who need our love and support. As the eyes of our hearts open, we see God's Light in everyone. Seeing that light and beauty in each other is a vital part of a real marriage.

Ideally, if one spouse becomes wrapped up with the world, the other can remind them that their concerns are not so important. In a spiritual marriage, we can remind each other to be human, to be travelers journeying together on the Path of Truth.

I sometimes think the main goal of marriage is to defrost our hearts. All our hearts are a little bit frozen, and marriage is designed by God to soften and open our hearts. The world is a constant challenge, and meeting that challenge is far easier with a partner. Before I married, I had a dream in which I was chipping away the ice in the freezer compartment of an old refrigerator. The refrigerator had no automatic defrosting, so the freezer had become filled with ice. Tosun Efendi told me that the dream meant that my marriage would defrost my heart. And, thank God, he was right.

As we learn to love each other, we are practicing love. God gave us each other and gave us the potential to love each other. God gave us the beauty of Creation so that we could learn to love. God gave us the ability to see the beauty in our life partners. The love we learn in loving each other gives us the capacity to love God. How can we love what is beyond comprehension and beyond our senses if we cannot love what we *can* comprehend? How can we love the One who is beyond all sense perception unless we can love what we see in front of us? Muzaffer Efendi used to say, "If you have never loved someone, you will never be able to love God."

As the great Sufi poets have written, God is the Beloved. For a dervish, this is one of the most important Attributes of God. We are here to love each other and to treat our spouses as our beloved. Then we can begin to understand our relationship with the Beloved.

▸ 18 ◂

Spiritual Poverty

Someone who follows the path of Sufism is also known as a *fakir*. The word *fakir* comes from the Arabic root for "poverty." There have been many Sufis who had almost no possessions. Those dervishes who are wealthy should not be attached to their wealth.

There are many kinds of poverty. There is material poverty, the state of those who have nothing and who may have to beg to survive. Those who suffer this kind of poverty are often dependent on others and on society. They are often seen as a burden and treated as second-class citizens.

One old sheikh commented, "Real poverty is fear of poverty." As dervishes we should learn not to fear anything in this world except God's displeasure. In particular we should not fear poverty, because if we fear poverty, we become a puppet of the world. But it is hard not to fear poverty. It is easy to say, "Don't fear poverty," but it is not easy to do.

One of my graduate students suffered from this fear. For her doctoral dissertation, she interviewed a number of women who shared her fear of poverty. Her dissertation examined the archetype of the "bag lady," a woman who lives on the street and carries all her possessions in bags or in a shopping cart. My student's deepest fear was that her life might fall apart and she would end up living like that on the street. For most of us it is a very unrealistic fear. We have friends and family and access to all kinds of social services. But the fear is there.

Years ago, when I was a student, I had a similar fear. I feared that if I failed to do well in my classes, I would not get a degree or a good job and I would end up poor or even homeless. As a result, I experienced underlying anxiety throughout my student years.

It takes courage to say, "Whatever You wish, O Lord. Whatever I have will come and go. My life is Yours to command." That is Islam. We talk about trust in God, but it is very hard to achieve it.

Muzaffer Efendi used to say, "Don't be so attached to your possessions. When you die, your family will divide them up and will probably sell most of your things. They will keep only a few souvenirs to remember you by. The rest will be sold or given away."

We are the custodians of our possessions for a limited period of time. Our possessions are not really ours. In reality we "own" nothing. Whatever we have is a trust, given to us by God. We get to take care of what we have in a responsible manner. We are like a governess who raises someone else's children. At least the governess knows that the children she is taking care of are not hers and they will leave her eventually. She will leave the house she is living in while raising the children and return home. The room she sleeps in is not her room, and the family she is with is not her family.

One of the older dervishes told this story. He had bought an old English-Ottoman dictionary published in the 1920s. The binding was gone, so he asked the bookseller to have his bookbinder make a new cover. The edges of the pages were frayed, so he also asked the bookseller to have the binder trim the edges. The bookseller replied, "No, that can't be done. We do not own books; they are not our possessions. The money you have given me for the book gives you the right to use this book. After you, someone else will use it. If everyone trimmed the pages, in time there would be nothing left of the book."

We are not living in "our" room or in "our" house. We will eventually leave it all behind and return to God. This is all temporary. Even our children are not ours. Like the governess, it is our job to love them and take care of them. But we don't "own" them, and they will eventually grow up and leave home. When we get too possessive of our children, it doesn't do them or us any good. No one possesses other human beings. As parents we need to be reminded that slavery has been abolished. We also have to remind ourselves to be less attached to everything around us. We are afraid of letting things go.

If we are lucky to live long enough, we will physically become poorer and poorer, more and more like a *fakir*. Little by little, parts of our life will go. We raise our family in a nice house and eventually the children move out and the house is too big, so we move to someplace smaller. We lose our physical abilities and can no longer practice the sports we loved. Our physical energy diminishes. So does our memory. We become poorer in many different ways.

We should cease accumulating more and more things. The older we get, the more we should pay attention to God and the less we should pay attention to the world. There is an old Sufi saying, "A dervish is someone who lives in the world, but does not belong to the world."

Spiritual poverty is contentment, the opposite of craving. Jesus‡ said, "Blessed are the poor in spirit: for theirs is the Kingdom of heaven."(Matt. 5:3, King James) The Prophet§ said, "I am proud of my poverty." He was poor in his love of the world, and rich in his love of God.

One sheikh said, "Real poverty is to be poor with God." This means being content with whatever God sends us and accepting happily whatever God brings. Then it doesn't matter what we do or don't have. It is the opposite of constantly running after more out of a sense of dissatisfaction.

Some dervishes have managed to live in true contentment, without craving. According to one Sufi story, there was a man who worked with his hands for a living. Every day he earned a single silver coin. He fasted every day, and when he received his wages at the end of the day he gave it all in charity. After the evening prayer, he would beg for food so that he could eat. He did that for twenty years.

That is the ideal of poverty. This man was not a beggar in the conventional sense. He worked and earned money every day, but then he gave away everything he earned.

Muzaffer Efendi told the story of a young man who lived in Mecca years ago. He wore rags and owned nothing. A wealthy man offered him a bag of coins, and he immediately refused, saying, "What are you doing? I don't need that money. I don't want it." The wealthy man replied, "Then give it in charity," and the young man agreed. A sheikh who witnessed this saw the young man begging for food that evening. The sheikh was shocked. He came up to the man and asked, "My son, wouldn't it have been better if you had kept some coins out of that bag so you wouldn't have to beg?" The young man answered, "I didn't know if I would live until this evening, so I didn't keep anything."

Our remembrance of death is one of the great tools to help us become less attached and less worried about this world.

Another young man who lived in Mecca prayed all day long at the Kaaba, the most sacred structure in Islam, and the direction all Muslims face in prayer. He habitually prayed near a sheikh and his dervishes. As time went by, the sheikh enjoyed the man's silent company and came to feel very close to him. One day the sheikh brought a bag of coins to the young man, saying, "This is *halal* (lawfully earned) money. It is from the sale of fruit from my orchards."

The young man pushed the bag back to the sheikh and said, "You understand nothing. I gave away 70,000 silver coins so that I could be here with God with no distractions. And you want to ruin that with this money?"

Years later the sheikh commented, "I have never been more embarrassed for myself than at that moment, and I have never had more admiration for someone else than I had for that young man."

Islam teaches us to love and serve the poor and not avoid or ignore them. Unfortunately, we live in stratified communities, surrounded by other middle-class people. The poor are pushed into ghettos where we can't see them.

One Sunday afternoon years ago, my oldest son fell from a tree and hit his head. We rushed him to the emergency room at the county hospital. Many of the people there were extremely poor. Some were injured, others were sick. Many were wearing torn clothing, deeply soiled by hard manual labor. They were clearly malnourished and living at a subsistence level. I had never seen people like that in town. We lived in different worlds, and I realized how segregated we are. We don't even notice the poor, who suffer from terrible nutrition and struggle for bare subsistence.

Serving the poor is extremely important. If God has blessed us with material abundance, we have an obligation to share it. The Prophet§ loved the poor. He would share his food with them, and he would visit and eat with them, often eating rancid olive oil and spoiled food because that was all they had.

We must overcome our fear of poverty. We need to be courageous and say to ourselves, "Material things will come and go. I will continue to work and save what I can, but the day may come when I may end up with nothing. Whatever God wills. It is not in my hands."

We need very little. The great Sufi sage Ibn ʿArabi◊ wrote, "All that you need from the world is something lawful to satisfy your hunger, something with which to cover yourself, and a roof over your head. Let these be the only things you ask from this world, nothing more."[1]

We confuse *wants* with *needs*. We are surrounded by possessions we don't need, but our egos hypnotize us into believing we must have them. Think of all the clothing we have accumulated. How many shirts do we have? How many pairs of pants? How many sweaters? And yet we all have quite a collection.

There were two saints who passed on at the same time. One of them was ushered into heaven before the other, even though the second saint had spent more time in prayer and contemplation. When the second saint asked why, he was told, "He had only one shirt and you had two."

Some understand poverty in the profound sense of non-attachment to material things. They live a wonderful, contented life. The great Sufi saint Ibrahim bin Adhem began life as the prince of Belkh, but after he became a dervish he owned nothing but the old, patched robes he wore. A beggar asked him, "How did you get to this sorry state?"

"I paid a whole kingdom for this. And it was a bargain at that price."

Another saint wore clothing of sackcloth, rough burlap cloth taken from sacks that goods came in. Someone asked him why he dressed so incredibly poorly. "I paid the world for this clothing. I was offered heaven for it, and I would not give it up, even for that."

We can come to love our spiritual poverty, simplicity, and non-attachment. To be a dervish means to become simple and unattached. It means to want God and to refuse to let our desire for the world interfere with our desire for God. A dervish's desire for God becomes his or her motivation for everything. The world can come and go; our longing for God is what sustains us.

We have to work at this. We have to become more conscious of all the attachments we have. We can't claim we are not attached to the world. Non-attachment is a goal to which we aspire.

We all start out attached to the world. It is important to be honest, to admit we like nice things and that there are many things we wish to have. Then we can examine our desires. Isn't our material desire the reason why we work? What motivates us to spend our time as we do? What are we seeking in this world? Are we seeking something from the world, or are we seeking God?

We have to explore our attitudes toward poverty. Do we understand spiritual poverty? Can we even begin to feel the joy and beauty inherent in it? Our attachment to the world may not go away completely, but we can become more conscious of it. Safer Efendi said, "The *nafs* is with us until we die. The old wolf no longer has teeth or claws. The wolf has no strength, but when a lamb passes by the wolf begins to pant." It is a serious mistake to say, "I am a dervish, so of course I am not attached to this world."

We were not born as dervishes. We have become dervishes because we want to grow spiritually, because we realize we need help. We don't *begin* at an advanced level; no one does. We all have to work to appreciate the virtue of poverty. And we can begin by asking ourselves, "What do I want? What am I seeking?"

I am not suggesting that we try to drop all our attachments or leave the world and join a monastery. Rather than trying to force ourselves to change, we need to observe ourselves and learn what we truly want, what we truly care for. We can learn to understand possessions and the part of us that wants them. We can also come to understand why our possessions will never satisfy us. That takes real contemplation.

Self-examination is difficult. When we see our attachments, for example, we tend to slip into one or two responses. One is to become critical of ourselves. "I am so material, so worldly. I have not grown on this path at all." Or we do the opposite—we rationalize: "I really need this for my work." "Society forces me to buy these things." "It is expected of me." "My family wants this."

It is a challenge to avoid judgment or rationalization and observe ourselves clearly. We can ask ourselves, "I do want this, but where does that desire come from? What would happen if I got it? What would happen if I didn't?" All too often we don't really examine ourselves. If we all tried to experiment with ways of becoming less attached, we could be role models for each other.

We have to water the seeds of appreciation of spiritual poverty. Eventually we can begin to taste the joys of those who have attained a state of contentment. Wanting more is endless.

If God wills, we will learn to be content with whatever our Sustainer gives us, to be grateful for what we receive, and to be generous with what we have. May we slowly become more attached to God and less attached to the world.

It is important to see how much we desire something. All too often we have strong desires, but we are not really conscious of them. We take our desires for granted.

When we look within, we should not say "*I* want." Instead we can say, "There is something in me that wants." Or, "A desire has arisen in me." Identifying with our desires can be a problem, because then we may become stuck with them. If we don't identify with wanting, we can come to realize that a desire has arisen in us and then we can ask ourselves, "Where did this come from? Just because I have a desire, that doesn't mean I have to fulfill it."

When we say "*I* want this," we have become identified with our wanting. It implies all of us want something and we *have* to have it. It is more accurate to say there is a voice in us that wants this, part of us that wants this. But is it a reasonable part or not? Can we discern what that voice is and where it comes from?

The old Christian concept of *discernment* is based on the idea that we have different voices within us. Some voices lead us closer to God and other voices lead us away from God. Discernment means to distinguish between them.

We can try to understand where our inner voices are leading us. Does a particular impulse move us *toward* God or *away from* God? Are we following the example of our Prophet§, or are we acting in contradiction to his teaching and his example? Are we avoiding something, or are we seeking something? For example, an impulse of generosity arises in us. And then an inner voice says, "The poor don't deserve charity. They will probably misuse my money." That voice is seeking to move us away from generosity. We can become conscious of these inner voices. Whenever we think of doing something charitable, we will almost certainly hear two opposing voices.

If we become more aware of these inner voices, we might notice that a certain voice sounds like our father or mother—perhaps even with the same intonation or turn of phrase. That voice is not us. It comes from teachings we heard when we were young, which we internalized. Another voice is the five-year-old in us. It is part of us, but certainly not all of us, nor the wisest or most mature part of us. Other voices are more dangerous and seductive.

During one of Muzaffer Efendi's trips to Europe, he visited a Catholic church in Switzerland. The priest showed him the art works in the church, including a picture of Satan. Satan was depicted as an ugly, threatening figure with a tail and horns. The priest said, "This is a picture of Satan." Muzaffer Efendi exclaimed, "No, that cannot be!" The priest objected, "How can you be so sure?" Muzaffer Efendi smiled and replied, "If Satan was that ugly, who would ever listen to him? No, he always assumes an attractive appearance. He is as glamorous as a movie star."

We practice discernment continually during Ramadan. We feel hungry and thirsty but we choose not to eat. During the rest of the year we often automatically rush to get something to eat or drink, without any reflection on our desires. One of the many benefits of Ramadan is that we stop and reflect when these desires arise.

When we identify with our thoughts or desires, we become caught by them. Most arguments occur because people become identified with their opinions. The more identified we are, the more upset we become when someone else dares to express a different opinion. The argument is rarely about the real merits of differing points of view. Each person has become committed to defending their ideas, actually defending their egos, and neither one seriously considers the other's ideas or arguments.

We should always be happy to question our own thinking and desires. We should be pleased if someone else questions them. We might learn something then. We are usually so convinced we are right that we refuse to really listen to others and learn from them. It would be better to commit ourselves to learning instead of committing ourselves to being right.

One of my colleagues[2] has written that there are two kinds of people in this world: *knowers* and *learners*. The knowers are those who are committed to being right. They fight to defend their own opinions, so they learn very little. They would prefer that everyone agreed with them. Then they would learn nothing, but they would be "right." The learners, on the other hand, are not defensive. They welcome differing opinions and contradictory information, because they are dedicated to learning. As dervishes we should be learners.

It is the same with our desires. Sometimes we have desires, and there is nothing wrong with that. One day I saw a Bentley. I thought, "What a lovely car." Then I thought, "Thank God no part of me wants a car like this for myself." We can look at a fancy car and appreciate it without lusting after it or envying the owner. It is like feeling hunger and thirst in Ramadan and telling ourselves, "I am not going to eat or drink until sundown," instead of getting caught up in our desires for food and drink.

One excellent practice to reduce our desires is to give away more. We can counter our wish to hold onto things by giving them away. As soon as we notice a desire for more clothes, we can give away some of the clothes we seldom wear—not with the object of making space in our closets, but as an expression of our understanding that we have much more than we need. This is not so much an act of generosity as an exercise to help us overcome our seemingly endless desire for more possessions.

The truth is, we are all stingy. A man once asked a saint, "How much of our wealth should we pay in *zakat* (the annual charity given at the end of the month of Ramadan)?" The saint asked, "For you or for those like me?" The man replied, "Everyone knows it is 1/40 of the money we have accumulated each year!" The saint replied, "That is for stingy people like you. As for those like me, we give everything."

Our lack of generosity is a sign of our lack of faith. It means we do not trust that God will continue to provide for us. We think *we* have to provide for ourselves, and we have to hold on to whatever we "have." That is our egos speaking.

May God grant us the opportunity to strengthen our faith through knowledge and conscious experience. We can open our eyes to Truth and Reality, or we can close them. Let us not act like blind people.

▸ 19 ◂

Generosity

There are three kinds of generosity. The generosity of the average person is to give to others a portion of what they have. The generosity of the elite is to give most of what they have and to keep only a small part for themselves. The saints give everything they have, not putting anything aside for the future, and relying solely on whatever God provides.

Generosity means we welcome the opportunity to give and we don't regret what we have given. Some of us give reluctantly. We know it is a good thing to do, but we find it difficult. As Muzaffer Efendi used to say, some people act as if their wallets are covered with nettles. When they reach for their wallets to give charity, their hands sting.

There are many wonderful Sufi stories illustrating the value of generosity. A man from Medina was traveling in the early days of Islam. He came to a city of new Muslims. The people asked the traveler where he was from, and he told them he was from Medina. They asked about a man from Medina named Ibrahim bin Abdullah, and the traveler said that he knew him. One of the townspeople exclaimed, "What a wonderful man he is. He made us all wealthy."

The traveler said, "I don't understand. He is not a wealthy man. How could he have made you wealthy?"

"It wasn't money he gave us. He taught us generosity. So now none of us go without."

Isn't that a fascinating idea? Generosity made them wealthy. Generosity can make us all wealthy. If we are generous with one another, no one will go without. I have often said to members of our Sufi community, "As long as any of us has a roof over our heads, none of us will become homeless. As long as one of us has food in the refrigerator, none of us will go hungry." We may not be wealthy, but we have more security than the wealthy who have no one to depend on if they lose their wealth.

Not giving is a sign of our lack of faith, a sign of our ego's attachments, or, more precisely, our attachment to our egos. First, we think, "It is *my* money." That is the first mistake. Then we think if we give "our" possessions we will not have enough. Again, that comes from lack of faith. We forget that God is our Sustainer and that whatever comes to us is from God.

Everything is God's. It is our job to be generous custodians of what God has given into our care.

If we make space, new things can enter. Every one of us can go through our drawers and closets and give away at least half of what we have. We wouldn't miss it, and there are people who need it. And, Islam teaches us that the one who gives will benefit more than the one who receives.

Muzaffer Efendi told a story about generosity that I have retold many times. Before Islam, one of the early prophets lived in a small town. He performed all the religious ceremonies for his people, from births to marriages to funerals. One day he married a young couple, and after the wedding feast the prophet was very sad, even though he normally loved to perform weddings. His friends asked him why he was so unhappy, and he said, "The destiny of this couple is very depressing. They are very happy now, but they are not meant to live out this night."

The next morning, the townspeople saw the young man in the market. The prophet was surprised and asked the young man if he could come to his house. The man said, "Of course." The prophet came along with some of his companions. The young wife greeted them at the door. The prophet entered the house and noticed that the couple's bedding was still on the floor of their bedroom. He flipped over the bedding with his staff and uncovered an extremely poisonous snake. The prophet asked the snake what had happened that night, and the snake said, "I crawled in here to get warm. When the couple got into bed they disturbed me, and I was just about to bite them when something grabbed me by the neck. I was held immobile all night."

The prophet said, "Aha. The snake would have bitten them both, but something changed their destiny." He asked the couple if anything special had happened that night. They couldn't think of anything until the wife remembered, "Just before bedtime, a poor man came to the door, and I gave him a cup of milk."

The prophet said, "That cup of milk saved your lives."

In a *hadith*, Hazreti Muhammad§ said, "Charity prevents catastrophe."

We may think that charity is a small thing, that it does not matter, but we cannot know the effects of our generosity. The more we give, the more we nourish our own hearts and souls, in addition to benefiting others.

There are many ways to be generous. Do we have the spirit of generosity? Can we feel our hearts nourished by generosity and take joy in it? We have to cultivate that feeling.

According to a *hadith*, "The right hand should not know what the left is doing." That is, the more anonymous our generosity is, the better. It is best if we don't know who is going to receive our charity and they don't know who has given it. Then there is nothing personal in it, and the recipient is not embarrassed by receiving charity.

241

CHAPTER 19

Muzaffer Efendi told the story of a man who came to his neighbor, who was a sheikh. The man said he needed five hundred gold pieces, which was a great deal of money in those days. The sheikh immediately gave him the five hundred coins. When the man left, the sheikh began crying. One of his dervishes asked the sheikh if he was sad that he gave the man so much money. The sheikh said, "No, not at all. I am crying because he had to ask. What kind of a neighbor am I? I did not know he needed the money, so he had to ask."

The truly generous see with the eyes of their hearts and hear with the ears of their hearts. They understand with the wisdom of their hearts, so they know what others need. The generous *want* to give, with no thought of reward.

How often do we think of others? Too often we only look at what is on our plate, and we don't even look to see if our neighbor's plate is empty or full. If we just think of our own needs, we will find it hard to be generous. We can try to remember that God has always provided for us, so we don't have to worry about what is on our plate. God will fill it as God has constantly filled our plates in the past. If we remember that God is our Sustainer, we can be generous without worrying.

According to a traditional story, man asked a sheikh about heaven and hell. That night he dreamed that the sheikh escorted him to a dining room filled with hungry men and women. The table was filled with delicious food, but the only utensils provided were long spoons that had to be held by the handle. No one could get the food directly into their mouths because the spoons were so long. The hungry guests kept spilling food on themselves in their efforts to feed themselves. The sheikh told the man, "This is hell."

Then the sheikh escorted the man to another dining room. This room was filled with hungry dervishes. It had the same delicious food and the same long spoons as the first room. The dervishes grabbed their spoons and began feeding the people seated opposite them, and everyone was fed. The sheikh commented, "And this is heaven."

There was once a dervish who had traveled for many years. In some Sufi Orders, the dervishes traveled as part of their training. They traveled to remind themselves that this world is not our permanent home.

Eventually the dervish found a wonderful sheikh and stopped traveling in order to stay with him. As much as he loved his sheikh, there was a part of him that felt he was better, because he had spent so many years traveling and his sheikh had lived such a settled life. The dervish felt he had learned to rely solely on God through his years of traveling.

The dervish fell in love with the sheikh's daughter, she fell in love with him, and they married. On their wedding night, he wrapped up some bread from the wedding feast. His bride asked him what he was doing. "I am putting this bread aside for tomorrow." She looked at him in shock, "What? Give that to me!" She gave the bread to her sister and told her sister to give it to the poor. "How can you keep something for the next day? Where is your faith?"

The young dervish realized that trust in God had nothing to do with traveling or not.

I am not suggesting we give away everything each night. But consider how much more we have than we need. It is good to realize that we *need* very little while what we *want* is endless.

Developing generosity is like developing our muscles: the more we exercise, the stronger we get. At the end of each day, we might ask ourselves if we practiced generosity that day. Did we give anything to others? It does not have to be something big. We have plenty of extra clothing. We have food. We also have time, which we can devote to others. Sometimes a sympathetic listening ear or a simple smile is priceless.

If we don't know whom to talk with, we can always contact our families. We all have family members we love and who love us. And most of them will welcome contact from us.

CHAPTER 19

We can think of many ways of serving others. As I said earlier, we can cultivate an attitude of generosity. We can learn to enjoy giving. For example, when we serve those we love—our children, parents, spouses—we derive real joy from it. In a way, it may even feel selfish, because we can gain more pleasure in giving to those we love than in getting something for ourselves. If we want to grow on this path, we might think of expanding that feeling so that we find the same joy in serving all of God's children that we find in serving our families.

It's okay to begin with the limited generosity of serving our loved ones, but we should go further. Generosity transforms us. The act of giving and the feeling of generosity are potent medicine for the ego, because the ego wants exactly the opposite. It says, "I want to give to myself. I want to serve myself and have others serve me."

I strongly recommend the practice of giving charity every day. I learned this practice from an Indian sheikh. Keep a charity box in your bedroom. Every night put all your change or a dollar or two in the box. Do this with a *bismillah* and say to yourself, "I am giving this money to charity." Even if the money does not immediately go to the needy, putting it aside for charity means that you are giving charity every day. It is your intention that counts. It is a wonderful blessing to give charity every day. I have felt the value of it in my own life.

There are many ways to be generous. We can give money to worthy causes. Better than that is to remember that charity begins at home. We should first look in our immediate environment to see if there are any around us who are in need. We can give our time as volunteers to charitable organizations. We can volunteer to work at a soup kitchen; every community has one. It has become very fashionable to volunteer at a soup kitchen on Thanksgiving, and we can see pictures of local politicians serving meals to the poor that day. But how about the rest of the year? Those soup kitchens—and the people they serve—need our help all year long.

244

Many years ago someone complained that the sheikhs of Baghdad were contradicting the laws of Islam in their *sohbets*. The Caliph became angry when he heard this and arrested all the sheikhs. His soldiers lined up the sheikhs and were going to execute them.

One of the sheikhs immediately stepped forward and cried, "Take me first."

The executioner exclaimed, "I have never seen someone so eager to die."

The sheikh replied, "I want to go first so that my dear brothers will have a little longer to live. That is why I stepped forward."

The executioner said, "I can't execute a man like you." He went to the judge and told him what happened. The judge said, "These men must be sincere Muslims. They cannot be guilty of distorting Islam. I will examine them personally."

The judge summoned the sheikhs and interviewed them at length. All their answers were rooted in a profound understanding of Islam. The judge went to the Caliph and the sheikhs were all pardoned. They were saved by sincere generosity.

We can develop generosity of spirit. We all know people who are naturally generous, who would be happy to help us if we needed their aid. We also know other people who are nice, charming, but somehow, we sense, not generous. They probably would not help us if we really needed help.

My sheikh used to say that our hearts are temples built by God to house God's Presence. But remember, the holy shrine of the Kaaba was filled with idols for many years before Islam. If our hearts are filled with our desires for the things of this world, there is no room in them for God. Just like cleaning out our closets, the first step is to clear out our hearts and make space for God.

We think we want God. Actually, we *want* to want God. That is a sign of faith, but it also indicates we have not yet cleared the rubbish from our hearts. There is a part of us that wants God. But when we look at how we act day in and day out, how much of our lives is focused on ourselves, our needs, our pleasures? How much do we focus on others and their needs? How much do we seek to serve God's Creation? Generosity cleanses our hearts, and God will only enter when our hearts are ready. We just have to prepare ourselves. God is always with us, but we are unaware.

Muzaffer Efendi often said, "Every time you repeat *la ilaha illa Allah,* you tear out a weed in the garden of your heart. When you have invited the Sultan to your house, you clear the house before he arrives."

Generosity can take many forms. Generosity includes saying a kind word, listening compassionately and patiently, thinking of the right thing to say or do. Basically, we need to think less about ourselves and more about others. Paradoxically, that will benefit us more than anyone else. But if we are motivated by the desire to receive, our actions are not generous. One sheikh commented that generosity actually flows from the poor to the wealthy. That is, the poor provide the wealthy the opportunity to give, which is the greater blessing.

Another aspect to generosity is to let others serve us so *they* can benefit by being generous. Some of us love to serve others but hate to be served. Then we deprive others of the opportunity of serving. We are not being truly generous. It is good to remember that the receiver is generous to the giver.

In every encounter let us think how we might be generous to the others. Sometimes it is to serve them, and sometimes it is to allow them to serve us. Sometimes we serve best by speaking, and sometimes we serve by being silent. To serve well, we have to open the eyes of our hearts so we can know what others need.

▶ 20 ◀

Taking Responsibility for Our Spiritual Lives

n Islam, all those who are adult and mentally competent need to take responsibility for their spiritual lives. Many seekers believe their teacher is the greatest or their religion or spiritual path is the best. Unfortunately, with this belief often comes the assumption: "My teacher/tradition is so wonderful that I do not have to work hard; my teacher or my tradition will do it for me." That may be a comforting belief, but it isn't true.

As I mentioned earlier, Muzaffer Efendi used to say that we all come to this path with our own containers—some have a cup, some have a bucket, and some have a barrel. The important thing is to fill our container. That is our job in life. He also said that some sheikhs are like a dripping faucet, and others are like a great waterfall. It is essential to put our own container underneath the source that God has sent to us—and to keep it there. That is our job as dervishes. We have to maintain that divinely blessed connection God has sent to us and fill our own container.

Even a slowly dripping faucet will fill our container—if we hold it there long enough. If we keep searching for a "better" source, going from one teacher to another, our container will never fill. We need to have patience and hold our container under the source of blessing we have been given.

We also have to do our best to make sure our container does not leak. This means being honest, sincere, just. It means following the morals and ethics of Islam—that is, leading an orderly life, one that can hold the *berekat*, the energy and blessings, of this path.

A sheikh is a physician of the heart. The lessons given by a sheikh are the "medicines" to cure the hearts and minds of their dervishes. Whatever our teachers have given us to do is what we should be doing. For that, we must listen deeply to what they say. Then we must be consistent in the practices given to us. It is easy to imagine that there are better teachers or better practices out there and fail to follow the path we have been given. That is the voice of the ego, which prefers imagination to real effort. Also, we may imagine that someone else is progressing faster, or is better off spiritually than we are. Our egos will constantly try to convince us of this; they will argue, "You are not getting the attention you deserve. That is why others are progressing faster." Our egos will always try to convince us that we are better and more important than others. First of all, that is not true. Second, we will never grow if we focus on others instead of doing our own work. Imitating someone else does nothing for our own spiritual development. And being jealous of others only leaves us worse off than we were before. Muzaffer Efendi advised, "Concerning wisdom and spiritual development, we should look upwards toward those who are more advanced than we are. We should be inspired by their example.

In material matters, we should look at those who have less than we do and be grateful for what we have."

Islam and Sufism are a way of life, not merely a collection of formal practices and rituals. Sufism is the subtle aspect of Islam and teaches us how to improve our character. The sheikh guides dervishes to this goal. If we want to reach an unfamiliar destination, we need a guide. I know your ego is telling you simply to get a map and follow it yourself. But there are no maps for this inner journey.

Inner States

Many of us have been blessed with inspirational experiences during *zikr* or in the presence of our sheikhs. These are times when we have felt filled with the light, love, and grace of God. But those experiences are always temporary. Like dreams, we have to wake up eventually and return to our everyday state of being. In Sufism, these inspired experiences are called *hal*. They are distinguished from more stable states, which are known as *maqam* or dwelling place. The term *maqam* also means a mode in music, such as major or minor. We only use these two modes in Western music, but in Eastern music there are hundreds of *maqam*. A musician can play countless pieces in the same mode. Similarly, we can have thousands of experiences and still remain in the same state of being.

Many dervishes have been deeply inspired by the presence of their teachers and experienced various spiritual states in their presence. It is a wonderful blessing. However, there is a danger in this. We may think our teachers do our work for us and that we do not need to take responsibility for our own spiritual lives. We have to fill our own lives with *zikr*, love, and service. No one else can do it for us. No one else can love or worship for us. A sheikh can teach the most wonderful truths, but these teachings are useless if we say, "How beautifully and wisely the sheikh speaks!" but fail to act accordingly.

A spiritual teacher is like a coach. Gifted athletes need good coaches to develop their skills as fully as possible. A good coach can help make an athlete's training far more effective, but the athlete still has to do his or her training. A coach cannot run a single mile or do a single pushup for an athlete.

One my teachers said, "God does 99 percent of the work for you. You really only have to make 1 percent of the effort needed to find God. However, you have to do 100 percent of that 1 percent!" Of course, God's Mercy may even add that last 1 percent. But God expects us to make sincere efforts.

The words of the Qur'an have inspired millions of Muslims over the past fourteen hundred years. But, unfortunately, there have been many millions who have called themselves Muslims yet were never transformed by those holy words. Tyrants, egotists, and fools have often turned the priceless words of Scripture into their opposites. Divinely inspired words alone are not enough. As the Holy Qur'an teaches, many people are like donkeys carrying holy books. No matter how precious the books, the donkey is untouched by what it is carrying. Too many of us are donkeys.

Regular prayer alone is not an end in itself, and it is no guarantee of spiritual growth. Many who call themselves Muslims have abused their families, neighbors, or themselves. The same is true for the followers of all religions. We need to be shocked out of our complacency. Superficial practice does little or nothing, no matter how wonderful our religion or spiritual path might be. As Hazreti Muhammadﷺ taught, "Some people pray and all they get from it is exercise. Some fast and all they get is hunger."

Let us develop the habit of trying to connect ourselves with God in our prayers and other forms of worship. The more awareness we bring to our spiritual practices, the more these practices will bear fruit.

Before we pray, we should try to put all our worldly concerns behind us. When we do this, we create an empty space in front of us, and we no longer put anything between God and ourselves. This is the real meaning of *fakir*: one who is poor in anything that distracts from God. We have to work at this. It is a very personal effort. We try to feel that we are in God's Presence. The virtue of *ihsan* means to pray with a sense of God's Presence. That is, even if we do not see God when we pray, we know God sees us.

When we recite "*la ilaha illa Allah*," we should make it an inner practice. *La ilaha* literally means "There are no gods." *Illa Allah* means "There is God." Muzaffer Efendi used to teach that *la ilaha* cleanses the heart. It reminds us that there is nothing divine or transcendent but God. (Another level of meaning is there is nothing that truly exists except God.) Ideally, this phrase cleans the temple of the heart of our attachments to and dependence on the transient things of this world. The second phrase, *illa Allah*, sanctifies the altar of the heart. It asserts that even though all we can see is the material world, God does exist; God is the Reality behind this apparent reality of Creation. And God is in our hearts.

When we say this holy phrase, we can open our hearts and focus on God, the One who created us. Mechanical repetition of this or any other holy utterance does very little. We must develop our own understanding of these words. For example, *la ilaha*—not the world around me, not my own personal concerns and problems; none of these things are permanent or truly important. *Illa Allah*—my God is in my heart. This is personal prayer.

Everything Counts

Our nervous systems register everything we say, everything we think, and everything we do. Our character develops positively with every kind word, every kind thought, and every kind action. Conversely, our character develops negatively with every unkind thought, every heedless word, and every angry act. However, Muzaffer Efendi used to say that we will not be punished for unkind thoughts unless we act on them. And when we do behave badly, if we sincerely repent and God accepts it, a good deed is recorded in place of the bad one.

Sufism is our personal path. Our path is based on our own thoughts and actions, on the quality of our life, day in and day out. We have companions along this path, and we have the guidance of our Prophet§ and our teachers, but we still have to walk every step ourselves. If we are taking a trip with others, we cannot expect them to carry us on their backs. God has given us two legs and the capacity to walk. How can we ask someone else to carry us on his or her back? This path rests on our own efforts.

God is the Beloved, the one who is closer to us than we are to ourselves. God is at the core of our being. God is in our heart of hearts. Whenever we say *la ilaha illa Allah*, we are connecting with our own heart, the heart that God gave us as a temple to house the divine spark within each of us.

We can become more and more filled with light and radiate that light to everyone around us. Some people illuminate others. Light, warmth, and love emanate from their eyes, their words and their actions. This light nourishes their loved ones, their neighbors, and the world around them.

No one else can do our spiritual work for us. The change we are seeking is a function of the time, sincerity, and patience we put into our spiritual practice. We will change if we carry out our practices patiently, with awareness, not mechanically. This will work. This path has transformed millions of people over the course of human history. Islam is not a new religion. It teaches the same truths that God revealed to humanity since the time of Adam‡. The Path of Truth is as old as humanity.

This Is *Our* Path

Our egos may tell us that this is not really our path, that it is the path of some peculiar people from the twelfth century. Years ago, a friend asked me why I didn't try something else. Why, my friend wanted to know, was I involved in this funny Sufi business? My ego had asked the same thing, far more eloquently, and more than once.

I answered, without stopping to think about it: "I could look for other spiritual teachers. There are certainly a lot of them out there. However, I honestly believe I have been placed on this path, and my only choice is to follow the path God has given me or to refuse to follow it. It is not a question of finding a better teacher or a more suitable path. If I leave the path I am on, I would be abandoning the priceless gift I have been given. If I do that, I am abandoning my own spiritual path for a fantasy that there might be something better out there. If God takes me from this path, that is another question. But God has put me here, and I pray I will remain on this path."

We all have the choice to follow this path or not. I recommend doing it. In general, it seems to be a good idea to do whatever God has given us to do.

Our egos will make all kinds of excuses. "I'll really devote myself to this path next month" or ". . . next year." "I will devote myself when all my work is done" or ". . . when I don't have to worry about money." Of course, this will never happen. There will always be work to do, and we will always feel we need more money. Our egos will always try to get us to put off devoting ourselves to this path until some point in the future. We can always find reasons and distractions.

Our egos will tell us this is not our path. The ego will argue, "The Qur'an is in Arabic, so it must be the path of the Arabs." Or, "This is a Turkish Order, so it is a Turkish path." If we are Turkish, our egos will argue, "This is a path for Turks from the seventeenth century, not for modern Turks." The answer to our ego is, "This is the path I have been given, and now is the time to practice it." We need to say to ourselves, "This is *my* path, not the path of others, not a path restricted to the saints of the past. And I can only come to understand it more deeply by following it to the best of my ability."

We understand as much as God gives us to understand. It is not that important to understand a great deal. It is far more important to practice whatever we do understand. It is not really that difficult. We all understand far more than we practice.

Our egos may tell us to wait until we have mastered Arabic. That is a wonderful excuse, because that will probably never happen. We have to practice now, with the resources and understanding we have now. It is a question of taking what we know and living it—making this our own path, taking responsibility for following it as best we can.

We must not go through the motions and mechanically recite the words without contemplating their meaning. Instead, we must make intention in a way that it becomes a real action: We can do more than just mouth the words. We can experience the words of prayer and the words of *zikr*. We can *mean* the words we recite. If we do that, these words can transform us.

Becoming Conscious

The more conscious we are, the more others will be affected by what we say, because we will mean what we say. It is very easy to go through the motions and remain unconscious when we speak or act.

Habit is one of the great enemies of consciousness. Habit is a mixed blessing. We have to develop habits; without them, we would have to relearn to tie our shoelaces every day and relearn to drive a car every morning. I would never get on the road if all the other drivers on the road were busy relearning their driving habits. I would much rather walk.

Our ability to button our shirts, use a knife and fork, type—these are all habits. We learn complex actions and store these patterns in memory, and it becomes easier and easier to perform what had at first been extremely difficult. On the other hand, habit takes us out of being present and aware of what we are doing.

There is an old Sufi saying, "The dervish is a child of the moment." This means we pay attention to tying our shoelaces whenever we put on our shoes. We are not thinking about our email or planning our evening activities. When we button our shirts or brush our teeth, or whatever else we may do, we remain present to the act itself.

We have all become addicted to multitasking. Our children watch television, study, and talk on the phone, all at the same time. Instead, we can cultivate being fully in the moment, not thinking about one thing while we are doing something else.

There is a strange modern notion of efficiency that tells us that as long as we are doing something mechanical or habitual, we should also be doing other things as well. We think we can save time by doing several things as once. We know it is dangerous to drive and talk on our cell phones, but most people still do it. When you drive, drive; when you talk, talk. Be present in whatever you are doing.

Whenever we try to do several things simultaneously, we are developing the habit of distracting ourselves. Then, when we are praying, we have trouble keeping our minds focused. It is not surprising that we are not focused during our prayers if we have been distracted all day long.

As a part of our spiritual practice in daily life, let me suggest something very simple: Do one thing at a time. Be more aware of everything you are doing. Practice being a child of the moment. We devote relatively little time to our prayers each day. If we spend most of our waking hours daydreaming or distracted, how can we expect to be in the present when we worship? Remember, Hazreti Muhammad§ taught, "Without the *presence* of the heart, there is no prayer."

Many of us are so busy that we feel we have to slip our prayers in between all our other activities and appointments. We rush to do our prayers during a commercial break in a TV program. Our prayers are sandwiched into our tight schedule instead of being treated as one of the most important things we do every day. Ideally, we should put everything else aside, take a moment to become more present, and prepare ourselves for prayer.

One of the Attributes of God is *ya Hadi,* the Guide. That divine quality is still alive today. God is the essence of all guidance, past, present, and future. God is available to us as our Guide on the Path of Truth. God is *our* Guide. If we think of God as only a guide to the great prophets and saints of the past, we are limiting this attribute of God. God is the Guide for each of us, the Guide for every creature— in the past, at this moment, and forever.

God is also *al Haq,* the Truth. How are we searching for the Truth in our own lives? This is a personal path, and we cannot be satisfied with the outer form alone, or with the words of others. We can try to pray as Muzaffer Efendi prayed. When he made *dua,* his prayer was not someone else's prayer, nor was it mechanical. His prayer was real, unique, and immediate. It came from his heart. Our goal should be to pray like that.

When we recite our formal prayers, we can try to make the words our own. When we say *Bismillah ir-rahman ir-rahim*, we can reflect on what it means to say "In the name of God, the most Merciful, the most Compassionate."

When we say *Al hamdu lillah*, we can contemplate what it means to say "Praise be to God." I love the churches in which the preacher and the congregation will cry out, "Praise the Lord!" Those words are powerful and inspirational for them.

Our ego tries to prevent us from being in the present and to prevent us from taking responsibility for our spiritual lives. The ego has tremendous power and sophistication, and it is our worst enemy. Do not ignore it. Sheikh Tosun Efendi used to ask us what would we do if our homes were invaded by a psychotic, escaped convict—a highly muscled killer armed with an assault rifle. Paying attention to this dreadful danger would be the most important thing in our lives as long as he was in our home; such a maniac has the capacity to destroy us and everyone we love. But Tosun Efendi pointed out our egos are even more dangerous: the psychotic's fists and bullets can only harm our bodies, while our egos can destroy our spiritual lives and permanently wound those we love. But this is only possible if we refuse to follow the guidance of *ya Hadi*.

As I mentioned earlier, one of my teachers pointed out that God provides 99 percent of what we need. We only need to do 1 percent of the work. However, we do have to do 100 percent of that 1 percent. For example, suppose someone gives you a beautiful new car. The car works perfectly—the engine, the ignition system, the steering system, etc. All you need to do in order to start the car is to insert the key into the ignition lock and turn the key. The car will not start by itself, nor will it start if you only insert the key half-way, or if you only turn the key half-way. We have to do 100 percent of the starting-the-car procedure.

The same is true in our spiritual lives. God's blessings provide 99 percent, and we only have to do 1 percent. But God expects us to complete our 1 percent.

Every Path to God Is Unique

Everyone's path is unique. On the one hand, we are all Muslims and we are all dervishes. We share the same religious and spiritual practices. We are all following the same path, and we can support and accompany each other on the path. We can and should be a spiritual family.

But on the other hand, our paths are unique because our lives are different. Have you ever marveled at how each pebble on the beach is unique, although they all have the same general form? The ways we love God are unique, and the ways we can serve each other differ. In a famous *hadith*, Hazreti Muhammad§ said there are as many paths to God as there are souls. We have to pay attention to our own spiritual path. It must be alive. It grows and changes, just as we grow and change. If we stop changing, we have lost this living path of ours.

This path is a journey. In any journey, we have to keep our balance with every step we take. If we fail to maintain our balance because we were balanced a moment ago, we are likely to fall. We have to remain in the present and keep paying attention. One level of meaning of this *hadith* is, we have to pay attention each moment. We have to remain aware of what we are saying and doing.

The steps we take today are not the same as the steps we took last year. The path we strive to follow is the path of Hazreti Muhammad§, which is the path of all the prophets. The path does not change, but the circumstances of life vary. Our spiritual path demands that we remain awake, vibrant, and alive. We cannot sleepwalk through life, simply going through the motions.

Our egos will keep trying to change what I have been saying. Our egos will try to distract us, keep us from listening closely, make us forget, and get us to interpret this into something easier, less demanding, and less effective. To follow our path, we have to answer these challenges.

Many of us judge ourselves harshly because we are not pursuing this path perfectly. But we never will be perfect. God does not expect perfection from us, only sincere effort.

Tosun Efendi told the following story about prayer. One day, the Prophet§ asked if anyone could do their prayers perfectly, without their mind wandering. No one said anything. Finally, Abu Darda, a close companion of the Prophet§, said, "If God wills, perhaps I might."

The Prophet§ said, "Just make two *rakats* [cycles] of prayer without your mind wandering and I will give you my cloak."

When Abu Darda began his prayers, the Prophet§ watched him extremely closely. Then, after Abu Darda finished the first *rakat*, the Prophet§ turned away. When Abu Darda finished, the Prophet§ asked him, "What happened?"

"Thank God, my mind did not wander at all during the first *rakat*. But as I was starting the second *rakat*, the thought came to my mind, 'He has two cloaks; which one would I get?'"

We Are Not Perfect

This story reminds us that we are never going to be perfect. We were not created perfect. We all experience distractions. We were created in need of God's help, mercy, and forgiveness. We need to call upon

God's Attribute *ya Ghafur*, the One who Pardons. In this Attribute, God has a special relationship with humanity, in which we relate to God by seeking divine forgiveness.

Being perfect is not an option for us. But we do not *need* to be perfect, and we should not try to *be* perfect. However, we should strive *toward* perfection. Our egos love to tell us that we have to be perfect, because then we will never make real spiritual progress. The ego wins because we will never succeed.

All we can do is make intention and do the best we can. That is all we can hope for. That is a lot; don't underestimate it! We can try to improve each day. We can try to be as conscious as possible and experience each moment more clearly. We should not be discouraged by what we cannot do, but be grateful for what we can do. And then ask God to forgive our shortcomings.

It is better to strive for *improvement* than to strive for an unreachable image of perfection. We can enjoy the Presence of God in our lives right now. God is not sitting on top of some distant Mount Olympus. Many of us think we have to wait for God's Presence, that we cannot experience God right now because we are not spiritually ready. But the time is now. We are as close to God as we ever will be. God tells us "We are closer to him [humanity] than his jugular vein." (50:16, Cleary) We may become more conscious of God's Presence, but we will never be closer to God than we are now.

From this point of view, the notion of progressing on a path is a delusion. How can we say that God is not fully present with us now? In a *hadith qudsi*, God points out, "There are seventy thousand veils between you and Me, but there are no veils between Me and you." We may think God is far from us, but that is not true.

We can savor our prayers and enjoy our experience of *zikrullah* with the feeling that God is close, that God can fill us with love and light at any moment.

My old Zen teacher once said that one of the most important elements in worship is to have a "bright mind." That means praying or performing *zikr* knowing that at any moment we can feel God's Presence—that God can "grab" us and transform us at any moment. Unfortunately, most people believe they are not ready or not worthy. If we believe we are not ready now, probably it will not happen.

Praying with a sense of God's Presence is *ihsan*, the sense that even if we do not experience God's Presence, we are firmly convinced that God is fully present, that God sees us and hears our prayers. We may feel veiled, but we know there are no veils between God and us.

We may often think, "I will be ready later; I will be worthy later." These are traps. Nobody is worthy, and everybody is worthy. We need to stop judging ourselves. We judge ourselves and compare ourselves to others. But we really do not know whether God will accept our efforts at worship. We do not know where we are spiritually. Only God knows. All our judgments are nonsense. So what can we do? We can follow the teachings of Islam and of Sufism. We can do our best to follow the example of Hazreti Muhammad§ and the examples of the saints.

We compulsively judge everyone and everything. We judge our friends, family, and neighbors. We judge other dervishes and our teachers. We judge other Sufi orders and other Sufi teachers. Just stop it. It is all imagination, and worse than useless. For one thing, our compulsive judgments distract us from doing our own spiritual work.

One answer to this tendency is to use the mantra, "Only God knows." We can use it whenever we think we know something, whenever we feel a judgment coming on. "Only God knows" is very effective. The traditional Islamic phrase is *Allahu alim*, "God knows best." We might also try the mantra, "I might be wrong." It is also extremely effective.

Only God knows whose prayers are accepted. Only God knows who is close to Truth. Only God knows where anyone is on the spiritual path. Only God knows what is going on in us or in anybody else.

God knows us better than we know ourselves, and no one else's judgment matters. Others may judge us even though they do not know us. So what? This path is between God and us. God is *al Alim*, the All-Knowing. This is another one of the ninety-nine divine Attributes.

Most of the events of our lives are beyond our control. We do what we can and leave the rest to God. My master Safer Efendi used the example of an airplane trip. The operation of the airplane is completely independent of our individual will. Our will does not affect when the plane will take off, how high it will fly, or when it will land.

The same is true of the rest of life. Most of our lives is not under our control and cannot be affected by our own actions. When we came into this world and when we will leave it are matters of destiny.

And yet, God does allow us free will. For example, we can sleep the whole time we are on the plane, or we can use that time to study or pray or read something interesting. We can sleepwalk throughout our lives or use our time here to accomplish something.

We don't know how long we have to live; we don't know how long our loved ones will live. We don't know how long we are going to keep our jobs or our homes. But we can use productively the time we do have. We can help others and act in ways that nourish us emotionally and spiritually—or not. That choice we can make.

In one sense, our choices are a function of our individual wills. In another sense, it is all God's Will. Both perspectives are useful and both contain truth. Both are ways of understanding life. It is like looking at a garden from two different angles. Each view shows us something different.

To Wake Before We Die

We often behave like sleepwalkers. We run on habit and rarely pay close attention to the world around us, and we will not grow on the spiritual path unless we become more conscious, more awake, and more heedful. One way to become more conscious is to become less attached. Our attachments can be tremendous distractions.

Non-attachment

Some years ago, one of my teachers told me the following story. He had given up a promising career as an architect in order to devote himself to the Path of Truth. He was studying with Frank Lloyd Wright, one of a small group of gifted young architects chosen to work with the master architect. When he met his sheikh, he left his studies with Frank Lloyd Wright in order to pursue the Path of Truth.

One day a senior dervish came to visit the sheikh. The senior dervish was an extremely wealthy businessman and brought the sheikh many expensive delicacies imported from the Middle East. The sheikh and his dervish ate together, taking great pleasure in these costly, exotic foods.

As he was serving them, the young man thought to himself, "I gave up my career to devote myself to this path. I gave up the world and my worldly ambitions, and now I see how my sheikh is enjoying the world, how attached he is to the things of this world."

At this point the sheikh turned, looked at the young man, and said, "My son, you do not understand nonattachment. Nonattachment does not mean that you fail to enjoy whatever God sends to you. Non-attachment means you don't miss those gifts when God takes them away."

In a *hadith*, the Prophet§ said we should eat of the best of foods, but in moderation. This is a model for all our activities: we should enjoy the world and live well, but in moderation. We can enjoy the world without becoming obsessed by it or addicted to it.

Using Our Precious Time

Think about all our little attachments, the ones that occupy so much of our lives. How do we spend our time? How much time do we spend on trivial distractions, and how much on valuable activities? Nothing in this world is permanent. Little by little, everything will go, including our health, our stamina, and our mental and physical energies. Let us use our capacities well while we still have them.

In his diary, the great psychologist B. F. Skinner wrote that he could still work when he was in his eighties, but he could only spend an hour of two of focused intellectual activity each day. If he frittered that time away, he lost his opportunity for real work that day. When Skinner was younger, he could work for hours every day without worrying about conserving his time and energy. In his later years, he had only one or two hours a day to work, and he had to spend that time wisely. Shouldn't we also think about spending our limited time wisely?

As we get older, our energy level becomes reduced, as does our ability to heal, to recover from illness or injury. Our body tends to become weaker with age, in part because we generally get less and less exercise as we grow older. There are some older athletes who still run marathons in their sixties and seventies. Our capacity for physical performance is still there, if we keep using it. But our resilience does seem to decrease over time.

If we love making music, we should enjoy it now, for we never know how much longer we will be able to play. Our sight and hearing gradually erode over time, and, they can be taken from us completely at any time. Our ability to make music is a gift that can leave us at any moment. The same is true for painting, cooking, reading, or any other activity that requires concentration and coordination. In a few years, or even sooner, we may not even be able to feed ourselves. As the sheikh said to his young dervish, the ideal is to enjoy the gifts God has given us and not regret them when God takes them away.

It is an excellent practice to contemplate what we might choose to give up ourselves before God takes it from us. Our egos want us to spend time on all kinds of worldly activities. We devote ourselves to the demands of the world—earning money, shopping, seeking fun and enjoyment. We might devote more time to seeking God.

Many people spend their working years looking forward to retirement, when they think they will finally do what they want to do. But why are we waiting for retirement? What have we put off in our lives? Perhaps we should begin now some of those activities. We might not be able to pursue them later. Among the things most people put off are activities that nourish our hearts and souls.

We don't know how much time we have. We may never make it to retirement.

CHAPTER 21

Prepare for the Future

Many things we love will be taken from us sooner or later. My mother, God rest her soul, dearly loved reading. It was the greatest passion in her life. When I was a child, we went to the public library every week and came home with at least ten books apiece. In her eighties, my mother developed Alzheimer's disease, and I suddenly realized she was no longer able to read. She would still sit with a book, but she didn't turn the pages. A huge part of her life had been taken away.

Nothing is guaranteed. We do not know what might be taken from us, or when. But most people do not prepare for the future. As dervishes, we are supposed to prepare for the life after this one, but we should also prepare for this life as well. We should think about what kind of person we would like to become. For example, if we want to know the Qur'an better, we can devote a little time to studying Qur'an every day. If we memorized just one verse of Qur'an a week, in two years we would have memorized 104 verses. All it takes is steady practice and maintaining our commitment to this goal. Let us think about how to spend our time well—and how to reduce those activities that are of minimal value in our lives.

Let us ask ourselves, "What truly nourishes me? What does God want me to do? What have I been created for?" All Creation exists to seek God, to come to love and know God. That is why we were all created. God tell us in the Qur'an, "I created ... humans but to worship Me." (51:56, Khalidi)

It is easy to become so wrapped up in our daily activities that we fail to look beyond them. But we can exercise a little self-discipline and spend at least an hour every day on something that nourishes us spiritually. We can spend an hour or more like this every evening instead of watching TV. There are many things we can do to enrich our inner lives.

When most people think of preparing for the future, they think of making investments or buying real estate. By preparing for the future spiritually, I mean building our future as dervishes and as human beings. Are we investing in our spiritual lives? It is all too easy just to mark time. Then, we stay at the same level; we don't learn anything new. In this, as in everything else, we either grow or we stagnate.

Muzaffer Efendi used to tell a parable of a kingdom in which a new king or queen was selected every year. At the end of the year, the old ruler was exiled to an island off the coast of the kingdom. The less intelligent kings and queens spent their year enjoying the power of ruling and the pleasures of the court. The more intelligent rulers sent carpenters and other artisans to their future home. They built a comfortable house and filled it with food and fine furniture. When their year was up, they were able to retire in ease and contentment. The foolish rulers found themselves living on a barren island.

My master asked us to consider our own future in the hereafter. Are we building for that future, or are we so enamored of the pleasures of this world that we forget that our time here is limited? He said, "We are in this world to earn the Hereafter."

What Is Most Important?

In a famous *hadith*, the Prophet§ said that if one day is the same as the day before, that day is a loss. We need to continue to grow and learn, every day. This does require a certain change of attitude—to focus on continually developing and not staying at the same level. What is more precious than the gift of time God has given us? We can't buy even a moment of time. We are ungrateful if we waste that gift. Why do we fritter away this precious gift by doing things that really do not matter?

Another way to decide what is truly important is to ask ourselves what opens our hearts. We could engage more in heart-opening activities, as opposed to activities that really do nothing for us, or worse, activities that close our hearts.

We can evaluate whatever we are doing by asking ourselves if it touches our hearts. For example, we can do more for others and less to entertain our egos. That will open our hearts. We can think less about ourselves and more about others. We can try to soften and open our hearts instead of amusing ourselves or feeding our egos.

How much of value do we retain after watching a TV program or surfing the internet? So many people spend hours every day in front of the TV or computer. But have we learned anything of real value? Are our hearts touched by what we watch on TV? An hour later do we even remember what we watched?

Even if we follow the news, what do we do with that information? Do we act on the information we receive? And if we fail to act on it, what good is it? We learn about terrible suffering in different parts of the world, but we don't even bother to make a small gift to charity to relieve that suffering. Which causes our hearts to harden.

It is a bad habit to keep ourselves busy with half-conscious activities. Watching TV is popular, because it doesn't require much of us. We do not have to pay attention when we watch.

Some people feel they need to watch TV after an intense day at work in order to relax. That may be true, but how long does it take to relax? It certainly does not take hours of watching meaningless programs. Also, we can come up with more constructive ways to relax after work, like listening to music or reading an inspiring book. Also, after a day of sitting at a desk, most of us would benefit far more from exercise than sitting in front of a TV.

When we hear something significant, are we truly present? The presence of the heart is extremely important. When we listen to our spiritual teachers, are we listening with our hearts, are we truly present? When we pray, are our hearts present?

In another famous *hadith*, the Prophet§ said, "O humankind, will you wake before you die?" He also said, "Take yourself to account before you are taken to account." That is, be aware of what you are doing. It is a profound spiritual practice to learn to be more present in all aspects of our lives, a practice of great value in both our worldly and spiritual lives.

Notes

Chapter 1

1. The *hadith* are the recorded sayings and traditions of the Prophet Muhammad§; the *hadith qudsi* is a subcategory of *hadith*: holy sayings in which the Prophet repeated what God revealed to him. There are many collections of *hadith*, and there is no standard form for citation, so I have followed most authors and not given citations for the *hadith* I have quoted.

2. This Sufi story is based on the recounting of the story of the Golden Calf in *Sura Taha* of the Qur'an (20: 83-98). The Qur'an is filled with stories of Moses‡ and Jesus‡ that are closely related to classical Biblical stories. Judaism, Christianity, and Islam are all "Abrahamic" religions. That is, all three are rooted in the monotheism of Abraham. In Islam, Jews and Christians are considered to be "people of the Book," people who follow revealed scriptures and divinely inspired Prophets.

Chapter 2

1. Prem Prakash, *Three Paths of Devotion: Goddess, God, Guru* (St. Paul, MN: Yes International Publishers, 2002), 103.

Chapter 3

1. The Italicized language in this verse comes from the Qur'an (28:88), as translated by Reynold A. Nicholson in *The Mathnawi of Jalaluddin Rumi* (London: Luzac, 1977), 3:3901–03, 05.
2. Sigmund Freud, *The Ego and the Id* (New York: Norton, 1923; repub. London: Hogarth Press, 1949). 708.

Chapter 4

1. James Fadiman and Robert Frager, eds., *Essential Sufism* (San Francisco: HarperSanFrancisco, 1999), 102.
2. 'Abd al-Qadir Al-Jilani, *The Secret of Secrets* (Cambridge, England: Islamic Texts Society, 1991), xlvii.
3. See Roger Brown, *Words and Things: An Introduction to Language* (New York: Simon and Schuster, 1958).
4. This quote is found throughout Zen literature; see http://www.sacred-texts.com/bud/zen/shodoka.txt.
5. *Baba,* which literally means "Father" in Arabic, Turkish, Farsi, and other languages, is often used to address a Sufi teacher or elder.
6. This story is taken from Robert Frager, *Heart, Self and Soul: The Sufi Psychology of Growth, Balance, and Harmony* (Wheaton, IL: Quest Books, 1999).

Chapter 5

1. See Brother Lawrence, *The Practice of the Presence of God with Spiritual Maxims* (Grand Rapids, MI: Spire, 1967).
2. The only *sura* that does not begin with *Bismillah ir-rahman ir-rahim* is *Sura Taubah.* Muslim scholars explain that this is because it is likely that the *Sura Taubah* is not really a separate *sura* but a continuation of the *sura* before it.

Chapter 6

1. Jalaluddin Rumi, *The Essential Rumi*, trans. Coleman Barks (San Francisco: HarperSanFrancisco, 1995), 205.

Chapter 7

1. Ibrahim Hakki Erzurumi (1703–1780) was a Turkish Sufi sage and encyclopedist. In 1756, he published his work *Marifetname* (*Book of Gnosis*), a compilation and commentary on geology, astronomy, mathematics, physiology, psychology, and Sufism. It is famous as the first treatment of post-Copernican astronomy by a Muslim scholar.
2. Reich, Wilhelm, *Character Analysis, The Function of the Orgasm* (New York: Touchstone, 1974) 300.

Chapter 8

1. Hazreti Ibrahim bin Adhem (718–782) is one of the best-known early Sufi saints. As a young man he became the sultan of Balkh, a city-state in what is now northern Afghanistan. He left his throne to become a penniless dervish. The major source of the stories and legends of Ibrahim bin Adhem is Farid al-din Attar's *Muslim Saints and Mystics: Episodes from the Tadhkirat al-Auliya' (Memorial of the Saints)*, trans. A. J. Arberry (London: Routledge and Kegan Paul, 1966).

Chapter 18

1. M. Ibn 'Arabi, *Divine Governance of the Human Kingdom: Including What the Seeker Needs and the One Alone*, trans. T. Bayrak (Louisville, KY: Fons Vitae, 1997), 224.
2. Fred Kofman, *Conscious Business: How to Build Value through Values* (Boulder, CO: Sounds True, 2006), 97–131.

Glossary

Unless otherwise noted, all non-English terms are from Arabic.

adab. Refinement, respect, etiquette, good morals, decency. *Adab* often means following a code of behavior; in Sufism, that is the code of one's Sufi Order.

Adhem, Ibrahim bin. A famous Sufi saint who gave up his throne as the sultan of Belkh to become a penniless dervish.

Aisha. The second wife of Muhammad§, whom he married after the passing of his first wife, Khadijah. She was also the daughter of his close friend Abu Bakr, who became the first Caliph after Muhammad's passing.

alif. The first letter of the Arabic alphabet. *Alif* also has the value of one, which signifies Unity, one of the niety-nine Attributes of God.

al Alim. One of the ninety-nine Names of God: the "All-Knowing." God knows everything that occurs, past, present, and future.

Allah. The Arabic word for God. (In the Middle East, Christian and Jewish speakers of Arabic also refer to God as *Allah.*)

ammaara. The Arabic root *amara* means "to command." This form intensifies the root meaning and can be translated as "to incite" or "to tyrannize."

angelic soul. In the Sufi system of souls or levels of consciousness, the angelic soul is the sixth level of soul. The angelic soul is in a state of constant Remembrance of God. This soul knew its Creator before we were born, and it has never forgotten.

animal soul. The third level of soul in the Sufi system of souls or levels of consciousness. The animal soul includes the capacities for movement, emotion, and motivation.

ayah. A "sign" or "proof," or a verse from the Qur'an (plural: *ayat*). Each verse is considered a divine message, a sign from God. Anything in the universe that gives news of God is also known as an *ayah.*

Baba. "Father" in Arabic, Turkish, Farsi, and other languages. *Baba* is often used to address a Sufi teacher or an elder.

barakah. Blessing, divine Grace, spiritual power that flows from God into Creation. *Barakah* is more concentrated in holy places and in saints. The root meaning in Arabic is "lightning."

barzakh. An isthmus; an intermediate state between life and death, between heaven and earth.

batin. The inner or spiritual dimension. The inner or esoteric meanings of the verses of the Qur'an. The opposite of *batin* is *zahir,* the outer.

Bismillah ir-rahman ir-rahim. "In the Name of God, the Most Merciful, Most Compassionate." This phrase is recited before reading the Qur'an. It occurs at the beginning of each Qur'anic *sura* except for one (*Sura Taubah*). It is also recited by pious Muslims before any daily activity.

dergah. In Persian, a shrine built at the grave of a Sufi saint. Another meaning is "portal" or "threshold." *Dergah* also refers to a Sufi lodge or center, as many Sufi masters have been buried next to their meeting places.

dervish. A member of a Sufi Order. The term comes from the Persian root for "needy," or "beggar." In the past, many dervishes have been ascetics who have taken a vow of poverty.

discernment. The virtue of wisdom or good judgment.

dua. An invocation in which we make requests of God. Muslims often ask God for forgiveness, healing, or answers to their prayers (for themselves or others). In Islam, *dua* is considered a profound form of worship.

ego. Latin for "I." Ego is one of three constructs in Freud's model of the psyche (along with *id* and *superego*). According to Freud, the ego mediates between the demands of the id and the realities of the outer world.

Efendi. Originally a title of nobility, meaning "lord" or "master." In the Ottoman Empire, it was used as the equivalent of the English "Sir." It is often used as a title of respect for a Sufi sheikh.

al Fattah. One of the ninety-nine Names: "the Opener"—of all that is closed, locked, or hardened. God opens all gates and all knowledge, especially the treasure house of the human heart.

fakir. From the Arabic root *faqr,* "poverty." A *fakir* is a Sufi ascetic. Traditionally, *fakirs* were wandering dervishes who had no possessions and lived on alms.

fana. Literally means "to pass away," "to cease to exist." In Sufism, *fana* refers to the loss of self, or the loss of our narrow self-image, the loss of a sense of separation from God. At this stage we fully follow God's will; we become servants of God.

hadith. Recorded sayings and traditions of Prophet Muhammad§.

hadith qudsi. A subcategory of *hadith,* these are holy sayings in which the Prophet§ repeated what God revealed to him.

Hajar. The second wife of Hazreti Ibrahim‡ (Abraham) and the mother of the Prophet Ishmael‡.

hajj. Pilgrimage to Mecca; the Fifth Pillar of Islam. The *hajj* must be carried out at least once in a lifetime by every able-bodied Muslim who can afford to go. It occurs from the eighth to the twelfth of the month of *Dhu al-Hijjah,* the last month of the Islamic calendar.

hajji. One who has successfully completed all the required rituals of the *hajj.*

hakim. Literally, "wise person." A title for a physician trained in Islamic medicine.

hal. In Sufism, a spiritual state. These states are temporary in nature, like flashes of lightning, and are considered gifts from God.

halal. Something lawful and permitted according to Islamic law (see *sharia*). This includes food that is permissible to eat because a) the food is lawful—for example it does not contain pork; b) if meat, it has been ritually slaughtered; c) the food was purchased with money that was lawfully earned.

halife. Turkish for representative; a sincere and dedicated servant. Muslim rulers who were considered to be the successors of the Prophet were known as *khalifa* (Arabic), or Caliphs.

halvet. "Solitude" in Turkish. In Sufism, *halvet* is a solitary retreat, usually lasting for forty days and involving spiritual practices performed under the direction of a sheikh.

Halveti-Jerrahi Order. Also known as the Jerrahi Order. A three-hundred-year-old branch of the eight-hundred-year-old Halveti Order, the Halveti-Jerrahi Order was founded in Istanbul in the eighteenth century by Pir Nureddin al Jerrahi.

al Haq. "Truth"; one of the ninety-nine Names of God. God's Truth is unchanging. It needs no proof and is impossible to deny.

al Hayy. "Life" or "Ever-living"; one of the ninety-nine Names of God. God is perfectly alive and the source of all life. All life rests on this Attribute of God.

ya Hu. Literally, "He." Often used in Sufi *zikr.*

Hazreti. (Turkish, from the Arabic *Hadrat.*) A title of respect similar to "His Holiness."

human soul. The fifth level of the soul in the Sufi system of souls or levels of consciousness. The human soul includes the attributes of compassion and service.

id. Freud's term for the part of the psyche that contains our unconscious drives and impulses.

ihsan. "Perfection" or "beauty." Acting with the knowledge that one is in the Presence of God; striving for perfection in worship by worshipping as if we see God, and remembering that even if we cannot see God, God sees us.

ihvan. Turkish pronunciation of *ihwan*, Arabic for "brotherhood"; a Sufi community.

imam. The person who leads prayers; the worship leader of a mosque, often the religious leader of a Muslim community. The term is also used to refer to a religious scholar.

inspired nafs. The third level of the self, in which the individual begins to experience the joys of prayer, worship, and service. However, pride and egotism are still present at this stage.

jihad. "To strive," "to defend one's life or religion." *Jihad* is often used in the sense of "struggle in the path of God." The term generally refers to our personal struggle against our shortcomings, against our ego.

Kaaba. The most sacred site in Islam, located in Mecca. Muslims all over the world face toward the Kaaba in prayer.

kalbi. Turkish for "from the heart" (*qalb* in Arabic), a style of chanting during *zikrullah*.

Kemal Baba. The senior Jerrahi dervish under Sheikh Safer and a close personal friend of Safer Efendi.

Khorasan. A large territory now lying in northeastern Iran, southern Turkmenistan, and northern Afghanistan. Khorasan was a major crossroads between Central Asia, South Asia, and the Middle East.

la ilaha illa Allah. "There are no gods; there is God." This is the most important expression in Islam. *La ilaha* can be understood to mean "nothing exists." *Illa Allah* means "there is God."

Malami. From the Arabic root *malama,* "to blame." In this Sufi tradition, the dervishes conceal their spirituality and often pretend to ignore religious practices in order to avoid attachment to others' opinions. Practitioners are called Malami or Malamati.

maqam. "Place of residence"; a stage on the Sufi path toward knowledge of God.

Mathnawi. Written by Jalaluddin Rumi, this six-volume extended poem is one of the most influential works in Sufism and in Persian literature.

mineral soul. The first level of the soul in the Sufi system of souls or levels of consciousness. The mineral soul refers to the basic structures that life is based on.

muezzin. The person who gives the call to prayer in a mosque. The call is traditionally given from one of the mosque's minarets.

Muzaffer Ozak. An eminent imam and Sufi teacher (1916-1985) who became the nineteenth head sheikh of the Halveti-Jerrahi Order in 1966; referred to in this text as Muzaffer Efendi.

nafs. "Self," "psyche," "ego," or "soul." It is often used in Sufism to refer to the *nafs ammaara,* the lowest level of the *nafs.*

nafs ammaara. The "tyrannical self," the narcissistic ego. The term is taken from the Qu'ranic reference *nafs ammaara bil su,* "the self is certainly compulsive with evil" (Qur'an 12:53, Cleary). At this level of functioning, the individual is almost completely self-centered and unprincipled.

narcissism. The personality trait of egotism, vanity, or self-centeredness. Freud believed that everyone develops narcissism from birth, but mature adults move from egotism to healthy self-love.

narcissistic self. In the Sufi system of levels of the self or of the ego, this is the first level, sometimes termed the "lower self." It is called the *nafs ammaara* in Arabic.

Nasruddin. A Turkish Sufi sheikh from the thirteenth century, who often taught through humorous stories and anecdotes.

pre-human soul. The fourth level of the soul in the Sufi system of souls or levels of consciousness. At this level, the intelligence is developed, but not the capacity for love and compassion.

qalb. The spiritual heart, the source of love, wisdom and compassion. The *qalb* is considered the seat of the soul.

Qur'an. The central religious text of Islam. The Qur'an is the word of God, revealed to Muhammad§ by the angel Jibreel‡ (Gabriel) over a period of twenty-three years. The Qur'an was compiled into a single book shortly after Muhammad's death by the order of the first Caliph, Abu Bakr.

rabita al kalb. In Turkish, "heart connection"; an inner spiritual connection between dervish and sheikh.

rakat. A cycle of prayer, composed of several parts. Each of the five daily prayers consists of two, three, or four *rakat.* First, the worshipper stands and recites verses from the Qur'an. The second part consists of bowing while standing with hands on knees. Third is kneeling and touching forehead and nose to the ground. Fourth is sitting on one's knees.

Ramadan. An Islamic lunar month during which Muslims fast each day from dawn to sundown. This fast is one of the Five Pillars of Islam.

regretful self. The second stage of the development of the self. At this level, individuals are conscious of their narcissistic, self-centered tendencies and the effects of these tendencies on their lives. But they are not yet able to change. This stage is also known as the "self-blaming" self. In Arabic, the *nafs lawwamma.*

Rumi. A great Sufi mystic and poet, and one of the great spiritual poets of world literature. Known variously as Jalaluddin Muhammad Balkhi or Jalaluddin Muhammad Rumi, he was born in Balkh, one of the major cities in Khorasan (see *Khorasan*). Rumi lived most of his life in Konya in Central Turkey, an area known as Rum, or Roman, because those lands were once ruled by the Byzantine, or Eastern Roman, Empire.

as Sabr. The Islamic virtue of patience and perseverance. One of the ninety-nine Names, or Attributes, of God.

Safer Dal. The twentieth head sheikh of the Halveti-Jerrahi Order from 1985 until his passing in 1999. Referred to in this text as Safer Efendi.

sahaba. Companions of the Prophet Muhammad§.

sajda. One of the positions of *salat,* in which worshippers kneel and touch their forehead and nose to the floor.

salat. In Islam, formal prayer done five times a day. The Second Pillar of Islam.

Satan. The major source of evil in the world. Satan (*Shaitan* in Arabic) swore that, until the Day of Judgment, he would mislead everyone except for the truly sincere worshippers of God.

self-critical self. See *regretful* self.

serene self. In the Sufi system of levels of the self or of the ego, this is the fourth level, also called the "contented self." At this level, individuals are content with their lives, rather than constantly striving for more (more wealth, more fame, more pleasure, etc.). In Arabic, this is called *nafs mutmainna.*

shahada. "To witness" or "to know and believe without any doubt, as if witnessed." The First Pillar of Islam is to recite before at least two Muslims, *Eshedu en la ilaha illa Allah; Muhammad rasulullah,* "I witness [that] there is no god but God, and Muhammad§ is a Messenger of God."

sheikh. "Elder"; a title of respect for an elder or a religious leader. In Sufism, it refers to someone who is authorized to teach and guide dervishes. A female sheikh is a *sheikha*.

sharia. The moral code and religious law of Islam, based on the teachings of the Qur'an and the example of the Prophet§.

silsilah. "Chain" or "link." Every Sufi Order has a "chain of initiation" that connects each generation of teachers, all the way back through the founder of the Order, to Prophet Muhammad§.

sohbet. In Turkish, "talk" or "conversation." In the Sufi tradition, a *sohbet* is a sheikh's talk about the Sufi tradition. It can be a spiritual dialog and also a meeting of hearts. Often more is transmitted than the words alone—including love, a heart connection, and mystical knowledge.

Sufi Order. A Sufi Order is known in Arabic as a *tariqa*, or a way, a path, or a method of spiritual practice.

sultan soul. In the Sufi system of souls or levels of consciousness, this is the seventh and final level of the soul. Also known as "the secret of secrets," this is the spark of God within us. It is transcendent, God's Presence within us.

sura. A chapter of the Qur'an, which has 114 *suras* in all. They vary in length from only 3 lines to 286 lines.

Sura Fatiha. The first *sura* of the Qur'an, recited at the beginning of each *rakat,* or unit, of formal prayer.

terawih. Special prayers held each night during the month of Ramadan.

tariqa. See *Sufi Order.*

Tosun Bayrak. The senior sheikh of the Jerrahi Order in America, leader of a Sufi community in New York, and author of more than ten books on Sufism. Tosun Efendi has been my spiritual guide for more than thirty years.

Tuğrul Inançer. Since the year 2000, the head sheikh of the Jerrahi Order. Referred to in this text as Tuğrul Efendi.

vegetable soul. In the Sufi system of souls or levels of consciousness, this is the second level of the soul. The vegetable soul includes the functions of growth and digestion.

al Wahhab. One of the ninety-nine Names of God: "the Bestower," who gives abundantly; the source of all good that comes to us.

zahir. The exterior or outer dimension of things. This includes the exoteric or literal meanings of the verses of the Qur'an. The opposite of *zahir* is *batin,* the inner.

Zamzam, well of. The well of Zamzam is located near the Kaaba (see *Kaaba*) in Mecca. It is considered a miraculously generated source of water, and its water is considered holy in Islam.

zakat. "Purification" or "growth." (In Turkish, *zekat.*) *Zakat* is considered an act of piety that purifies the possessions of the one who gives, and blesses him or her with further prosperity. All Muslims who have accumulated wealth during the year are required to give roughly 2.5 percent of their accumulated assets to be distributed to the poor and needy. The Fourth Pillar of Islam.

zikr. Turkish, from the Arabic *dhikr,* "recitation" or "remembrance." *Zikr* often refers to *zikrullah* (see below).

zikrullah. Remembrance of God. Prayer is considered *zikrullah,* as are the Sufi rituals in which several of the divine Names are chanted.

Bibliography

Al-Jilani, 'Abd al-Qadir. *The Secret of Secrets.* Translated by T. Bayrak. Cambridge, England: Islamic Texts Society, 1991.

Asad, Muhammad, trans. *The Message of the Qur'an.* Gibraltar: Dar al-Andalus, 1980.

Attar, Farid al-din. *Muslim Saints and Mystics.* Translated by A. J. Arberry. London: Routledge and Kegan Paul, 1966.

The Bible, King James Version. New York: Oxford Edition, 1769; *King James Bible Online*, 2008. http://www.kingjamesbibleonline.org/

Brown, Roger. *Words and Things: An Introduction to Language.* New York: Simon and Schuster, 1958.

Cleary, Thomas, trans. The Qur'an. Bridgeview, IL: Starlatch Press, 2004.

Fadiman, James, Robert Frager. *Essential Sufism.* San Francisco: HarperSanFrancisco, 1997.

Frager, Robert. *Heart, Self and Soul: The Sufi Psychology of Growth, Balance, and Harmony.* Wheaton, IL: Quest Books, 1999.

Freud, Sigmund. *The Ego and the Id.* New York: Norton, 1923; repub. London: Hogarth Press, 1949.

Ibn 'Arabi, M. *Divine Governance of the Human Kingdom: Including What the Seeker Needs and the One Alone.* Translated by T. Bayrak. Louisville, KY: Fons Vitae, 1997.

Kofman, Fred. *Conscious Business: How to Build Value through Values.* Boulder, CO: Sounds True, 2006.

Khalidi, Tarif. The Qur'an. New York: Viking, 2008.

Lawrence, Brother, *The Practice of the Presence of God with Spiritual Maxims*. Grand Rapids, MI: Spire, 1967.

Prakash, Prem. *Three Paths of Devotion: Goddess, God, Guru.* Saint Paul, MN: Yes International Publishers, 2002.

Reich, Wilhelm. *Character Analysis*. Translated by Vincent Carfagno. New York: Farrar, Straus and Giroux, 1949.

Ringer, Robert. *Looking Out for #1.* New York: M. Evans and Company, 2005.

Rumi, Jalaluddin. *The Essential Rumi*. Translated by Coleman Barks. San Francisco: HarperSanFrancisco, 1995.

———. *Mathnawi.* Vol. 1. Translated by Reynold Nicholson. London: Luzac, 1977.

Index

Related Quest Titles

*Heart, Self, and Soul: The Sufi Psychology of
Growth, Balance, and Harmony,* by Robert Frager

*Practical Sufism: A Guide to the Spiritual Path Based on
the Teachings of Pir Vilayat Inayat Khan,* by Phillip Gowins

*Sufism and the Way of Blame: Hidden Sources of a
Sacred Psychology,* by Yannis Toussulis